Rangers

v Celtic

Rangers
v Celtic
The Gers' Greatest Old Firm Victories

Jeff Holmes

First published by Pitch Publishing, 2019

Pitch Publishing
A2 Yeoman Gate
Yeoman Way
Worthing
Sussex
BN13 3QZ
www.pitchpublishing.co.uk
info@pitchpublishing.co.uk

A CIP catalogue record is available for this book
from the British Library.

ISBN 978 1 78531 568 8

Typesetting and origination by Pitch Publishing
Printed and bound in India by Replika Press Pvt. Ltd.

List of Matches/Contents

Introduction

Rangers Football Club means so much to hundreds of thousands of followers the world over. For generations, supporters have picked up the red, white and blue scarf at a young age and followed in the family tradition. Happily wandering down the Copland Road just as their forefathers did. It's that kind of club.

As someone once said, bluenoses are born, not manufactured.

And that means Follow Following when Rangers play pre-season friendlies down south, Scottish Cup ties in the north of Scotland, or European matches in far-flung parts like Vladikavkaz, some 4,000 kilometres from home.

But there is one fixture more than any other that is always guaranteed to get the juices flowing. Since the first encounter in May 1888, it has taken on a life of its own. Now, more than 130 years after the first meeting, Old Firm games are as keenly contested as ever, and that intensity shows no sign of abating.

So, what makes this fixture different from, say, the Merseyside or Manchester derbies, or its equivalents in either Madrid or Buenos Aires?

First of all, it's 'our' big game, and while it's not quite a matter of life and death, as the late, great Bill Shankly once suggested, it's not a kick in the backside off it.

The match means so much to so many people, and win or lose, it's about far more than bragging rights. That's just paper talk.

If Rangers are on, say, a seven- or eight-match unbeaten run against Celtic, then that manifests into power. When we were winning nine titles in succession, the football power in the city rested south of the River Clyde. Even if Rangers weren't playing their greatest football, managers like Walter Smith always found a way to beat Celtic. He had their number. His sides normally did just enough, and it wasn't always down to good fortune.

And then there are the resounding victories, such as the 5–1 mauling in August 1988, when it was a great time to be a bluenose. Mind you, has there ever been a bad time? But Rangers were 5–1 up a little over an hour into the game that day, and that was the way it ended, much to the chagrin of the great many supporters who sensed a mauling. To this day, some speak with forked tongues about 'letting them off the hook'. They wanted double figures – complete and utter humiliation.

The Old Firm match is part power grab, part religious, part territorial, part political, part lots of things. It brings out the best in people, the worst in others. With both clubs having such massive fan bases, then we can expect all kinds of views and emotions, from the sublime to the ridiculous. But even the most moderate among us still craves victory in this fixture over just about any other.

When it comes to the players, some can handle it, while others are found wanting. In a nutshell, it separates the men from the boys.

Rangers great Sandy Jardine once described the Old Firm game as 'like no other'. He added: 'The build-up starts from the beginning of the week and you train harder and think about the game a lot more than normal. All players are affected. If you're not, you're made of stone.

'Then there's the pre-match tension. It's like nothing else. Players who are normally free from bad nerves are jumpy, or stay very quiet. As you change in the dressing room the atmosphere seems to creep under the door and set you tingling. You can hear the crowd building up and the singing gets louder, more intense.

'The occasion really gets to you. In fact, it's almost a relief to get out on to the pitch and get the game started. Much better than in the dressing room. Once the game is underway it's so hectic that you just have to push everything else out of your mind. The game is fast and there is little time to think.

'I've heard a lot of words that describe the Old Firm game: endeavour, excitement, tension, glamour, drama, frustration, joy. Yes, they're all pretty appropriate.'

My greatest memories as a Rangers supporter are of matches against Celtic. Victory in this fixture always means so much more than any other game. From my first Old Firm encounter, in the early 1970s, to the final match of the 2018/19 campaign, I've enjoyed/hated every single one, and I plan to go on enjoying/hating these fixtures until my number is called. Hang on, maybe they are more important than life itself!

Anyway, enjoy reading this list of cracking Rangers victories.

Jeff Holmes

August 2019

Rangers 3 Celtic 1

Saturday, 18 February 1893
Glasgow Cup Final

FOOTBALL supporters venturing in the direction of Hampden Park can pop into a once famous old Glasgow ground as they make their way along Cathcart Road. Cathkin Park – former home of the great Third Lanark – still exists in ghostly form just a mile or so from the national stadium.

You can stand on the terrace, lean against a red crash barrier, and imagine you've travelled back in time. How about to Saturday, 18 February 1893? In your mind's eye you will be witnessing a little piece of football history. Well, just about. Technically, the Cathkin Park that remains is the second incarnation, with the original just across the road, but why let the facts …

That day, Rangers chalked up their first ever victory over Celtic, their great Glasgow rivals. Ten thousand spectators filed into Cathkin expecting to see a clever Celtic side continue their dominance of the Light Blues. It had been five years since the formation of the Parkhead side and they'd hit the ground running, leaving Rangers, and just about everyone else, trailing in their wake. Thus, backcourt bookies had made the Celts red-hot favourites to land their third successive Glasgow Cup.

Rangers, on the other hand, had yet to win the old trophy despite reaching the first final against Cambuslang. Mind you, they had looked impressive while disposing of Northern, Linthouse, Queen's Park and Glasgow Thistle en route to this latest final.

Rangers must have taken heart from seeing Celtic lose just their second competitive game of the season the Saturday before, when Paisley side Abercorn won the Scottish League match 4–2 at Underwood Park.

With the kick-off just a few minutes away, members of the Glasgow committee found it difficult to hide their disappointment at the turnout, but there were a number of reasons for it. First of all, the weather. It was a dreich afternoon, which had no doubt kept many a supporter indoors. The admission money was also higher than normal, while many fans regarded the result a foregone conclusion.

The Rangers players could do nothing about admission prices or the weather, but they could have a good go at sorting out number three!

When Celtic captain James Kelly led his team out from the pavilion, a few of his team-mates appeared a little subdued. Half the crowd reckoned the Abercorn result had taken the wind from their sails, while others perhaps thought an easy win lay before them.

Regardless, it was the Rangers that set the early tempo, and a contemporary match report stated that 'the daring, dashing play of the Light Blues was something to behold', but could they keep it up for 90 minutes?

The initial pace was certainly hectic, thanks to the work put in pre-match by trainer Johnny Taylor, and while the players would go on to lift the cup with verve and style, Taylor was hailed as a major reason for Celtic's downfall. The players looked incredibly fit, worth its weight in gold on such a heavy pitch.

That said, Celtic certainly didn't fold like the proverbial pack of cards. They battled gamely but simply failed to get into their stride, not only at the start, but throughout the game. Combination and close passing, which had carried them to many a victory, were conspicuous by their absence, partly due to their inability to adapt quickly to the soft ground, but mainly because the Rangers half-backs had the measure of their opponents and their tackling was spot on. Not a Parkhead man could put his foot on the ball but there were two Gers men immediately on top of him.

The half-back line of Robert Marshall, Hugh McCreadie and David Mitchell broke up any attempts Celtic had at passing it around. The Celts might have exhibited something less than their true form, but never before had the Rangers played up to them so staunchly.

The Ibrox men certainly gave their critics – and there were many – something to chew on, and exposed the weaknesses of the Celtic forward line. Suddenly, Madden, McMahon and Campbell were considered human, as the Rangers half-backs and backs snapped at their ankles the moment they received the ball.

Rangers all but won the game in the way they set out their formation. Captain David Mitchell coached his team superbly from the first minute to the last, while the cries of their 'touchline men' could be heard throughout the ground.

The Rangers' style was cool, clever and confident. They made winning the ball in the middle of the park a priority, and when they did so they wasted not a single moment, but lashed the ball on, and raced after it for all they were worth.

Neil Kerr turned in a real man-of-the-match performance, and defied those who had called him 'chicken-hearted' in the run-up to the game. He was gameness personified. He had the beating of Dan Doyle, he bagged the second goal, and he fed Davie and McPherson with some delightful passes throughout an entertaining contest. After such an intelligent performance there was talk of a Scotland call-up for the Rangers centre-forward.

The sound defence of Reynolds and Doyle prevented the Celts from an even heavier disaster. Their half-backs failed them, bar Kelly, and Rangers gave neither Dunbar nor Maley any chance to tackle, so fast and open did they continue to keep the play. And when they got within range of Joe Cullen in the Celtic goal they let fly, so that even Doyle and Reynolds weren't given time to tackle.

Cullen lost the first goal rather easily, but John Barker's play deserved it. Barker's was one of the reputations the final improved. He had a dashing, light, free-and-easy style that pleased the eye.

Although the Rangers were going brilliantly, and deserved more than their lead of a goal at half-time, still everybody was waiting for the Celts to rise; but they were doomed to disappointment, for they didn't respond or ever rise to the occasion.

If it was possible, Rangers looked even sharper at the start of the second half. They kept up the pressure on Celtic and, if the truth be told, had them completely mastered, so much so that long before their second goal, they missed out on one of the easiest opportunities ever to score. A shot came off the bar and stopped on the line, the sodden turf holding it in its place, and with Cullen out of his goal, it remained there until dramatically cleared by a defender.

Celtic had a couple of chances but David Haddow, in the Rangers goal, was very assured, and saved well on a couple of occasions. In fact, he also saved a fierce drive by heading it away! Haddow was a class, cool keeper, and it's a surprise that he only ever played once for Scotland.

There was one other save of note for Rangers – but it wasn't made by Haddow. With Haddow off his line, John Campbell looked set to score for Celtic, but he didn't reckon on the acrobatic qualities of defender Jock Drummond, who was able to 'knee' the shot to safety!

It was not till 15 minutes before time that the Celts showed anything like their true form. They pinned the Rangers back for a spell but the game was all up long before then. Rangers, from a corner, managed a second goal, scored by Kerr, and not long after, midfield ace John McPherson thumped home a third. Celts managed a consolation seconds before the final whistle.

There is no doubt the best team won. Rangers were better all over the park and in Mitchell they had a player who tackled, passed and coached superbly. It was one of his best performances in a Rangers jersey.

Haddow was safe and sure. Hay sound, not a showy player, but with a large soul. Drummond was solid, while Marshall had the measure of Willie Maley. Another reputation strengthened.

McCreadie mastered Madden, and while few people would have thought Rangers could master Celtic in defence, they did.

In attack, Kerr was fantastic, and was backed up superbly by Barker, whose only fault was a penchant for straying offside. Hugh McCreadie and McPherson supported the forwards well.

The game was conducted in a sportsmanlike spirit. It was a final in which Rangers had all the glory, but Celtic no shame.

It was the pleasure of Baillie Primrose to accept the trophy for the winning team. After being presented with the handsome trophy, the Rangers official said that there was no team which Celtic would rather see win the cup, a comment which was endorsed by President Glass of Celtic.

The kindred interchanges of mutual good feeling were a fitting climax to one of the best and friendliest finals ever witnessed.

Rangers: Haddow, Hay, Drummond, Marshall, A. McCreadie, Mitchell, Davie, H. McCreadie, Kerr, J. McPherson, Barker.

Celtic: Cullen, Doyle, Reynolds, Maley, Dunbar, Madden, Campbell, McMahon, Kelly, Towie, Blessington.

Referee: Mr Hay

Attendance: 10,000

Rangers 5 Celtic 0

Saturday, 2 September 1893
Scottish League

JOHN Barker was the local lad made good. Named after his father, a fitter in one of the thriving shipyards around Govan, he was born just a stone's throw from Ibrox. The talented left-winger joined Rangers from Govan senior side Linthouse in 1892 and made an immediate impact on Gers supporters. Barker would remain at Rangers for four years before leaving to help with the formation of another local side, Middleton Athletic.

He had been in good form as Rangers made an unbeaten start to the 1893/94 league campaign, and when Celtic visited Ibrox Park at the start of September, it was to Barker and fellow striker John Gray that the Light Blues supporters looked to for the goals against their Glasgow rivals.

And the Scotland international didn't disappoint, becoming the first Rangers player to score a hat-trick in an Old Firm league game for Rangers – and he achieved it in Rangers' first league win over Celtic.

Ibrox Park hosted a tremendous crowd for the match, as everyone wanted to see the battle of the previous season's champions and runners-up. The importance of the contest was enhanced by the position of the clubs in the present standings. Both teams were unbeaten from three matches, with Celtic a point ahead at the top of the table.

Punctually to time, Gray of the Rangers set the ball in motion against the sun and wind and it was soon apparent that they were playing with confidence, despite Celtic having the first real chance of the game when Campbell shot over the bar from close range.

The next opportunity fell to Rangers, who were awarded a corner, but Dan Doyle cleared the danger. However, the Celtic full-back could do nothing to prevent Rangers taking the lead soon after. Cullen stopped a corker of a shot from McPherson but James Steel nipped in to clip home the rebound.

Rangers squeezed on the gas and after good lead-up work, they were two up, Barker finishing in style. Five minutes later, Rangers were three to the good when Gray headed home a perfect Steel cross.

Gradually Celtic improved and started to string together some passes, but they couldn't find the net and it was Rangers who went in three goals up at half-time.

On resuming play, both teams fought out a dour struggle in midfield, although the Celts were first to open up the opposition defence, courtesy of Blessington, who found Cassidy, only for the Celtic forward to shoot inches past the post.

It was a warning shot to the home side.

There were chances at either end as the game opened up, and had Celtic found a little more cohesion up front, they could have given Rangers a fright or two. Time after time they broke away, only to be checked by the home side's full-backs.

Once again, though, play swung in Rangers' favour and each time the ball was played forward, the Rangers strikers looked capable of scoring. Seldom had they been seen in a better light. Their combination was perfect, and they appeared far fitter than their opponents. The final quarter of the match belonged to the home side and Barker scored twice to compound Celtic's misery – and claimed a hat-trick in the process, although not the match ball!

The Rangers defence was impregnable in the second half, while the Celts, nettled at their impending defeat, worked desperately hard to get something from the game. They had chances, but just couldn't find a killer final ball.

In stark contrast, every one of the five goals scored by Rangers was soundly earned, and they received many plaudits for the quality of their forward play. They went at it hammer and tongs from beginning to end, and every goal scored seemed to inspire them with redoubled energy. Not an opportunity was lost, no hesitation displayed. If the goal was within shooting distance, bang went the ball, and five times it flew past Celtic keeper Joe Cullen.

Rangers were superb all over the park, but weaknesses were apparent in every line of their opponents – weaknesses that the Light Blues exploited to the max. But the chief failure for the visitors lay in the half-back line. The three that wore the green jerseys didn't have the speed, the skill, nor the pluck to check the dashing Rangers.

Only one man in the Celtic rear division deserved praise, and that was Doyle, who worked like a Trojan. All to no purpose, though, as the Celts sustained the biggest beating of their career. 'It will be two wet days and a dry one before the people get over their astonishment at this unexpected and overwhelming collapse,' claimed one newspaper reporter.

After the game, the league table showed Rangers in top spot, with six points from four games. Celtic were a point behind, while Rangers were also the highest scorers in the division with 13 goals.

But sadly that 5–0 mauling would turn out to be the high point of Rangers' league campaign, as come the end of the season they would be locked in a battle with St Bernard's to see who could finish third!

With two league games remaining, Rangers needed two wins, and the first of these was against St Mirren at Ibrox. Nothing other than a win would do but the Paisley side had been showing great form, and despite missing a trio of top players who were off with Scotland on international duty, both teams started at a high tempo and Rangers led by the only goal when the teams retired for refreshments at the break. In the second 45, the home side were rampant and scored four times without reply. It was a blow to the Paisley Buddies, who had to be content with a sixth-place finish.

For Rangers, though, it was two points, and with one home match remaining, this time against Edinburgh side St Bernard's, the prize for the victor was third spot behind Celtic and Hearts. After such a positive start to the season, it had gone downhill pretty quickly for the Gers, and their campaign now hinged on this final game.

Rangers and St Bernard's had already tried to play the game but it had been abandoned just nine minutes from time when the referee decreed that 'darkness had taken over'! At the time of the stoppage, Saints had been leading 2–1 and playing in a manner which suggested they would more than likely hang on to their slender lead.

Meanwhile, there was something of a revolt going on down Ibrox way. The players had met in secret to discuss asking for more money, and presented their thoughts to the board of directors. They wanted £3 per week during the playing season, and a wage of £2 per week in the close season.

It was said the demand 'all but flabbergasted the committee', and when they recovered – no doubt with the use of some quality smelling salts – they quickly rejected the players' request. There wasn't a club in Scotland who could afford to pay more money than Rangers, and the reporter bringing us the news had a feeling that the players would come to their senses in time for signing their new contracts, and on the same terms as before.

Three days before the final league match, Britain's oldest club, Notts County, travelled to Ibrox to take part in a challenge match. And, if nothing else, the result and performance showed the Scottish League in a good light. Rangers were on top from start to finish and won 3–1, playing, in the process, some attractive football. Notts had their moments but the final scoreline was kind on the Englishmen.

A contemporary publication wrote, 'When allowance is made for the fact that the Rangers at the present time are in very poor form, one cannot help marvelling that a club like Notts County should this year have secured the highest honours in English football.'

It was being reported on several fronts that Rangers half-back Andrew McCreadie was a transfer target of Sunderland. It seemed a bit more than wild speculation as the player had failed to agree terms for the new season with the Ibrox hierarchy. Other reports suggested he was about to join Stoke City or, heaven forbid, Celtic!

When the match against St Bernard's was eventually played, Rangers produced a standard Jekyll and Hyde performance and lost 2–1. It meant St Bernard's finished third in the table and Rangers fourth. A league campaign that had initially promised so much delivered just eight wins from 18 matches, which wasn't a great backdrop for players demanding a rise! Mind you, the Glasgow Cup was secured for a second successive season, and fans still had a Scottish Cup Final to look forward to.

Rangers: Haddow, Smith, Drummond, Marshall, A. McCreadie, Mitchell, Steel, H. McCreadie, Gray, McPherson, Barker.

Celtic: Cullen, Reynolds, Doyle, Curran, Kelly, Dunbar, Davidson, Blessington, Madden, Cassidy, Campbell.

Referee: Mr Davenport

Attendance: 18,000

Rangers 3 Celtic 1

Saturday, 17 February 1894
Scottish Cup Final

THE first Scottish Cup competition was staged just 12 months after the formation of Rangers – yet it was a full 20 years later that the Light Blues won it for the first time.

Queen's Park (on ten occasions), Vale of Leven (three times), Dumbarton and Renton had all annexed the silverware in the intervening years, and Celtic's first victory arrived just two years before this maiden Old Firm final.

To get to their third national final, Rangers had defeated Cowlairs (8–0), Leith Athletic (2–0), Clyde (5–0) and Queen's Park (3–1) along the way, yet they were still deemed by a great many to be second-favourites to lift the trophy.

But who ever cared about backcourt odds?

For the 17,000 supporters who witnessed this battle, they would never forget; and for those who didn't, they can imagine the scene. A more depressing day has hardly ever dawned upon a final than that of this great occasion. There is no doubt the adverse weather affected the gate, and though £750 was still a fair amount to draw in, it would have been far greater had the sun been present.

Nevertheless, Hampden was still busy, and what it lacked in numbers was made up for in enthusiasm, because never before were two teams encouraged with greater heartiness by their followers than these two. Rangers had the balance of the shout in their favour, with the 'neutral' evidently leaning to their side.

Referee Marshall's verdict, given early in the forenoon, that the ground was playable set all doubts at rest, and accordingly pilgrim football fans from every quarter, and by every kind of conveyance, flocked to the scene of the tie.

The ground, though playable, was not in a condition for fine football. It was thought to favour the Rangers, and it did. The Celts, as usual, stuck to their close passing, and would not, or could not, lash the ball on like their opponents.

As the teams stepped out – first the Celts, led by captain McMahon, and then the Rangers by David Mitchell – the jauntiness of their going was interfered with by the soft ground, which in parts reached up to their ankles.

A roar proclaimed that the fray had begun, Celts kicking off. The pace set by them was a cracker, and for 20 minutes or so every man went at it hammer and tongs. It couldn't last, though the Celts in those opening exchanges definitely had the better of the Rangers.

Two men beat them in the early moments, and these same two men beat them at the finish. The defensive play of Nick Smith and Jock Drummond was a sight to behold. They were more powerful, dashing and effective than their opposite numbers, and Smith, from his first kick to his last, played as if his life depended on the result. Everything he attempted came off. One of those days when the young Ayrshireman could do no wrong.

Celtic forward James Blessington was a constant threat to Rangers, but Smith checked the eager striker's play with some timely blocks. In fact, he was also outdone by a keenness to get his side in front during the early exchanges.

Celtic should have scored first, and it was Blessington who got a fine shot on target only to see Rangers keeper David Haddow save brilliantly.

One of the main problems of the first half for Rangers was the selfishness of John McPherson. He stuck to the ball like a leech, and would not part with it, and it was only after he was 'floored' by an opponent that he started to offer it to team-mates.

That said, McPherson did have one good individual run, at which point Joe Cullen's goal should have fallen, for two Rangers players were in acres of space, but could only look on as Cullen clawed away McPherson's shot.

That no team could score in the first 45 minutes was down to the stout defending of both clubs. Dan Doyle was the shining light of the Celts, Drummond ditto of the Rangers.

When the second half began, the Rangers, as they did against Queen's Park, came away with their usual vigour. And when push came to shove, the Celts were not equal to it.

Rangers opened the scoring, and while Hugh McCreadie's goal was a clever effort, it was also a lucky one, poking home among a host of feet.

The Celts had reached the end of their tether, and several of their players – namely Campbell, Maley and Kelly – were run to a perfect standstill. James Kelly, in particular, was a beaten man. The hero of a hundred fights had to concede the midfield battle to Andrew McCreadie, although his were worthy shoulders.

The method of the Rangers showed itself in this half. Whereas the Celts' forwards lay abreast, the Light Blues were arranged in higgledy-piggledy – and perfect – fashion. Gray was seen lying, like Cassidy, well upon the Celts' backs, McPherson away behind Steele, and Barker again lay out as a sort of skirmisher.

Whether by luck or design the ball always came first to a Rangers foot, and when he parted with it he did so to the advantage of his side. Three solid men the Rangers had in the engine room. These were Marshall, McCreadie and Mitchell. This trio blocked, tackled and placed in such style as to have the Celts' forwards at every turn. They had McMahon and his partners' tempers roused, their confidence destroyed.

McCreadie was the pick of the three. He was faster, fairer, trickier and cuter than the rest. In comparison the Celts' midline were weak, although Maley could be excused as he looked ill.

John Barker's goal, Rangers' second, showed up the Celts' defence in all its feebleness. He slipped prettily past Curran, and with the most beautiful of shots, scored the goal of the game.

Celtic's fate was sealed, and despite the best efforts of forward duo McMahon and Campbell, they still couldn't get the better of Smith and Drummond. The fact is it would have taken miraculous work to beat these two, for they were outstanding all afternoon.

Celtic's misery was compounded when McPherson whipped in a third goal. It was the icing on a particularly sweet cake, and although the Parkhead side did get a late consolation, it failed to alter the destination of the cup.

As the Rangers players made their way back to the pavilion, they first had to get past an army of loyal admirers, such had been their stranglehold on this game. The result was a clear and correct index of the play.

Celts could not adapt to the sticky ground. Rangers did, and every one of them stayed the pace, and often made it, too. Rangers had several individual heroes in their midst but it was their collective talents and spirit that won them the cup.

There was talk afterwards that the Scottish international selectors could do far worse than choose the entire Rangers half-back line for the forthcoming match against England. McCreadie, Marshall and Mitchell, the Rangers captain, had done everything asked of them and it was felt that their ability to play together would be a real asset to Scotland against the Auld Enemy.

Centre-forward John Gray might not have got his name on the score sheet, but his overall play was first class and a great asset to the clever combination play Rangers displayed. John Barker was also praised for his relentless work rate, while only bouts of selfishness had prevented McPherson from being spoken of in the same exalted tones.

Celtic might have won the Scottish League in season 1893/94, but the press were adamant that the Scottish Cup winners just shaded it when talk turned to naming the team of the season.

But in the midst of the general rejoicing down Govan way by the vast army of Rangers admirers, a correspondent for the *Scottish Referee* sports newspaper insisted that it should not be forgotten that to one man belonged no mean share of Rangers' grand victory.

That man was Johnny Taylor, trainer of the club for several years. No one knew better the mode and extent of the self-denial necessary to put a team into a final tie with the prospect of 90 minutes of the hardest running and kicking. That the Rangers were judiciously handled during the past fortnight, the ordinary spectator of Saturday's match must have been satisfied. Never before had we witnessed a team last the full 90 minutes with such tenacity of purpose amid such a punishing game. Even when Celtic started their attempts to force the game early on, they were met with solid defence, and the forwards didn't stop running all afternoon. Taylor deserved his moment.

Rangers: Haddow, Smith, Drummond, Marshall, A. McCreadie, Mitchell, Steele, H. McCreadie, Gray, McPherson, Barker.

Celtic: Cullen, Reynolds, Doyle, Maley, Kelly, Curran, Blessington, Madden, Cassidy, McMahon, Campbell.

Referee: Mr J Marshall (Third Lanark)

Attendance: 17,000

Celtic 0 Rangers 4

Saturday, 24 September 1898
Scottish First Division

TWO for the price of one here as we chart Rangers' first ever league double over Celtic – and the implications the victories had for the club at the end of a most historic season.

For a change, the weather was glorious, so no grounds for complaint on the score of soft surface, greasy ball, high winds, etc. In fact, one could've been forgiven for thinking many of those making their way to the ground were heading to a picnic, such was the warm glow coming from the sky.

And then there were the brakes-men, spanking along in their 19th-century supporters' vehicles, with banners glittering and fluttering in the summer breeze.

It was no doubt the excellent afternoon, coupled of course with the prospect of a thrilling contest in the east end, which contributed to a packed ground.

There were 45,000 spectators inside Celtic Park, the majority of them, it would appear, hoping for a home victory.

They would ultimately be disappointed.

Despite Rangers chalking up five wins from their opening five league games, even the staunchest follower of the Light Blues might not for a moment have imagined their favourites, at Parkhead of all places, could be capable of such a comprehensive win; in fact, it's extremely doubtful if they entertained the notion of a Rangers win at all.

But while tradition was in favour of the home side, it was the Rangers back line that turned in such a combined, powerful game that the possibility of an away win was on the cards early on. The shooting of the visiting forwards was also in marked contrast to that of their opponents. And with regards to the half-backs, there was simply no comparison. In a positional sense, as well as tackling and passing, the Rangers trio of Mitchell, Neil and Gibson were masters to the pupils of the Celts' midfield. Men against boys.

Robert Hamilton was the perfect centre-forward, for with far less work on the ball than Campbell, he got to the goal in half the time, and then couldn't he just shoot? The Ranger was grandly assisted by Miller and McPherson, with Miller being one of the most useful men afield. Campbell, with far less power than Bell, was as effective, and it must surely be a matter for satisfaction to Rangers that, whereas Bell cost the Celts some £300, Campbell cost Rangers less than a third of that.

Rangers were forced into a pre-match switch due to Jock Drummond's sudden indisposition. But not to worry, as Nick Smith turned in a fantastic performance.

As far as the goalkeepers were concerned, Matthew Dickie more than held his own with Dan McArthur, to whom no fault was due for his loss of four goals. Weak all-round play lost Celtic this match; strong all-round play won it for Rangers.

Referee Dixon is to be highly complimented on his independence, impartiality and ability. The bulk of his decisions went against Celtic, but that was due to the fact that the 'run' was against them and not the referee.

The Rangers goals were scored by Robert Neil, from the penalty spot, John McPherson, John Campbell and Jimmy Millar, while the gate receipt, which amounted to £1,405 14s, was a new record for a Scottish League match. It was a matter for congratulation that the huge crowd of over 40,000 witnessed the game in comfort and security.

There were a couple of minor pitch invasions on the day, but these were connected to a rather inept performance by the home side rather than want of accommodation.

Celtic: McArthur, Welford, Storrier, Goldie, Hynds, King, Bell, Gilhooly, Campbell, McMahon, Fisher.

Rangers: Dickie, N. Smith, Crawford, Gibson, Neil, Mitchell, Campbell, McPherson, Hamilton, J. Miller, A. Smith.

Referee: Mr Dixon

Attendance: 40,323

Rangers 4 Celtic 1

Monday, 2 January 1899
Scottish First Division

BY the time the second Old Firm league match of the season came around, Rangers had recorded 16 successive wins and had just the match at home to Celtic and a trip to Shawfield, to face Clyde, remaining.

If they won both games, Rangers would emerge from the league campaign with a 100 per cent win record from their 18 matches: a record that could certainly never be eclipsed, and perhaps only matched.

Preston North End had enjoyed a fantastic campaign in the English League First Division in season 1888/89. It was a 12-club competition and they remained unbeaten, but unlike Rangers, they had four draws, and their total for the season was 40 points from 22 games.

In season 1897/98, Celtic had a good time of it, winning 15 and drawing three games, but Rangers were determined to go one better. There was talk that Celtic were bent on breaking the Rangers' record, and it was also an equally common rumour that the Light Blues were just as determined to maintain and also enhance what had already been achieved.

When the game got underway, Rangers took the bull by the horns and it's fair to say the contest was won and lost in the first ten minutes, although the Celts did not relinquish their objective without a few parting kicks, so to speak.

It was the sudden way in which Rangers opened that threw their opponents off balance, and won them the match; and it may be said that with the exception of very few passages, the men from Parkhead were completely eclipsed.

It wasn't a brilliant game by any manner of means, but Rangers did exactly what was necessary to win the game. They weren't overstretched and won comfortably in the end. It was just regrettable that towards the finish, when Rangers were playing what could only be described as exhibition football, one or two Celtic players reverted to bully-boy tactics. This was especially the case with Battles, whose undue attention to Hamilton left marks and bruising on his leg, and made him a doubtful starter for the impending Glasgow League match against Partick Thistle.

If Battles made his mark in this way, then Hamilton made his in a far more positive manner. The popular centre, born in Elgin, grabbed his third league hat-trick of the season, which took his tally to 21 in 17 games.

Hamilton was in his very best form, as his goalscoring indicated, but the selectors gave cause for concern by naming their 'other' Jimmy Miller in the left-half berth in place of David Mitchell, and although not so polished a player as David Mitchell, Miller's breaking-up tactics were not far short of his partners' – Neil and Gibson. In fact, it was so effective that Celtic's clever pair, Somers and Gilhooly, were seldom dangerous. It had been a gamble, but it paid off.

John Campbell scored Rangers' other goal, the second of four, which was the result of a magnificent drooping shot sent in from the touchline, with McArthur jumping a little too soon and allowing the ball to go over his head. Campbell was also on top form and tricked King and Davidson time after time.

From start to finish Celtic were indeed a beaten team, Bell being the only forward in their 11 who was in anything like the form shown by the opposing forwards. Their defence, too, was weak, Davidson especially making several bad mistakes, worst of which was in standing claiming offside for McPherson while Hamilton stepped in to score the third goal.

Although losing four goals, Dan McArthur deserved a word of praise for a brilliant personal display, but for which Rangers would have certainly ended with a similar total to that which they had inflicted upon Hibs (10–0).

Having cleared the Celtic hurdle successfully, Rangers looked to end the league campaign with victory over Clyde at Shawfield, and though it was unlikely the Bully Wee would succeed where all others had failed, Clyde had long been known as surprise packets, capable of upsetting the applecart. Rangers were advised to take no risks, and they didn't. They won the match 3–0 and were ahead of Clyde on every front.

Goals by Alex Smith, Jimmy Millar and Robert Neil, from the spot, did the trick, and while the title may have been wrapped up a few weeks earlier, this win saw Rangers become the first Scottish team to finish a league campaign with a 100 per cent win record.

And it's a record that no one since has come close to equalling.

The Glasgow League was staged at the end of the Scottish League and Rangers opened with an 8–2 win over Partick Thistle at Firhill, just 24 hours after beating Celtic. Hamilton played with an injury to his treasured right foot – and again scored a treble, this time using his weaker left!

Rangers: Dickie, N. Smith, Crawford, Gibson, Neil, JE Miller, Campbell, McPherson, Hamilton, J. Miller, A. Smith.

Celtic: McArthur, Davidson, Storrier, Goldie, Battles, King, Gilhooley, Somers, Divers, McMahon, Bell.

Referee: Mr J. McPherson (Cowlairs)

Attendance: 30,000

Rangers 5 Celtic 1

Saturday, 12 May 1900
Glasgow Merchants' Charity Cup Final

IT was another season when the Old Firm dominated, and this was illustrated in the share-out of the available silverware, with Rangers winning the Scottish League and Glasgow Cup, while Celtic had been crowned Inter City League champions and were Scottish Cup winners.

Now, these two giants were going head to head in the final of the Charity Cup at Hampden Park in a bid to secure the last trophy of the campaign.

Rangers had finished third in the Inter City League – a competition for clubs from Glasgow and Edinburgh – but had been buoyed by the opening of the second Ibrox Stadium (the current ground), so they were up for the battle. It was the 11th meeting of the season between these great clubs and Celtic held the upper hand in terms of wins.

But it was the form of Rangers that suggested Celtic would start red-hot favourites to win the final encounter, especially as they had just recently beaten Rangers home and away in the Inter City League.

Celtic were without their regular keeper, Dan McArthur, and also Orr, both of whom had received injuries in the previous round against Queen's Park. Rangers, on the other hand, replaced Hyslop and Graham with Miller and Campbell, but these changes were made of their own volition as both of the latter were on trial for the following season.

The ground was in splendid condition although there was a strong wind blowing, which troubled the players a good deal. Rangers won the toss and elected to play with the wind, and right from the start they adopted a fast, dashing game, which gave Celtic no end of early problems. This led a good portion of the crowd to believe that the form book was in the process of being shredded.

The Celtic defence stood up to the early onslaught, but as wave after wave of attack bore down on them, cracks began to show, and when Alex Smith shot for goal, Barney Battles was forced into a mistake which led to him putting the ball into his own net. 1–0 to Rangers.

Celtic, when they did break free from the pressure, insisted on taking the same route to goal every time, and this was lapped up by Rangers midfield trio Gibson, Neil and Robertson.

The tie was over at half-time, though, as further goals from Campbell and Gibson handed Rangers a 3–0 interval lead. There was no way back for the Parkhead side.

In the second half the Ibrox men continued to have the better of the exchanges and when Hamilton broke away to score a fourth goal, the destination of the cup was settled.

Celtic continued to work hard, but their finishing in front of goal was weak, and only a defensive error allowed Hodge in to score a consolation. However, Miller scored again for Rangers to return the gloss to the final scoreline, while Celtic's miserable afternoon was compounded when they missed a late penalty.

Of the Rangers it would be hard to pick out a failure. The two up for possible transfer, however, Miller and Campbell, transformed the front rank, which never moved to more deadly effect, and it looked like both players would be kept on. The finish was most exciting, and Matthew Dickie earned the handshakes of his Ibrox mates for his brilliant saving.

The only negative to come from the game was the apparent insistence of both defences to overuse the offside rule. As a charity match, some commentators reckoned this completely spoiled the occasion for the vast majority of those who paid their entrance fee. It seems some folk were still at odds with the rule, even though it had been law since 1863, although it was changed in 1925 from three defenders to just two.

After the Charity Cup Final, one scribe penned the following passage: 'It may be good fun for the players to outdo each other either by kicking out, walking at snail pace for goal-line balls, or playing at "hide and seek offside", but if, when doing so, they disgust and disappoint the public, these players had better have a care lest they be left on the field to enjoy this so-called sport with an array of empty benches or an attendance of small boys who enjoy juvenile larks and freak football.

'Although down three goals at half-time, there was no reason why Celts should have played but one back in order to throw Rangers offside. Had they pursued the usual and manly method of playing all together and all onside, then we think 5–1 would not have been the result at the end of this foolish and farcical exhibition.

'Two blacks do not make a white either, and so we condemn Rangers' adoption of the same tactics. It's no argument whatever, from a public point of view, to say that they were justified, or that what is "sauce for the goose is sauce for the gander". What we impress on both finalists, and on all football players, is the duty they owe the public to play what the public pay to see, and we trust in future this will be done.

'It was the most childish and uncharitable finish to a season's football we have seen for many years, and we solidly and seriously hope it will be many more seasons before we see it again.

'We also express the hope that in their own interest as organisations the directors of both clubs will administer a word of warning to their players, from whose wages a contribution to the charity funds would not be a bad corrective for putting the offenders onside. This question of playing "trick" football, too, is not beyond the province of the SFA or League to deal with. For if the game of football be played in such ludicrous style, then they as bodies may well entertain a fear for their own existence, as well as for that of the game they govern.'

Revenge had obviously been rankling within the Rangers players, judging by the stern, resolute and determined manner in which they went about their business. It might have been a 'charity' final, but there was little, if any, charity shown by the Light Blues. There was no mistaking their superiority over Celts, although what surprised most folk in attendance was their remarkable freshness.

They played as if they were beginning the season after a course of salt baths and underdone steaks at Millport rather than at the end of a season with the marks and traces of a full season's 'penalty' kicks on their tender shins. Rangers thus regained possession of the cup they had not won since 1897, when they were so uncharitable to Third Lanark as to beat them 6–1 in the final.

Another problem arose. Many suggested that due to it being the eleventh meeting of the teams that season, that the repeated meetings were neither good for the clubs nor for Scottish football. However, organisers were certainly happy with the 15,000 attendance, which meant a good sum of £1,027 would be donated to Glasgow and western institutions, although one newspaper reporter commented: 'As in previous years, we hope to see the fund distributed on non-sectarian lines. Charity knows no distinction of class or creed, and for this reason, amongst others, it is well entitled to be regarded as the crowning grace of all. £950 was last year's total, so we have beaten that and yet kept the matches within one short week and within the regular season.'

It's interesting to note that both Nicol (Nick) and Alex Smith were from the tiny Ayrshire village of Darvel, although they were unrelated. Nick signed for Rangers in season 1893/94, and once he had settled in at Ibrox, recommended his friend Alex, whom he thought would be capable of making a real impact at the club. Both had played for Darvel Juniors and had a solid grounding. And he wasn't wrong.

Alex was three years younger than Nick, and was a dashing left-winger in the mould of the great Alan Morton. He was just 18 when he signed for the Gers and would remain at Ibrox for an incredible 21 years, playing 642 competitive games for the Light Blues. Smith also scored more than 200 goals for Rangers.

He won 25 honours while at Ibrox, including seven league titles and three Scottish Cups. His stunning wing play was also noted by his national team and he played 20 times for Scotland, as well as representing the Scottish League on a further 14 occasions.

When he finished playing in 1915, at the age of 38, he returned to his native Darvel, where he worked in a lacemaking business in which he was a partner.

Rangers: Dickie, N. Smith, Drummond, Gibson, Neil, Robertson, Campbell, McPherson, Hamilton, Miller, A. Smith.

Celtic: Docherty, Storrier, Battles, Russell, Marshall, King, Hodge, Gilhooly, Campbell, McMahon, Bell.

Referee: Mr Tom Robertson (Queen's Park)

Attendance: 15,000

*Rangers 2 Celtic 2

Saturday, 26 October 1901
Glasgow Cup Final

WASN'T this book solely for Old Firm wins? Sure was, and while this match might have finished all square, it didn't stop Rangers collecting the trophy. Confused? I bet, so let's start at the beginning.

At the time, the teams were so evenly matched it was almost impossible to pick a winner, so when it ended all square, some suggested a fix, although perhaps no one bothered to tell Rangers centre-forward Robert Hamilton, who hit the post with a ferocious shot in the last minute. That said, match fixing was apparently a real issue in those days, but there was no carve-up here, no seeking a replay for extra gate money. It was a good old-fashioned cup tie – the 14th Glasgow Cup Final – and it was packed with incident and drama.

It brought together the two outstanding clubs in Scottish football and Ibrox looked picture-perfect, the spacious grounds lined with eager, expectant faces, and the welcome sunshine brightening up a truly magnificent scene.

It was unfortunate for Rangers, the cup holders, that several of their players were not fully fit for such an important game. The talented Neil Gibson, who was suffering from a knee injury, was one, and had initially hoped to look on from the enclosure, while Nick Smith and Robertson played because the club wasn't in a position to give them a rest.

Celtic, like their opponents, did not make a final selection until a few minutes before kick-off, but their dilemma was somewhat easier. Watson or Battles? The first-named found favour with the directors, and soon the keenly anticipated tie was in progress.

Early in the game it looked as if the Parkhead men were about to fall softly before their great antagonists, despite showing occasional signs of nimbleness and smartness, mostly in the forward and half-back areas. McMahon and Campbell worked their socks off up front for the visitors, while the omission of John McPherson seemed a hefty mistake by the Rangers selectors. McPherson's work rate in the middle of the park was certainly missed. And with Gibson less than fully fit, Drummond's forays up the park were limited, although he stuck to his task manfully.

It was perhaps a little surprising then that Rangers found themselves two goals to the good inside the first 15 minutes. Goalscorers Finlay Speedie and John Wilkie seemed to settle the destination of the cup, but the Celts did not lose heart and their uphill fight eventually brought its rewards. Mind you, in the final, final analysis, their heroics would be to no avail.

After Willie McOustra had headed the first goal the Celts played like demons, and when John Campbell equalised from a penalty kick, it was anyone's game.

The second half was not so fiercely fought, but there was still some brilliant football on display. Rangers had the better chances, but Celtic were also dangerous, and some excellent defending retained parity.

Celtic keeper Rab Macfarlane twice found Lady Luck smiling upon him. On both occasions he was beaten all ends up, but each time the ball struck him on the way into the net and had its course diverted.

No fault could be found with the Rangers defence. Gibson battled bravely to overcome his injury handicap and was bailed out once or twice by the excellent Drummond. Nick Smith, James Stark and Robert Neil also had a successful afternoon's work.

Alex Smith, Speedie and Wilkie played grandly in the front ranks, Speedie's only fault being his weakness in finishing. Hamilton performed well, and with a touch more luck could have won the cup late on for Rangers.

At the gate, the sum of £821 0s 9d was taken. With 5,000 boys at 3d, and members and season ticket holders, this represented an attendance of close on 38,000. The stand money, which was divided between both clubs, amounted to £246 0s 6d.

The social after the match was held in the Alexandra Hotel, Bath Street, and was attended by most of the afternoon's star turns. Song and sentiment passed away a few happy hours, and the various officials and players parted with the hope that a similar happy experience would be theirs the following week.

But no sooner had the last of the taxis departed for their different destinations than stories were emerging of a potential problem with the replay. After the final whistle, directors from both clubs met to fix a venue. The clubs couldn't agree and it was suggested the association be asked to adjudicate. Celtic claimed the replay should take place at Parkhead, while Rangers insisted on Ibrox. Both sets of officials were adamant on the point. One thing they did agree on, though, was that no matter the venue, a great game lay in store.

The basis of Rangers' claims lay in the Glasgow Association fixing the final for Ibrox in the first place, contending it should be played there till a finish, no matter how many draws. They also asserted that all precedent was against the claim of Celtic, and pointed not just to the Scottish and other finals, but to the last occasion on which the two clubs met in the same competition at Cathkin Park in 1896, when, after a 1–1 draw, the match was replayed on the same field till a finish. If the Glasgow Association decided to upset this precedent, then the Rangers were prepared to have the matter tested.

Celts insisted the replay must go ahead at Parkhead because, prior to the decision of the association at its last meeting, a private arrangement was made between Celtic director Mr O'Hara and Mr McKenzie, of the Rangers, that in the event of a draw the tie would move to Parkhead. However, many believed that if such an understanding did exist, then the Rangers, in good faith, should stand by it. That was a sticking point, but at no time did Rangers acknowledge such discussions had ever taken place.

As a way out of the difficulty, a neutral venue was suggested, and the excellent Glasgow Exhibition ground offered to the clubs. Purpose-built for the 1901 Empire Exhibition, in what is now Kelvingrove Park, it was considered a viable alternative.

An important factor to be considered was the capacity of the venue. Unless the Glasgow Association was prepared to charge one shilling for entry, then the host stadium had to be capable of holding at least 40,000, which would allow the tariff to be fixed at sixpence, something that *had* been mutually agreed before the first match.

According to the rules of the association, the GFA made no provision for altering the venue in the event of a draw, the understanding and precedent being that the final tie should be played on such ground until one of the teams won.

As to whether the association could recognise a private arrangement between the clubs altering its original decision as to the ground, it was a moot point, but it was that very point which was up for discussion at a hastily convened meeting a few days later.

Sadly, the meeting failed to break the deadlock, with both Old Firm clubs, and the Glasgow Association, as sharers in the gate proceeds, refusing to accept compromise of any kind.

Rangers were still holding out for Ibrox, the Celts for Parkhead, but ultimately a decision had to be made and the association decided upon Ibrox. The judgement was based upon the previous decision, and also warranted by past precedents established in previous years.

The Celts evidently anticipated the association would stick to its initial decision, for the moment a judgement was delivered the club tendered, by letter, its resignation from the competition. Thus they became the third club in the short history of Scottish football to scratch from a competition. Vale of Leven were awarded the Scottish Cup in 1879 after an injury-hit Rangers refused to appear for the replay. They had asked for a change of date, but it was refused.

Five years later, Vale refused to take part in a Scottish Cup Final replay for the same reason and on both occasions the cup was awarded in the absence of the scratchers.

In a surprise announcement the day after the meeting, Rangers said they would be willing to play on a neutral ground provided the Glasgow Association sanctioned it. All concerned awaited an announcement by the Celtic directorate, but nothing was forthcoming.

They say time is a great healer, but a week after Rangers' offer, both Celtic and the GFA were still refusing to budge. If anything, the rift between the pair had widened, and with no sign of a compromise in sight, the association decided to present the trophy and winners' badges to Rangers.

Rangers: Dickie, N. Smith, Drummond, Stark, Neil, Gibson, Robertson, Wilkie, Hamilton, Speedie, A. Smith.

Celtic: Macfarlane, Watson, Davidson, Moir, Marshall, Orr, McOustra, Livingstone, Campbell, McMahon, Quinn.

Referee: Mr J. Baillie (St Bernard's FC)

Attendance: 38,000

*Rangers were awarded the cup.

Rangers 2 Celtic 0

Monday, 1 January 1923
Scottish First Division

WHEN is a football match not a football match? When you can't see the action for a thick blanket of fog! That was the case when the Old Firm met at Ibrox on New Year's Day 1923, and by the close of play, supporters leaving the stadium were calling it 'phantom football'!

Arguably the most important fixture on the league calendar was reduced to farce when the ground was enveloped in an eerie, dense fog. It was impossible to see from one side of the field to the other, and from the press box it was nigh on impossible to estimate the crowd; in fact, had it not been for sporadic cheers it would have been difficult to imagine there were any people present at all.

It was a great pity, because the Ne'erday contest was one which was as traditional as the First Foot greeting itself and was keenly anticipated for many weeks beforehand, long before the annual holiday arrived. So it was unfortunate that following ten days of wet weather, fog developed and ultimately spoiled the annual duel.

To make it more infuriating, as the 1pm kick-off time approached, there was nothing in the air except sunshine, bar a slight mist. What happened afterwards was probably unprecedented, a bank of fog rolling up from the river and completely covering the ground. It was a difficult situation for the officials, but the referee decided to start proceedings.

The playing surface was little affected, and when the players emerged from the tunnel, only the spectators in the immediate vicinity of play could tell what was going on. It was invisible football, and what took place was mere surmise.

No player was visible ten yards from either boundary line, and the ball could not be followed from the moment it was kicked upfield by a player. Shadowy forms were seen running around at intervals, but what the run of play was very few people knew. Thanks largely to a lack of any real crowd noise, it was ascertained at half-time that no goals had been scored.

The fog had lifted slightly when the second half started and the range of vision increased. It was not long before Rangers took the lead. Two minutes had gone when Danish striker Carl Hansen scored a lovely goal, and ten minutes later Sandy Archibald more or less put the game beyond doubt when he scored a second for Rangers. It was perhaps due to some form of divine intervention that the period visible to many supporters included both goals!

That Rangers won by a couple would seem to indicate they were the superior team. To say definitely that they were would be drawing upon one's imagination, for it was quite impossible to follow the play with any degree of accuracy. Certainly most of the game was fought out in the vicinity of the Celtic 18-yard box, and in the few brief moments when it was possible to really see what was transpiring the goals of Hansen and Archibald were outstanding incidents.

From a spectator point of view, however, the game was a pure farce, and no good purpose would be served by entering upon any detailed criticism. The result must speak for itself, and that result gave Rangers a pair of points, which consolidated their position at the top of the table.

In the 29 years that these two clubs had been playing one another, difficulties had been encountered, but it was remarkable that none of the engagements, though played in the most uncertain period meteorologically, had been interrupted.

The situation was well handled by the officials, but it is doubtful if under similar conditions, play would have been permitted at all in any but a New Year's Day Rangers–Celtic engagement.

Soon after the game had started several hundred spectators, evidently deciding that the event was a farce and not value for money as a spectacle, made their way to the pavilion and demanded their money back. Their numbers were quickly augmented, and soon a big mob had gathered. Matters looked ominous for a bit, but mounted police were called to the scene and took up guard. Best of all, the fog began to lift slightly, and many of the dissatisfied went back to see what they could see of the game while others chose to leave the ground.

When asked later about the trouble, Bill Struth insisted it was impossible to offer refunds as almost 10,000 had paid for 'half-time admission', and while attempting to give the incident the respect it deserved, described the trouble as 'infinitesimal'.

The win extended Rangers' lead at the top of the table to a couple of points over Dundee, who drew 0–0 at Pittodrie, but the Light Blues had three games in hand. Celtic were languishing in seventh spot, some seven points behind the league leaders, and this latest Old Firm reverse did them no favours whatsoever.

Carl Hansen, the plucky little striker from Copenhagen, signed for Rangers after showing up well playing against the Light Blues on their tour of Denmark in the summer of 1921. Bill Struth was fascinated by the skill, speed and tenacity of the lad who had just turned 23 and offered him a trial.

Hansen impressed while on trial and was offered a contract. He jumped at the chance. It was the winter of the same year before he came over to Scotland. As the first professional player in Denmark he'd encountered a few problems, but nothing which couldn't be overcome, and Rangers, having paid £20 for his services, were delighted to welcome him to Ibrox.

His impact on the Scottish scene was nothing short of explosive. Struth eased him in and Hansen made his debut against Queen's Park in the first round of the Lord Provost's Rent Relief Fund Cup. Rangers won a tight match 3–2 and Hansen scored a debut-day hat-trick. The Rangers supporters in the 7,000 crowd at Hampden took to him instantly.

His next outing was against Partick Thistle in the semi-finals of the same competition and the little Dane scored again, as did Sandy Archibald, as Rangers won 2–0. Celtic awaited Rangers in the final at Hampden Park and once again Hansen showed no nerves in front of 25,000 by scoring the opening goal from the penalty spot. Tommy Cairns added to that goal and Hansen had his first winners' medal in Scotland.

He made his league debut on Boxing Day against Dundee at Ibrox and scored in another Gers win. There was no stopping this young lad. In his ten other league appearances before the end of the season he scored a further seven times, but Rangers finished runners-up in the league to Celtic by a single point. In their last ten league games, Rangers won eight, but goalless draws against Aberdeen and Clyde proved costly.

Hansen looked set to play a pivotal role in the Rangers team for the 1922/23 season, but suffered the cruellest fate in just the second match of the campaign against Third Lanark, which ended in a 5–1 win for the Light Blues. The talented little Dane had scored twice but in his haste to net a third, bounced straight off goalkeeper Brownlie, and thumped into the post. The result was a broken tibia, and Hansen was a 'guest' of the Western Infirmary for a fortnight. His recovery was arduous, though, and he wasn't fit to play again until the New Year's Day win over Celtic – which not many folk saw because of the fog! The goal, however, was the first scored in an Old Firm game by a foreigner.

Hansen managed ten league appearances in season 22/23 and his six goals helped Rangers win the title by five points from second-placed Airdrie, with Celtic a further four points behind in third.

Sadly, the injury all but finished Hansen's career in Scotland and he made just a couple more appearances the following season. Hansen had been very popular in Glasgow and supporters mourned the fact that the 'Little Shoemaker' (his nickname due to his father's trade) had failed to fulfil the enormous potential they knew he possessed.

When he returned to Denmark, he wasn't allowed to play for two years due to his professional status, and managed one season with his old club B1903 before hanging up his boots.

During the Second World War, Hansen was arrested and sentenced to four months' imprisonment for harassing a German. He served his full sentence in a German concentration camp at Neumunster, a small town in northern Germany, just a few miles from the Danish border. As a member of the Danish Resistance, Hansen despised the Nazis, but due to geographical reasons, Denmark was largely sympathetic to Hitler.

Rangers: Robb, Reid, McCandless, Nicholson, Dixon, Muirhead, Archibald, Cunningham, Hansen, Cairns, Morton.

Celtic: Shaw, J. Murphy, W. McStay, Gilchrist, Cringan, J. McStay, McAtee, Gallagher, Cassidy, McFarlane, McLean.

Referee: Mr T. Dougary (Bellshill)

Attendance: 50,000

Rangers 4 Celtic 0

Saturday, 14 April 1928
Scottish Cup Final

ONE of the most important matches in our history, and a game that gave 11 footballers the opportunity to become legends in the eyes of the Rangers support.

It had been 25 years since the Light Blues had lifted the national trophy, or as some folk put it, a national disgrace!

For a quarter of a century, the club had been the butt of many a music hall joke, with a string of funny men promising theatregoers 'boundless wealth when the Rangers eventually win the cup', or that Celtic favourites Patsy Gallacher and Willie McStay had more Scottish Cup badges than they had room on their waistcoats for, and that if the Rangers players asked nicely, Patsy or Willie would give them one. The gags were seemingly never-ending.

It was the 50th Scottish Cup Final (the competition being suspended during the Great War), and, despite previous shortcomings, there was an air of optimism in the Ibrox camp as they made their way to Hampden for the showdown meeting. When they arrived at the national stadium, supporters of both sides were milling around in their thousands. By kick-off, just over 118,000 had squeezed into the ground, half decked out in blue and white, and the other half in green. As the captains, Meiklejohn and McStay, shook hands, and the referee tossed the coin, excitement reached fever pitch. McStay called correctly and elected to shoot with the wind, no doubt hoping to conjure up a healthy enough lead that would give the Parkhead side the upper hand at the break.

Before the teams went out Mr William Maley expressed his wish for a good sporting tie. 'If Rangers win I will be the first to congratulate them,' said the Celtic manager.

Celtic were red-hot pre-match favourites to add to Rangers' Scottish Cup woes, and they were first to carve out an opportunity, but Gers' keeper Tom Hamilton saved Adam McLean's effort. The Ibrox goal had several further narrow escapes as Celtic used the wind to their advantage. A five-minute spell before half-time constituted Rangers' most trying time of the afternoon, and Hamilton played a real hero's role. It was a delighted Light Blues that reached half-time with their goal intact.

The second half was a different matter altogether. Rangers soon took command and Alan Morton, Andy Cunningham, Jock Buchanan and Jimmy Fleming went close.

But in the 56th minute arrived the pivotal moment of the game. From a Morton cross the ball was fired in by Fleming – and Celtic keeper John Thomson was beaten. Willie McStay stuck out a hand and referee Willie Bell had no hesitation in pointing to the spot.

A penalty kick to Rangers – but there were no takers. Not a Ranger stepped forward to take responsibility. Sensing a lack of confidence amongst his team-mates, Meiklejohn quickly offered his services. The ground fell silent. Twenty-five years of hurt preceded this kick. Score, and the Light Blues would be favourites to go on and lift the elusive trophy. Miss, and the consequences could be dire. As if operating in slow motion, the 27-year-old Rangers half-back placed the ball on the penalty spot, took one look at Thomson in the Celtic goal, and looked at the referee. He sounded his whistle; Meiklejohn started his run-up, and he kicked the leather with total precision, way beyond the reach of the Prince of Goalies. 1–0 to Rangers, and up in the air went 60,000 bunnets.

With their tails up, Rangers rattled into their opponents and an Archibald shot shook the bar, before Fleming flashed one narrowly past. Ten minutes after Meik's opener, Bob McPhail was in the right place at the right time to thump the ball past Thomson. Game over?

Two minutes later, Archibald let fly from 25 yards and the agonising 25-year wait was over. Thomson misjudged the flight of the ball and it was soon nestling in the back of the net. But Archibald wasn't finished and with ten minutes remaining, McStay cleared straight to the feet of the Fifer and he brought it down, steadied himself, and drove it like a rocket past Thomson.

Gers' full-backs Dougie Gray and 'Newry' Bob Hamilton had been standouts for Rangers in the first half, while Meik was solid in the middle line, holding Celtic legend Jimmy McGrory in the hollow of his hand. Fleming was full of running up front, as was McPhail. This pair of strong-going, fearless forwards did much to harry the almost always worried, and later overworked, Parkhead rear half-dozen.

Sandy Archibald, his two goals apart, did a lot of running and, with a lively Alan Morton, contributed his quota to this glorious Ibrox victory.

Afterwards, Meiklejohn said, 'I am too pleased to be able to express my true feelings. When we were awarded the penalty, and I stepped up to take it, I have never felt so anxious in my life. It was the most terrible moment of my football career. I had time to think what it might mean if I missed, and I can tell you I was glad when I saw the ball in the back of the net.'

Asked why regular taker Bob McPhail hadn't taken the penalty, Meiklejohn said, 'Bob told me he wasn't taking it because he had been missing them. He had missed two and when a man does that, his confidence is shaken.'

But McPhail was at his captain's elbow just before the kick, and one could have been forgiven for thinking that he, and not Meiklejohn, would take the kick. That, apparently, was the plan.

At last, 'at long last', as Joseph Buchanan said at the cup present-ation ceremony in the Queen's Park FC Reading Room, Rangers had laid their Scottish Cup bogey to rest.

And who will say that the Ibrox side were not worthy winners, Bailie? Even the most perfervid Celt will admit that their side was comfortably beaten.

Called upon to accept custody of the Scottish Cup on behalf of the Rangers, ex-Bailie Joseph Buchanan expressed his delight. He was more than glad that at last the spell was broken. But he wished to say that during their 25 barren years, they never became downhearted or pessimistic. He was particularly pleased that the victory had been achieved over Celtic, their greatest rivals. It had always been their ambition that when they eventually reclaimed the cup, Celtic would be their opponents in the final.

Bailie Buchanan referred to the game as a grand, determined struggle between giants, a struggle worthy of the reputation of the clubs and the magnificent patronage. These Rangers–Celtic encounters did much to popularise the game; and long may that friendly rivalry continue.

Celtic were unfortunate to get our boys on their toes, continued the Bailie. You will agree that on play we deserved to win. When Celtic's time comes again we will congratulate them as heartily and sincerely as they have done us.

Mr Tom White, replying for Celtic, was, as usual, short, humorous and to the point. With a merry twinkle in his eye, he said, 'I am glad to have lived to see the day Rangers won the Scottish Cup.' This brought a laugh, as did 'After seeing this latest performance of the Rangers, I begin to wonder if Celtic will ever win it again!'

He expressed himself as being pleased and delighted that they had attained their ambition. Rangers won very well indeed; what worried him in the last ten minutes was whether his side might concede more goals. But Rangers only had their due, and he hoped that the following year they would have a crowd of 150,000.

The 118,115 people who had attended that afternoon proved conclusively that the game was not going backwards.

The heroes of the hour then dressed in their finest attire and took once again to the field to be photographed with the cup.

Afterwards, there was a triumphal return to Glasgow restaurant Ferguson & Forrester's, where, in a brightly decorated room – blue and white flags, Union Jacks and Royal Standards – directors, managers and players dined together, with ex-Bailie Buchanan in the chair.

And it was a job getting through the crowds of exuberant Rangers fans all the way from Hampden to Buchanan Street. A sight of the cup in captain Meiklejohn's car was the signal for a massed raid, hands through the opened windows and handshakes galore. At Gorbals Cross hundreds surrounded the captain's car, and stopped its progress for some minutes. A day to remember for all connected with the Rangers.

Over 50 cables and telegrams were received at Ibrox from well-wishers, as old Rangers supporters in Pennsylvania and Toronto cabled congratulations on the great victory.

The hoodoo had finally been laid to rest.

Rangers: T. Hamilton, Gray, R. Hamilton, Buchanan, Meiklejohn, Craig, Archibald, Cunningham, Fleming, McPhail, Morton.

Celtic: J. Thomson, W. McStay, Donoghue, Wilson, J. McStay, McFarlane, Connolly, A. Thomson, McGrory, McInally, McLean.

Referee: Mr A. N. Other

Attendance: 118,115

Celtic 3 Rangers 4

Wednesday, 1 January 1936
Scottish First Division

THIS was indeed a glorious Rangers triumph on an afternoon when Celtic also played their part, but ended up completely mesmerised by the standard of football on offer from the visitors.

A rain-drenched crowd of around 50,000 turned up at Parkhead and witnessed Scotland's greatest rivals take part in a game that would go down in the history books as a classic.

Not for a single moment did it fail to thrill. Celtic took the honours in the first half, Rangers in the second – only more so, and that being the case, victory went to the better all-round team on the day. It really was super stuff.

Rangers were two goals behind at one stage in the first half, but took the bit between their teeth and gave an exhibition of comeback stuff that has seldom been equalled.

In the opening 45 minutes, one or two of the Light Blues, such as Whitey McDonald and Winning, were not completely at ease against the fast-moving young Celts, but in the latter part to a man Rangers pulled together and hauled themselves back into contention.

At times their teamwork was perfect. In the closing stages their passing especially was a treat to behold on such a sodden and tricky surface. Their inspiration could be traced to the brilliant coaching of the veteran Davie Meiklejohn, who all but played himself to a standstill.

And then there was the 'Real McPhail', Barrhead Bob, another old hand who gave his forward colleagues the cue. McPhail was his old forceful self, ripping the Celts' defence wide open with his far-flung passes and occasionally boring through the middle of the Celtic defence on his own.

Alex Venters, too, was a grand foraging forward, and Jim Fiddes, contenting himself with getting the ball across, swung it over to such purpose that three of his side's goals came directly from his boot.

Willie Lyon was Jimmy Smith's master in the first half, but big Jimmy gave the ex-amateur a stark lesson after the interval. Simpson was sorely troubled by McGrory to begin with, but certainly won the battle of the 'Jimmys' later on. Defensive honours go to Jerry Dawson and Dougie Gray – to the keeper for some marvellous first-half saves and to the right-back for never putting a foot wrong throughout the entire 90 minutes.

Celts started like an express train. A Jimmy Delaney goal in three minutes had them in front, but Smith headed the equaliser seven minutes afterwards, although for the next 20 minutes or so the Light Blues were badly outplayed.

McGrory fired a spectacular counter in 17 minutes, and as we reached the half hour, the same player again sent the Parkhead faithful into raptures by sneaking a cute third.

It was from this point that Rangers rallied. Down, but certainly not out, McPhail reduced the leeway eight minutes before half-time, and a 3–2 score in favour of Celts at the interval was just about right.

Practically the whole of the second half was a battle between the Celtic defence and Rangers' attack, and attack triumphed because of its superlative quality. McPhail headed the equaliser in 66 minutes, and six minutes before the end Smith did likewise for the winner.

Celtic could have no complaints at losing to such a team. They were given an inspiring lead by Jimmy McGrory, and played some delightful stuff in the first period, but were never in the hunt after the break.

Jim Foley gets a big hand for his goalkeeping. Joe Kennaway at his best could not have touched him. The home backs and halves started grandly, but were eventually reduced to mediocre proportions, with only Lyon maintaining a high standard to the end.

Of course, the weather did its worst to ruin the big game. Yet despite the depressing elements there were many great one-on-one struggles, some cracking football played and lots of end-to-end highlights.

Pity the party was disturbed by a too demonstrative element in the 50,000 crowd. There were two minor pitch invasions, which were promptly subdued by the police, and faction fights were frequent on different parts of the terracing. Many casualties were reported. The thrill of the game was too much for some. Ambulance men were continually at work. Stretcher cases were numerous, and many of these were to be traced to the fiery corners. Heads and hands were swathed in bandages – the results of blows. Yet at no time was there any danger of the crowd getting out of control.

In the final analysis, the result was just perfect for the Light Blues, and it promised a thrilling title fight to the finish, with Aberdeen, Celtic and Rangers almost dead level. Rangers were right on the heels of Celts and within striking distance of the Dons, who were lucky to nab a share of the spoils against Dundee at Dens Park – but they still topped the pile.

A late season collapse would see Aberdeen finish sixth, and Rangers crowned champions once again. The Light Blues remained unbeaten throughout the months of January, February and March and that was sufficient to see off the threat of, and overtake, Celtic. Rangers finished three points clear of the field and just four goals short of the ton.

Smith and McPhail shared 54 league goals, while Venters chipped in with 17 mainly from the inside-right position.

One of the men responsible for the downfall of Celtic that day signed for Rangers in 1927 from Airdrie, for what was then a considerable sum of money. Around £5,000 changed hands and Bob McPhail moved to Ibrox. It would prove the bargain of the century!

McPhail gave an early indication of what was to come when he scored twice in the 4–1 Charity Cup semi-final win over Celtic at the end of his first season as a Ranger.

He was a fantastic talent and had already displayed his considerable skills with Airdrie, helping them to a rare Scottish Cup success in April 1924 when they defeated Hibs 2–0 in the final at Ibrox. His partnership with Hughie Gallacher was the stuff of legend. McPhail was just 18 years old and it was a sign of big things to come.

The talented inside-left had a brilliant work ethic but his astonishing eye for goal was something to behold. He developed an uncanny understanding with Alan Morton and then Davie Kinnear in the Rangers front line and it was invariably highly productive.

He earned the rather uncomplimentary nickname of 'Greetin' Boab' for berating team-mate Torry Gillick one day and the tag stuck. But he was also known as 'Gentleman Bob', and that was the more accurate of the two.

McPhail scored 230 league goals for Rangers, a record which stood for over 50 years until Ally McCoist came along and claimed it as his own, and it's a record that will surely now stand the test of time.

Gentleman Bob played with some fantastic strikers during his time at Ibrox, including Sam English and Jimmy Smith, but it was his own longevity and consistency which was remarkable. His record of six Scottish Cup wins while at Rangers is shared only by Celtic's Jimmy McMenemy and Billy McNeill, and is another record sure to remain for a long time.

Bob McPhail was a genuine Rangers legend, and his place in the club's Hall of Fame was all but guaranteed from the moment the idea was first mooted.

And the next legend to be installed would have been McPhail's team-mate, the talented Davie Meiklejohn, arguably the greatest player ever to play for Rangers.

If ever there was a man reared to lead the Light Blues, it was Meiklejohn. Born and raised in Govan, Meik never strayed too far from Rangers' great stadium. He lived within a ten-mile radius of Ibrox his entire life, and was one of a long line of great Rangers skippers, and probably the finest of the pre-war generation.

A tactically astute defender, and Bill Struth's main man on the park, he was a vital member of the highly successful Rangers sides of the 1920s and 30s. The late Willie Thornton, a Rangers legend himself, paid Meiklejohn the ultimate tribute when he called him 'the greatest player I ever saw'. Signed from Maryhill Juniors – for a small fee and a corrugated iron fence – Meik spent 18 years at Ibrox before retiring in 1936. During that time he amassed an astonishing haul of silverware, which included 12 league championship medals and five Scottish Cup badges.

Meiklejohn made a total of 635 appearances for Rangers, and while he always came across as a fair and balanced player, opponents would cross him at their peril, because he was a Ranger through and through and the club meant the world to him.

Celtic: Foley, Hogg, McGonagle, Morrison, Lyon, Paterson, Delaney, Buchan, McGrory, Crum, Murphy.

Rangers: Dawson, Gray, McDonald, Meiklejohn, Simpson, Winning, Fiddes, Venters, Smith, McPhail, Turnbull.

Referee: Mr J. Horsburgh (Bonnyrigg)

Attendance: 50,000

Rangers 5 Celtic 1

Wednesday, 22 May 1940
Glasgow Merchants' Cup semi-final

THIS wartime fixture – and thumping Rangers victory – was overshadowed slightly by the behaviour of certain players and a large section of the visiting support.

Prior to kick-off, there is little doubt that the Celtic players had their orders: 'Stop Alex Venters – by hook or by crook.' And that's exactly what they did, although by full time, it hadn't stopped Rangers handing out a footballing lesson to the Parkhead men.

Throughout the game, Venters was targeted by two Celtic players in particular, but weak officiating from a rookie referee saw to it that their crimes went largely unpunished.

And as the game entered its closing stages, Venters – the man of the match – kicked the ball away in frustration when the referee stopped the game. Mr Provan ordered the talented inside-forward to retrieve it, but he refused, and told the referee that whenever he walked off the pitch to get the ball, he was targeted by stone-throwing thugs on the terracing nearest to where it lay. That part of the ground was occupied by a rowdier element of the Celtic support, so Venters wisely decided against going anywhere near them.

But that wasn't good enough for the referee, who one wag suggested was 'acting like a little Hitler' in ordering the player to retrieve the ball. The referee sent Venters off, which was harsh on a player who had been kicked from pillar to post throughout a torrid 90 minutes.

The Light Blues sprung a pre-match surprise when they announced the inclusion of Jimmy Caskie, on loan from Everton. It would be the Possilpark man's only appearance for Rangers that season – although he would become a fully fledged Ranger shortly after the war ended.

The big difference between the teams was in attack, where the Rangers had more guile, more tricks in their locker, while Celtic appeared somewhat disjointed.

The game was only 14 minutes old when Rangers took the lead. Dougie Gray sent a teasing ball into the Celtic penalty area, and Caskie showed a fine sense of opportunism to turn the ball home.

Celtic then had a great chance to equalise, but Gray popped up on the line to clear with keeper Jerry Dawson beaten. Willie Lyon then missed a glorious opportunity when presented with an open goal. He dallied in the box, deciding which foot to use, and that gave Jock Shaw just enough time to clear.

Six minutes from the interval, Rangers forged two ahead. Venters let fly from 20 yards and while Smith looked to have the shot covered, the leather struck Lyon and was diverted inside the post. It was cruel luck for Celtic, but deserved on the run of play.

Five minutes after the resumption, Dawson was called into action to claw away a corner kick, but Joe Carruth was on to the loose ball in a flash and knocked it past the goalkeeper, although the score was disallowed for offside, which was a real let-off for Rangers.

Celtic had resumed the game on the offensive and the sense of frustration at the disallowed goal seemed to spur them on. In fact, within minutes of the disallowed goal, a stand-up fight involving two players from either side took place in the middle of the park. While the first half had been relatively 'crime-free', a noticeable level of needle had crept into the game after the break. Punches were thrown but the referee decided no further punishment other than a good scolding was necessary (which made his later decision to send Venters off all the more harsh).

This whipped the crowd up into a frenzy and approaching the hour mark, they saw Willie Thornton add a delightful third goal for Rangers. The lightning-quick centre fired home after a nice through ball from Venters split the Celtic defence.

Five minutes later Thornton was again on target when he outpaced Lyon and raced through to score a fourth, and just seconds later Caskie finished the scoring for the home side with his own second of the game.

Shortly after Caskie's goal, Paterson grabbed a consolation for Celtic via the penalty spot.

Five minutes from the end Venters suffered the ignominy of being sent off, although it seemed a dreadfully harsh decision. The player, with head bowed, walked slowly towards the pavilion, although less than a minute later he was followed by John Divers.

The following day, the papers – which extended very few column inches to football during the war – chose to lead on the fallout from the game, rather than an excellent performance by Rangers and their five-star victory over Celtic.

One newspaper commented: 'The dismissal of Venters and Divers was the culmination of a series of incidents that were completely at variance with the sportsmanship of football. In the first half there was some ankle-tapping, some sleekit stuff by certain players. Tempers were a bit on edge and they flared to a fiery state early in the second half when four players, two from each side, engaged in fisticuffs. The spectacle was anything but nice. Grown men behaving like ill-tempered children, some fighting, others adopting a belligerent attitude, and a few with cool heads struggling to separate those who had brought the game to the level of a dogfight.

'It struck me as strange that the players who behaved in such a disgraceful manner should belong to clubs who, more than any other perhaps, are emphatic in their instructions to their players on how to behave.'

No one escaped the wrath of the pen. The referee was criticised for failing to take a firmer grip on proceedings, and failing to make an early example of those persistent offenders.

A correspondent of a daily newspaper said: 'It was regrettable that so many in the crowd seemed to enjoy the scene, more regrettable that some of them should take an active part by the despicable action of stone throwing.'

The game was attended by 21,000, which raised £942 for good causes, and that should've been the end of the matter, but it wasn't.

One Scottish newspaper journalist was so disgusted by the conduct of a number of the players and supporters that he took it upon himself to publicly flog the offenders, reminding everyone that in this time of war, football was to be viewed as an entertainment, and not some sideshow of ugly tribalism.

He added: 'The Glasgow authorities have been highly generous in their attitude to football considering the limitations imposed on the game by Whitehall, and Wednesday night's carry-on was a shameful abuse of the privileges. Fighting among players and spectators, stone throwing from the terracing, thousands shouting and bawling like half-crazy people. A fine measure of thanks for favours granted.

'To my way of thinking the Scottish Football Association must make an exhaustive enquiry into the whole affair. It is not sufficient that they treat Venters and Divers as two players reported by the referee. They were the two who were ordered off, but there were others who similarly should have received marching orders.

'The SFA, for the good of the game, and to show the authorities they will not stand for such disgusting conduct, must be firm and resolute in their attitude.'

The correspondent added: 'Venters and Divers were ordered off, but the most offensive player on the field wasn't even cautioned. It's often the way that the man who plants onions never has a smell on his breath. Only those who eat 'em. The usual suspects caused the bother and perhaps it was a blunder to put a new referee on to this tie. It needed a man who knew his "men".

'The police have warned both clubs and the SFA that if assurances against a repetition of these scenes are not forthcoming they may prohibit such games in future.

'Anyhow, despite the hullaballoo, I'm informed there will be no large-scale inquiry. Indeed, the matter probably won't come before the Emergency Committee for a month yet. Because at the moment there is no such committee. A new one will be selected after the first council meeting of the SFA.'

Mind you, it looked as though the matter might be irrelevant as a huge question mark hung over the future of wartime football in Scotland.

A leading manager said: 'Even if the government permits us to carry on, it's questionable if we would be able to. We cannot cope with the heavy financial losses much longer, while the government's latest measure suggests it will be next to impossible to secure players, never mind spectators to watch them.'

Rangers and Clyde were apparently the only debt-free Glasgow clubs, while there was talk of some clubs dispensing with the services of their managers to cut costs.

Rangers: Dawson, Gray, Shaw, McKillop, Woodburn, Symon, Waddell, McPherson, Thornton, Venters, Caskie.

Celtic: Smith, Hogg, Thomson, MacDonald, Lyon, Paterson, Carruth, Lynch, Divers, Shields, Kelly.

Referee: Mr J. L. Provan (Chapelhall)

Attendance: 21,000

Rangers 8 Celtic 1

Friday, 1 January 1943
Southern Scottish League

IT'S not every Saturday you get the opportunity to stick eight past your greatest rivals, but that was the case on New Year's Day 1943. Both clubs were more or less at full strength and there was no suggestion before the match that either of the teams would be so superior as to even contemplate achieving what still stands to this day as a record Old Firm score.

Contemporary commentators were hoping for a clean, sporting contest that would be remembered for all the right reasons – and they almost got their wish. For more than half the match, spectators had enjoyed as clean a contest as anyone could have wished for, although when Malcolm McDonald and Matt Lynch, of Celtic, were ordered off, the dynamics of the game changed, and it was easy to have sympathy for the Celtic manager, who had prepared as prudently as possible for the contest, only to have his game plan shot to pieces by the expulsion of two of his players.

That said, cut out the incidents that led to the ordering offs – which were NOT as a result of foul play – and the traditional year's opener at Ibrox met all the requirements. Of the result, within just ten or 15 minutes, there never seemed any doubt that Rangers would bag both points and continue their quest for a fifth successive league title.

And before Celtic were forced on to almost persistent defence by being hopelessly weakened, Rangers were leading 4–1, and by then both points were booked for Ibrox.

Twice in the first four minutes Rangers scored through Jimmy Duncanson and Willie Waddell. Celts fought back to a one-goal margin, Davie Duncan scoring, and so at half-time it was Rangers who held the upper hand, but only a single-goal advantage.

The visitors were quickly into their stride at the beginning of the second half and Jimmy Delaney took full advantage of their ascendancy to draw matters level – or so he thought. The goal was ruled out for offside, and as quite often happens in those circumstances, Rangers went up the park and extended their lead.

Torry Gillick, who was guesting for Rangers, was bang in form and registered a third goal for the Light Blues, but in doing so followed through and struck his head off a post. Immediately, he was advised to leave the field, but stubbornly declined. With no substitutes permitted in those days, Gillick insisted he was going nowhere.

For a short period, at least, the numerical advantage lay with Celtic, as Gillick was at times wandering around the field in a state of shock. But in the 56th minute came the first incident, described in newspapers the following day as 'deplorable'. Fully 50 yards from goal, George Young sent a free kick into the Celtic box and the ball missed just about everyone before deflecting into the net off Waddell. Malcolm McDonald, the Celtic full-back, questioned the referee's award of a goal and was almost immediately ordered to the pavilion. Thus began a full-blown midfield 'conference', in which the entire Celtic side took part. McDonald insisted a Rangers player had been offside when the goal was scored, but the referee stood firm. Celtic were reduced to ten men.

After a little delay, the game was restarted but within three minutes the Celts were yet another man light, Matt Lynch this time receiving his marching orders. A free kick was given against the talented right-half and he, too, had words with the referee, although it was his wagging finger which left the match official with no option other than to send him for an early bath. As Lynch walked off in the direction of the pavilion, you could visibly see the heads go down amongst the remaining Celtic players.

As an aside, it's said that the Rangers striker Jimmy Duncanson was so annoyed with the unjust circumstances in which Lynch was despatched from the field that he sent a handwritten note to the football authorities pleading for clemency for the Celtic player.

The second sending off ended the match as a viable contest and despite the nine men of Celtic battling on gamely, they lost a fifth goal when Waddell strolled through the centre of their defence in brilliant style to smash the ball high into the net.

Rangers were then awarded a penalty kick, which Young converted superbly, and the still-dazed Gillick, operating apparently as if by instinct, netted twice in as many minutes to secure his hat-trick, although stories of him not being fully aware of this achievement until he got back to the dressing room are said to be wide of the mark.

Thankfully, the incidents surrounding both sending offs failed to have an adverse effect on the conduct of the crowd, and there was no call on the police, as had been the case in previous fixtures.

The attendance of 30,000 was one of the smallest recorded for such a big game, and while there was talk that the fixture had lost some of its appeal, that certainly wasn't the case for Rangers fans!

As a result of the record score, the league positions were practically unaltered. Rangers and Hibs were still equal on points, with Morton the best of the challengers. Celtic were tenth in the 16-team league.

That same afternoon, and in one of the greatest shows of irony, Johnny Crum scored SIX goals as Morton routed St Mirren 8–0 at Cappielow. The forward had previously been released by Celtic as the directors believed him to be past his sell-by date. The great Stanley Matthews played for the Greenock side that afternoon and set up six of the goals!

As a postscript to the big match, Celtic, in spite of the scoreline, might still have been grateful that Willie Thornton was abroad on military duty at the time of the match. He returned to Scotland the day after the contest and played for Rangers against Queen's Park, on 4 January, before heading back to the continent. Rangers won 5–2, and Thornton was on target. Torry Gillick should have played centre-forward in this game but was apparently only too happy to give up his place to Thornton.

It was said that Rangers' forwards were just irresistible against Queen's, thanks a good deal to the (Scot) Symon service which would have delighted the hearts of any bunch of forwards. The driving force of Venters and artistry of Thornton put a strain on their defence which could not be withstood, especially when combined with the contribution from Waddell, Duncanson and Johnstone. Thornton left straight after the game to return to his unit.

Torrance 'Torry' Gillick was a supremely skilful inside-forward who wrote his name in the history books as the only player to be signed twice by Rangers manager Bill Struth.

Gillick, from Airdrie, played for one of Glasgow's most prominent junior teams, Petershill, as a youth and signed for Rangers as a winger at the age of 18 in 1933, but it wasn't long until his services were being utilised in the centre-forward position, although his flexibility was a great tool for Struth.

He was razor sharp in front of goal and his record of 187 goals from 347 games is testimony to that prowess. As well as possessing a sharp mind and fantastic skills, he was also a nuisance to opposition defenders and barely gave them a moment's peace if they tried to start an attack by knocking the ball across the back line.

Gillick was only at Rangers for two years (1933–35) and left after winning a Scottish Cup medal to join Everton for a then joint record fee of £8,000 (Sam English had joined Liverpool for a similar fee just a couple of years before). Gillick was just 20 when he agreed to join the Merseyside club. He was capped five times by Scotland while plying his trade at Goodison Park, and was also part of the Everton side that won the English First Division championship in 1939.

Ten years after leaving Ibrox, Struth brought Gillick back to Rangers, and he had developed into a dashing forward with excellent ball control. He soon became an important feature of Rangers' great post-war side.

He had another five highly profitable seasons as a Ranger before leaving to join Partick Thistle where, at the age of 36, he still showed he could play a bit.

In total, he won one league championship medal, two Scottish Cup badges and two League Cup medals during his highly successful two-pronged Rangers career. He stayed with Partick Thistle for a single season and retired to look after his thriving scrap metal business. Gillick died in December 1971, ironically on the same day as another Rangers great, Alan Morton.

Rangers: Dawson, Gray, Shaw, Little, Young, Symon, Waddell, Duncanson, Gillick, Venters, Johnstone.

Celtic: Miller, M. McDonald, Dornan, Lynch, Corbett, Paterson, Delaney, McAuley, Airlie, McGowan, Duncan.

Referee: Mr W. Davidson, Glasgow

Attendance: 30,000

Rangers 4 Celtic 0

Saturday, 1 January 1949
Scottish League Division A

UP until the day of this match, just five Rangers players had scored hat-tricks in competitive Old Firm games. Jimmy Duncanson wrote his name into the record books by becoming number six. And what a fine treble it was too.

Rangers – as a unit – were fantastic. They played some terrific football and took the match to their opponents at every opportunity. But this game wasn't played on a stretch of smooth-rolled turf on a beautiful spring day. It was a Ne'erday game, played in typical January weather, with the pitch an uneven surface of frozen snow and the foothold treacherous even for the most skilful player, which made Rangers' performance all the more astonishing.

From the moment the great Willie Thornton edged Rangers ahead in just three minutes, the home side put on a tidy all-round exhibition of football, and he and several of his team-mates rather cockily made light of the ground handicap by indulging in passing of the most intricate kind.

Celtic on the other hand were much more direct in those opening minutes. The longer the game progressed, however, the more apparent it became that the visitors were far behind Rangers in skill and teamwork, and in most cases incomparable as individuals.

The left wing of Duncanson and Eddie Rutherford was a tremendous success. The outside-left gave Roy Milne, the Celtic right-back, a roasting, and his partner made a triumphal return to the inside position he adorned for so long before switching to help his club as an outside-left.

And, of course, there was always Thornton, pirouetting, swerving and dummying – completely at his ease. For once the right wing of

Rangers was an auxiliary and not the main part of the attacking machine, although still highly effective, and ready to take the lead at a moment's notice.

But Celtic couldn't take it personally, because no team would have held Rangers on this form, although perhaps one of their own players might have made their task much more difficult. Step forward Charlie Tully, whose attempts to dictate the type of game his side should play were ill-advised. His team-mates tried to caution him about attempting to dribble the ball in his own penalty box but Tully throughout was in one of his irritating, petulant moods.

The revenge Ian McColl took on Tully for the latter's joy day at his expense earlier in the season was absolute; the tall right-half had not played a finer game. His constructive skill was as evident as his stoutness in defence, and with Sammy Cox also in an attacking mood Rangers' forwards were served as they seldom had been for many months.

The match was probably won and lost just before the half hour, when Duncanson scored the first of his three goals. That said, the opening goal – Thornton's – was a masterpiece of timing – and a great deal more. Willie Paton sent a searching ball up the wing and Willie Waddell could've been forgiven for stopping in his tracks and realising that chasing a lost cause was a waste of energy. But he kept going, got possession of the ball inches from the line, and his cross was headed home by Thornton, who leapt higher than both Celtic defenders. It was a lesson for watching youngsters.

Rutherford had a foot in Duncanson's first and second goals in 26 and 43 minutes, and he took the corner kick from which the inside-left scored the final goal two minutes from time. The lack of confidence to which the Celtic defence had been reduced was in evidence when Duncanson completed his hat-trick a couple of minutes from the end. Rutherford sent over the corner kick and Duncanson, completely unmarked, stepped forward and headed into the net.

Celtic appeared to make their best efforts when they were three down, and many thought they were unlucky to be denied a goal on the hour, but a free kick was given against Gallacher when he charged Brown over the line as the goalkeeper held a lob from Paton. The charge seemed fair: the goalkeeper was on his feet and almost invited the challenge. Changed days indeed!

Rangers were back on top of the table, a position they were more accustomed to, and they were there on merit. At one stage of the season they had given the impression of being unsettled, but had enjoyed an excellent December, and produced genuine championship form. After defeating Celtic they were hot favourites to reclaim the title.

Celtic's recent form had suggested they were in with a chance against Rangers, but they were well and truly beaten by a team of power, purpose and perseverance, allied to skill of a high degree.

The foundation of Rangers' excellent first-half teamwork was laid by four men with fine ball control and intelligent application. In the two wing-halves, McColl and Cox, and the inside-forwards, Paton and Duncanson, there was a mobile square in which each of the quartet went about his job with almost telepathic understanding.

Just about every time Rangers went upfield, particularly when Waddell and Rutherford got into their stride, they looked like scoring. One was given the impression that had Celtic scored, Rangers would have ran up the park and countered it. Perhaps a simplistic view, but the Ibrox side really were in total control of this game from start to finish.

The manner of the defeat and difference in ability and all-round play between the teams must have given the folk at Celtic plenty of food for thought. They were lying eighth in the table and there was much work to be done at Celtic Park.

Jimmy Duncanson might have been the star of the show with a sensational hat-trick, but one man who went quietly – and effectively – about his business was Ian McColl, a true Rangers great.

The Alexandria-born 'midfielder' was at Ibrox 15 years and played well over 500 games. During his time wearing the famous jersey, he was a part of SEVEN league title winning sides, and collected a further seven major honours.

McColl was part of the great Rangers sides after the Second World War, a period when they ruled Celtic, and shared the glory with Hibs, who boasted their Famous Five forward line, although Rangers had their Iron Curtain defence of Bobby Brown, George Young, Jock 'Tiger' Shaw, McColl, Willie Woodburn and Sammy Cox. In the period directly after the war, until 1953, Rangers and Hibs shared all seven available titles.

In those days the formation was 2–3–5 – which was two full-backs, three half-backs and five forwards (two wingers, two inside-forwards and a centre-forward made up the five).

McColl played right-half, alongside the great Willie Woodburn, and just in front of George Young – one of the greatest ever Rangers and Scotland defenders.

In a ten-year period, Rangers averaged less than a goal against per game, an indication of just how strong they were defensively, and especially over such a long period of time.

McColl was a perfectly capable defender, but it was his ability to get the ball down and play football, often turning defence into attack, which made him a standout amongst his generation. He won 14 caps for Scotland and was a shoo-in for the Rangers Hall of Fame.

However, his star was waning slightly in the wake of the 1958/59 season, and with Scot Symon building a new team it looked as though McColl might be surplus to requirements. (Ironically, McColl had taken Symon's place when he joined Rangers!) But our Ian was recalled to the team for the 1960 Scottish Cup Final as a replacement for the injured Harold Davis – and what a swansong! Rangers beat Kilmarnock 2–0, and he was outstanding. McColl didn't play again, but became manager of the Scottish national team. During his five years in charge at Hampden, he twice oversaw wins over England – once each at Hampden and Wembley, the latter of which saw a stunning individual performance by Jim Baxter, who scored both goals in a match watched by 100,000. The victory was all the more remarkable considering Eric Caldow broke his leg during the game and his Rangers team-mate, Davie Wilson, was forced to play left-back.

He also guided the Scots to a stunning 6–2 win against Spain in Madrid, and had a winning percentage of 59.3 per cent – the second-highest of any Scotland manager.

Walter Smith recalled watching McColl in action: 'Ian was fantastic for Rangers as part of the famous Iron Curtain defence. I watched him play for the club when I was a boy, and he later had a successful career in management. Anyone who plays over 500 matches for Rangers has made a significant contribution to the club.'

Rangers: Brown, Young, Shaw, McColl, Woodburn, Cox, Waddell, Paton, Thornton, Duncanson, Rutherford.

Celtic: Miller, Milne, Mallan, Evans, Boden, McAuley, Weir, Johnston, Gallacher, Tully, Paton.

Referee: J.B. Smillie (Law)

Attendance: 85,000

Rangers 4 Celtic 1

Saturday, 1 January 1955
Scottish League Division A

'THEY will still be calling January the 1st "Hubbard Day" in a hundred years,' wrote one newspaper columnist the day after the little South African had wiped the floor with Celtic at Ibrox.

And many years later, Sir Alex Ferguson – who was at the game supporting Rangers – would insist that wee Johnny's first goal was the greatest he had ever seen!

Eighteen minutes had elapsed when Hubbard, stationed 40 yards from goal, cut inside to take a pass from Billy Simpson. He eluded Haughney, who had tracked back with him, with grace, ran the ball past Jock Stein, looked up and saw goalkeeper Bell dashing towards him. With an easy action he dummied him, left the Celtic keeper floundering on the turf and carried on to tap the ball home. It was a thing of real beauty.

Hubbard was one of the most consistent Rangers players of his generation. There are many who will say they never saw him play a bad game, and while that might be a bit of a stretch, this was certainly an afternoon when he showed real class.

The fact he scored three of Rangers' four goals after Simpson had collected the first entitled him to a great deal of credit, but it wasn't the mere scoring of goals that stirred the crowd. The way he took all three was an object lesson to all young footballers hoping to reach the top.

Aside from his first goal, his penalty kick, too, was a gem with all the cunning and craft of the first. Hubbard chose the spot where he wanted to place the ball and very deliberately he succeeded.

Anyone not at the game and reading of the great prominence of Hubbard could be excused for thinking it was a one-man show, but it was a long way from that. Not all of the Rangers players reached the excellence of Hubbard, but, collectively, they outshone Celtic in teamwork and finishing punch. George Niven once had to imitate a contortionist to turn a great shot by Boden over the bar, but that really was the only time his goal was in any danger.

The entire Rangers defence was sound, with George Young outstanding, and, in the absence of Ian McColl, Willie Pryde took his chance well. Willie McCulloch and John Prentice hardly compared with the opposite wing, and there was not a better ball player than Simpson, always a completely confident and troublesome centre.

Celtic's chief fault was that time and again they produced football moves that looked like doing damage, but far too often they dilly-dallied. They also disagreed with the award of a penalty to Rangers, but the referee had no hesitation in awarding it. The incident was the only unpleasant one in a grand sporting game, during which not a single player required the attention of the trainer.

Though Rangers had in Hubbard and Simpson the best forwards on the field, this well-deserved victory was not so much the outcome of superiority in attack as of far greater competency in defence. There was a compactness and a coolness in the performance of Young and his defensive colleagues that provided a striking contrast with the nervous, almost panic-stricken, display in the Celtic rear lines.

The crowd of 65,000 were anticipating a great match and, accordingly, were as well behaved as any Rangers–Celtic attendance before them. Both teams began proceedings as if the ball was something they had never seen before. In the first five minutes almost every outfield player was guilty of an error of judgement, as if they were suffering from some tremendous strain.

The first to pay the full price for his blunder was Stein, who in the ninth minute grotesquely sliced a clearance straight to the feet of Derek Grierson, who promptly and accurately gave Simpson a scoring chance which he took with glee. The centre-forward's footwork was neat and precise, and he flashed the ball well away from Andrew Bell to give the Light Blues the lead.

For the rest of the match Stein was unsure of himself, and resembled a rookie instead of the experienced defender he was. Twice, at least, he and Bell became so confused that although not a Ranger was within speaking distance of them they almost scrambled the ball into their own net. Hubbard was quick to realise that if he could add his skill to that of Simpson in the middle of the field, they could take full advantage of the Celtic confusion.

There was no such alarm at Rangers' end even though for most of the first half Celtic had a monopoly of the ball and were, chiefly because of the tremendous urge of Bobby Evans, the likelier looking team to score.

However, after half an hour Young was forced to put a stop to Jimmy Walsh with an illegal tackle. Willie Fernie chose to take the resultant free kick and he fairly tricked the opposition defence. He sauntered up to the ball in lazy fashion, as though he were looking for the head of a team-mate. Too late, Niven realised the Celt's true intention and he could do little or nothing but watch the ball, hit with unerring accuracy, reach the net at the junction of the crossbar and his right-hand post.

But if the first half had been far from distinguished, the second by comparison was almost rich in entertainment, although most of that entertainment came courtesy of Hubbard and Simpson, and at the expense of Haughney and Stein.

It was level pegging at the interval, and on resuming, Celtic, chiefly through Evans and Peacock, introduced a sprightliness that hitherto had been lacking. Although for the first 15 minutes or so following the turnaround, the run of play had favoured Celtic in the outfield, Rangers, with Simpson playing intelligently with his mates up front, gave the impression of being the more dangerous.

Prentice in 68 minutes added a grey hair or two to his opponents' heads with a tremendous shot which rebounded from a post with all Celtic in despair. Five minutes later Hubbard took his own particular way of creating even greater despondency with that delightful goal.

That counter raised the match from the level of mediocrity, and placed it on a pedestal of greatness, and the effect it had on Rangers was incredible. With happy abandon they went about the job of driving home their advantage, and ten minutes from time the Simpson-Hubbard combination was once more effective.

Simpson, out wide on the left, broke away, and Stein failed in his efforts to impede him. Simpson looked up and his pass was so precise that Hubbard, intelligently placed in the centre, had merely to direct the ball into a gaping goal. The South African was Johnny-on-the-spot and Bell stood not an earthly.

The Rangers supporters went daft with excitement; the Celtic fans headed for the exits. At their end, there were great open spaces on the terracing before the fourth goal came along in the final minute.

Grierson was chopped down by Evans and the referee rightly pointed to the spot. It was a grand gesture on the part of skipper Young to give Hubbard a chance at a hat-trick, and the little fellow certainly took full advantage of the opportunity to crown a great day's performance.

One of the outstanding features of the contest was the highly successful play of Simpson. The Irishman, in the past, had been accused of slowness and awkwardness. Here he participated in tactics that made him look fast and anything but awkward.

Obviously no little thought had been expended on how to get the best out of him, and Rangers had perfected a move capable of splitting open the best of defences. This master stroke consisted of Billy first-timing the ball to a mate and darting forward to get hold of a quick return pass. Stein was caught out with it, and seldom indeed could the centre-half reach the centre-forward for a tackle.

It has been said many times that there is no move in football that cannot be countered. This one by Simpson and his mates is one that will cause many headaches in a game before the answer is found.

Even allowing for the ineptitude of Celtic's inside-forwards all credit must be given to Young for his powerful defensive play. A continuance of this form and the big fellow will once more be considered as an international proposition.

Season 1954/55 might not go down in history as one of the most successful in Rangers' long and illustrious history, especially with a third-placed finish in the league, but on 'Hubbard Day' the fans had plenty to cheer about, and they let the little South African know.

Rangers: Niven, Little, Cox, Pryde, Young, Rae, McCulloch, Prentice, Simpson, Grierson, Hubbard.

Celtic: Bell, Haughney, Meechan, Evans, Stein, Peacock, Boden, Tully, Walsh, Fernie, Collins.

Referee: Mr C. E. Faultless (Giffnock)

Attendance: 65,000

Celtic 1 Rangers 5

Saturday, 10 September 1960
Scottish League Division One

THIS game marked a watershed moment in the history of Rangers. It was the afternoon when the 'Baxter effect' took hold of the Light Blues for the first time, and transformed the side from a team of tireless, non-stop runners – who still possessed an abundance of skill – into one capable of dictating games from the middle of the park.

It could also be argued that Jim Baxter was single-handedly responsible for making the left wing of Ralph Brand and Davie Wilson tick like never before and it was something the Celtic rearguard simply couldn't cope with.

For more than an hour of this encounter it was anybody's game at Parkhead, but after Rangers scored their second goal on 65 minutes they romped home in stunning fashion. It wasn't that Celtic collapsed, but rather that Rangers struck irresistible form.

One of the main obstacles to Celtic's progress was Harold Davis. By shrewd anticipation he intercepted many balls intended for John Hughes, on whom Celtic were quite clearly pinning their hopes of a breakthrough. When the big winger did take possession of the ball he was fiercely tackled by the growling Bobby Shearer and gradually forced out of the picture.

But Davis was the main man in defence; the Iron Man of Ibrox was man of the match AND he scored the best goal of the game. Davis could look back on this Old Firm match with pride – for at long last he had been 'accepted' by the Rangers fans.

He had taken many knocks from the terracing critics since taking over from Ian McColl in the Ibrox midline. They jeered him and said he wasn't Rangers class. But Harold, who was told he would never play again as a result of wounds received in the Korean War, ignored the jibes and the jeers and became a key man in the Ibrox defensive set-up.

Within two minutes of the start of the game Rangers scored. Davie Wilson swung in a corner kick and Fallon punched the ball straight to the feet of Alex Scott, who shot into the net. In brisk retaliation by Celtic, Hughes just missed the goal and Stevie Chalmers hit first the crossbar, then the post. Rangers led by a single goal at the break.

If the opening minutes of the second half were furiously contested, the final third belonged to the men from Edmiston Drive.

After 65 minutes Celtic's John Kurila, who had trailed Jimmy Millar very successfully, took on both the centre-forward and Wilson. In the end he battered the ball against Wilson, from whom it rebounded to Millar, who rounded Duncan Mackay before beating John Fallon at the second attempt.

Rangers, now playing with the confidence of a team holding a two-goal lead, really settled to a game and bamboozled Celtic with their crisp and accurate football. Baxter was immense in the middle of the park.

In 78 minutes, Millar, out on the right with Scott, crossed a ball which Fallon mishandled. Brand was on hand to take full advantage and knock it into the net. And just six minutes later, and with Rangers 3–0 to the good, Wilson took a pass from Brand and scored Rangers' fourth with consummate ease. Enter Harold Davis, and the big man bulleted home a header from a corner by Scott.

With the seconds ticking away, and the majority of Celtic supporters already halfway home, Chalmers beat Rangers keeper Billy Ritchie from close range to nab a consolation.

Referee Mr Phillips had an excellent game and was always firmly in command. Yet so honest were the exchanges that he had only once to rebuke a player, Millar, who apparently felt he had been unfairly penalised for a tackle on Jim Kennedy and showed dissent.

Rangers had a wonderful team that season, and it would be the start of a period of domination for Millar, Brand and co. The match in question was only the second of a long and arduous league campaign but Scot Symon's men couldn't have got off to a better start, winning their first five matches and scoring 23 goals in the process. Despite losing the sixth game narrowly to Dundee, who had a good side in the early 1960s, they won 11 out of their next 13, which put them on course for the championship.

In the end, Kilmarnock pushed Rangers to the last day of the season, and only a resounding 7–3 victory over, ironically, Ayr United in their final game – with Scott on target three times – would finally clinch the title by just a single point from the Rugby Park side.

This was Rangers' greatest league win at Celtic Park since the inception of the fixture in season 1890/91, and it squared the account for the season, with both sides on two wins apiece.

The secret of their victory lay in the grand half-back line of Davis, Bill Paterson and Baxter, while they possessed, in Jimmy Millar, the star forward of the day. The result got the Light Blues back on track and their confidence was restored. It had taken a battering at the start of the campaign when they suffered two defeats to Celtic inside a week (League Cup and Glasgow Cup). But it's amazing the tonic an Old Firm win provides to a team perhaps not in the best of health. And not just any old 1–0 or 2–1, but a stunning 5–1 away-day success.

And, as an added bonus, both sets of supporters were also on their best behaviour, with the police insisting it was their quietest Old Firm afternoon for many a year.

Davie Wilson was one of Rangers' biggest stars at the time, and was also without doubt one of the finest wingers ever to don the light blue. His shock of blonde hair helped him stand out from the crowd, but he did his talking on the pitch – and boy, could he play football.

But the Glaswegian star revealed that one of the club's biggest assets at that time was the relationship between the players. He called it 'first class', and it was no doubt the catalyst for great success on the park.

He said: 'We had a great spirit within the squad and everyone got on well with one another. I had a fantastic rapport with the other guys and we always looked forward to playing together.

'It didn't matter who played in the team, because we always had the belief that we would win. We were the best team in Scotland, and we enjoyed every moment of it. In fact, we were one of the biggest clubs in Great Britain, and even Europe, because the least we seemed to get from the European Cup in those days was the quarter-finals.

'I don't think there was an awful lot of difference between the standard of football then and now, although the players are probably much fitter these days. The full-backs are able to get up and down the park much more now.

'The season we went to Russia, 1961/62, I played 58 games and scored 30 goals, which wasn't too bad for a winger! When I was a young boy, I used to practise all the skills and techniques over and over again. I became so accurate that I scored more often than not, and that was probably because I always knew exactly where the goals and goalkeeper were.

'I normally hit the target, and that was down to the hundreds of hours practising as a young lad. I had also spent many hours crossing balls into the box and by the time I was with Rangers I could stick the ball on a threepenny bit, or rather Jimmy Millar's head, not that he had a head like a threepenny bit!

'Ralph Brand, Jimmy and I used to stay behind at the Albion training ground most days and would practise for hours on end. Davie Kinnear, our trainer, would shout at us to finish up, but the manager, Scot Symon, would tell him to leave us alone, as we were working on certain things.'

Wilson played almost 400 competitive games for Rangers, and scored 155 goals – and the talented winger also won nine major honours with the Gers, in the days when the Rangers ruled the roost.

One of Rangers' unsung heroes was Bill Paterson, who had signed for the club two years previous from Newcastle United. Paterson was tall and stylish, but was often criticised by some supporters for being more of a ball player than a crunching centre-half. He was good pals with Harold Davis off the pitch, and that close relationship also showed on the pitch as the two players developed a good understanding and always played well together.

Celtic: Fallon, Mackay, Kennedy, Crerand, Kurila, Peacock, Conway, Chalmers, Carroll, Divers, Hughes.

Rangers: Ritchie, Shearer, Caldow, Davis, Paterson, Baxter, Scott, McMillan, Millar, Brand, Wilson.

Referee: Mr H. Phillips (Wishaw)

Attendance: 43,000

Rangers 4 Celtic 0

Tuesday, 1 January 1963
Scottish League Division One

JIMMY Millar was the toast of Ibrox after a stunning display put Celtic to the sword in this New Year's Day cracker. But it was the day after the match before it was revealed that the Light Blues' centre-forward had dragged himself from his sickbed to play and score the goal that really finished off the Parkhead side.

Millar had woken up shivering on the morning of the match and right away he knew the signs ... flu. He had breakfast and travelled from his Edinburgh home three hours earlier than usual in an effort to shake off the bug.

When he arrived at Ibrox trainer Davie Kinnear took over and after some pills the flu bug was mastered and Jimmy made it on to the field – and on to glory! His goal in the 69th minute settled the game in Rangers' favour and from then on Celtic were completely outclassed.

The adrenaline kept Millar going the entire 90 minutes and when he returned to the dressing room after his triumphant display, he all but collapsed in a heap. His work was done.

Let there be no mistake about it, Rangers, at the end of the day, were the easiest of winners. Celtic had quite a lot of the play, but once either Pat Crerand or Billy Price, both good class wing-halves doing all that was expected of them, parted with the ball, the fire was drained from the Celtic team.

The Parkhead forward line, as they had done for a long time, lacked the killer touch, and although they occasionally got in a shot at Billy Ritchie, they really never looked like scoring.

What a difference with the Rangers attack, every one of whom was goal-minded, and ready at every opportunity to have a go. Mind you, sometimes too ready when a pass to a better-placed team-mate might have paid off.

The first goal came along in the 12th minute. Alex Scott, operating on the most treacherous part of the pitch, placed a short corner to Harold Davis. The wing-half neatly beat an opponent and shot. The ball struck Crerand, rose high in the air and dropped into the net.

Celtic's supporters, by their singing, did not seem too worried. But they were silenced midway through the second half. Ralphie Brand, out on the left, crossed a hard, vicious ball. Frank Haffey pushed it out but Millar was on the spot to hook it into the empty net. It was a cool and classy finish.

Rangers took complete control and within two minutes they were three up. John Greig and Brand inter-passed for 40 yards and completely upset the Celtic defence before Greig cracked in an angular 18-yarder that gave Haffey no chance.

Celtic were down and out, and their supporters started the retreat from Ibrox – and thousands of them missed the final goal. Bobby Shearer found Davis with a delightful pass, and the half-back cleverly beat Jim Kennedy and cut the ball across goal. It reached Wilson who slashed it home past Haffey. It was all too easy in the end.

The great players in the Rangers team – apart from Millar, whose club loyalty played such a vital part in the victory – were Jim Baxter and Ronnie McKinnon. The latter was a rock and had the measure of John Hughes, who eventually moved to outside-left.

Sadly, Baxter was at odds with the Rangers management at the time and although supporters were hoping he might stay at Ibrox for the rest of his career, he moved to Sunderland in 1965.

But still, Rangers had the teamwork, the pace and the punch, and on this showing – just halfway through the league season – they were on course to win the league championship.

It was a sporting game, the only discordant note being in the first half when referee McKenzie, a highly capable official, found it necessary to speak to McKinnon and Hughes, when the pair were needling one another.

Still, that 14-minute spell – from the 66th to the 80th – was all the Rangers needed to flex their muscles and show their superiority. The match was put to bed in that short period.

Millar, Greig and Wilson severely punished a defence that had been vulnerable throughout and in which more than one player did not appear to enjoy his job.

Rangers played all the football on a ground which was iron hard and slippery and which was believed to be unplayable, if only for the fact that it was dangerous for even the most skilful player. The least successful Rangers player was Shearer and that was because outside-left Frank Brogan was far and away the most impressive Celt.

The result put Rangers a single point in front of Partick Thistle in the First Division table. Aberdeen were five points behind the Gers, while Celtic languished 11 points behind the league leaders in sixth place. By the end of the season, Celtic would have fought their way up to third spot, but presented no real threat to Rangers, who won the title by six points from Kilmarnock.

If Jimmy Millar received the bulk of the praise at the start of this piece, then Ralph Brand should be the star turn at the end. For while Rangers have had many famous pairings down the years, like McCoist and Hateley, Smith and McPhail and Stein and Johnston, for Rangers fans of a certain vintage it was Millar and Brand all the way.

In simple terms, Brand is one of Rangers' greatest ever goalscorers – 206 goals in 317 games is a phenomenal return. And while we're at it, eight goals in eight internationals for Scotland tells its own story.

Born in Edinburgh in 1936, Brand was signed for Rangers by Bill Struth in 1952, after impressing the boss with a terrific display for Scotland Schoolboys against their English counterparts at Wembley. It would be a further two years before he made his debut for the Rangers first team but, when he did, the inevitable goals – which would become a big part of his DNA – followed.

He formed one of the most lethal partnerships in Rangers' history with the talented Jimmy Millar and the duo would regularly stay behind after training to work on their combination play, but Brand recently recalled the moment that was to change his life forever.

He said: 'When Bill Struth signed me, Rangers were the club to play for. There were a number of clubs in for me from south of the border – big clubs too – but the only team I ever wanted to play for was the Rangers, and that's the truth.

'And that was down to an uncle of mine, who came from Glasgow. He would come through to Edinburgh to visit the family and would inevitably bring through a Rangers scarf or tammy, or other bits and pieces. I was only a young lad and I loved when he came through for a visit. Rangers were ingrained in me from a very early age and I knew there and then who I would play for if I ever made the grade as a footballer.

'Being signed by a man with the pedigree of Bill Struth was mind-blowing. I was one lucky young man and I never forgot that. For me, it was a dream come true to play for my boyhood idols and I cherished every moment that I wore the famous blue jersey.'

Brand played his last match for Rangers in April 1965, when he scored the only goal in a 1–0 win over Third Lanark in the last league game of the season. He was sold to Manchester City in August that year for £30,000, but two years later he moved to Sunderland before finishing his career at Raith Rovers. He retired in 1970 and became a taxi driver in Edinburgh.

He still looks back on his time at Rangers with great fondness, though, even if he doesn't watch much football these days. 'It's not the same now. There aren't any players like Willie Henderson or Jimmy Johnstone to really entertain the supporters, and that's a great shame. I used to love watching wingers keep the ball and dribble. They were the real source of entertainment.'

Brand's partner Millar was also born in Edinburgh and arrived at Ibrox after a stint at East End Park, where he had made his mark in a good Dunfermline side. He cost £5,000 when he signed for Rangers in 1955. He actually arrived at Ibrox as a half-back, a position he would also fill on numerous occasions for Rangers, but soon became known as a fearless centre-forward, and arguably the most courageous Rangers ever had. He was also the first ever substitute used by Rangers.

Rangers: Ritchie, Shearer, Caldow, Davis, McKinnon, Baxter, Scott, Greig, Millar, Brand, Wilson.

Celtic: Haffey, Mackay, Kennedy, Crerand, McNeill, Price, Chalmers, Murdoch, Hughes, Gallagher, Brogan.

Referee: Mr A. McKenzie (Coatbridge)

Attendance: 55,000

Rangers 3 Celtic 0

Wednesday, 15 May 1963
Scottish Cup Final (replay)

THE Scottish Cup and Ralphie Brand went hand in hand in season 62/63. The dynamic inside-left scored in every single round, claiming a dozen goals in seven matches as Rangers lifted the national trophy for a 17th time.

Davie Wilson and Jimmy Millar also hit hat-tricks on the road to Hampden but it was Brand who grabbed all the headlines.

Well, most of them, as it seems everyone in the city wanted to see the replay, and so it was that more than 120,000 spectators squeezed into Hampden for the midweek replay – and what a show the players put on.

There were still many supporters locked outside when the 'Ground Full' signs went up, and when referee Tom 'Tiny' Wharton got the action underway, both sets of supporters were convinced it was going to be their night.

But there would always be one set of supporters heading home with a scowl on their faces, and with Brand in unstoppable form there was little chance of it being those decked out in red, white and blue.

After a goal against Airdrie, four against East Stirling and strikes against Dundee (in both games) and Dundee United, Brand was on target against Celtic in the original staging of the Scottish Cup Final. That tie had drawn 129,643, meaning a quarter of a million had watched both games!

The only point of the game that Rangers failed to master Celtic was for a few minutes at the start of the second half, but only because the game's chief architect, Ian McMillan, decided it was time for a quick rest! The veteran inside-forward's recall to the top team had led to a feast of fine football in the first half. Billy Price, in so many matches that season the inspiration of Celtic's attacks, was so harassed in trying to counter wily old fox McMillan that he devoted little time to aiding his forwards. It was Price who urged Celtic on to their second half effort, and no doubt because McMillan had temporarily faded from the play.

Wee Willie Henderson was on top form against Jim Kennedy. He revelled in the pass thrust inside the back by McMillan. The outside-right's cross after Millar had passed down the touchline was swept past Haffey in the seventh minute by Brand, and only tremendous defending by Billy McNeill, Celtic's best player throughout, denied Rangers a second goal until the last minute of the first half.

When it arrived, it was as a result of John McNamee trying to help his forwards and forgetting that a wing-half's primary duty is to defend. He was far from his best when Millar passed to Brand who, as Duncan Mackay retreated, closed in and shot. Haffey could not hold the fast, low shot and Davie Wilson followed up to fire into the net.

Celtic's best scoring chance occurred in the 55th minute when Price chipped cleverly to John Hughes, who delayed so long in shooting from only ten yards that two Rangers players blocked his shot. And that was about it for Celtic.

Once Brand's left foot, from 25 yards, had surprised Haffey with a shot which dropped as it came to the goalkeeper and bounced over the line, Rangers toyed with their opponents.

It is difficult to recall a Celtic team with so many players both timid and lacking in skill. The forward line, Chalmers apart, were ridiculously easily brushed off the ball by players who had no physical advantage.

The skilful thrusts of Baxter, alongside the industry and guile of Shearer, McMillan, Millar and Wilson, left Rangers streets ahead of their opponents, and therefore there was only one possible outcome to the match – and it happened.

The only disappointment for Rangers supporters was that there was no demonstration of success by the victorious team. Once the cup had been presented all the players disappeared into the pavilion in accordance with agreed procedure.

But that didn't mean the supporters weren't able to celebrate along with their favourites, because a crowd of more than 500 gathered in St Enoch Square an hour after the game to cheer the victors when they arrived at the St Enoch Hotel.

The Rangers team stood on the balcony above the hotel entrance displaying the cup to the crowd below, and traffic in the square was delayed for almost an hour as the supporters cheered and sang their songs.

Although the match drew one of the largest attendances ever recorded at a midweek game in the city, several hundred people, the majority wearing Rangers scarves, didn't get into the ground. They were left outside when gates at the west end of the ground were closed shortly before the kick-off.

Some were able to get in later at the east end of the ground, favoured mainly by Celtic supporters, where gates were still open 20 minutes after the start, but the others left disappointed. A few who tried to scale the wall surrounding the ground were pulled back by the police.

More than 500 police were on duty to control the crowds inside and outside Hampden, and to direct the long queues of cars and buses travelling to and from the ground. The large car park in Queen's Park recreation ground was reported full before the game began, and others were also packed.

The cup victory was not only the climax to a glorious season for the Ibrox club, but it also meant they equalled Celtic's record of 17 wins in the competition. There was no doubt it had been a glorious season for Rangers, who easily won the Scottish League championship.

But it was their Scottish Cup record in modern times which stood comparison with the best. Since 1930 they had appeared in 12 finals and won the lot.

In the first match at Hampden, it was the Celtic keeper Frank Haffey who had broken Rangers' hearts. He produced half a dozen wonder saves to deny the Rangers forwards time and again. All of his saves could easily have produced goals – and even when he was twice caught out of position, one was kicked off the line and Henderson hit the crossbar.

When Brand, Millar or Wilson broke through, the huge Haffey frame was an imposing sight on that goal line, for whatever they slammed at him with venom, he clutched with hungry claws. He stood between Rangers and the Scottish Cup.

That said, Rangers also threw it away. Expectedly, they were the more mature, intelligent side, and in spite of some close attention, they made numerous chances – and missed just about the lot.

Rangers were by far the cleverer side. They were always trying to create something, while Celtic depended on long, hopeful balls down the middle to John Hughes most of the time. This suited Ronnie McKinnon, who enjoyed his best match since moving to centre-half.

McKinnon was marked as one of Rangers' pre-match weak links by many of the critics – the other was freely given as David Provan, but both were outstanding. Provan had a magnificent game, controlling the sparky little Jimmy Johnstone cleanly and skilfully – and stroking the ball forward to Baxter, Brand or Wilson in intelligent fashion.

On the left side of defence Bobby Shearer overcame his lack of speed by crafty positioning, forcing Frank Brogan to play at half speed. This lack of free running on the Celtic wings left inside men Bobby Murdoch and Johnny Divers too much foraging to do, thus allowing Greig and Baxter to dictate the blueprint to attack from midfield.

Rangers' main first half problem was the isolation of Henderson. For long spells he was merely patrolling the line, partly because George McLean couldn't command the ball, draw the opponent, and move it to the winger – and also because wee Willie, unlike Davie Wilson, didn't burst his way into the game.

Nearing the interval the match was urgently in need of a goal, and it duly arrived, and Henderson was the architect. He slipped past Kennedy to the line and deliberately shot across a low ball to the near post for the waiting Brand to flick home. Rangers piled into attack and that was when they were lowered to earth with a bump.

Right on the interval, Mackay cleared a long ball upfield. The Rangers defence was caught out of position and Murdoch swiftly sent Hughes through on the blind side of McKinnon to shoot hard at Ritchie. The ball stopped on the line and Murdoch followed up to score.

Rangers could have won the cup in the dying seconds. Of course, they didn't, but the folk who deserved most sympathy were the thousands on the drenched terracing wearing knotted hankies on their heads. They had nothing but soaked clothes to show for it.

Rangers: Ritchie, Shearer, Provan, Greig, McKinnon, Baxter, Henderson, McMillan, Millar, Brand, Wilson.

Celtic: Haffey, Mackay, Kennedy, McNamee, McNeill, Price, Craig, Murdoch, Divers, Chalmers, Hughes.

Referee: Mr. T. Wharton (Glasgow)

Attendance: 120,273

Rangers 2 Celtic 1

Saturday, 24 October 1964
League Cup Final

THE brilliance of Jim Baxter was often highlighted as the catalyst for so many great Rangers victories, and quite rightly too, but it would be tough to imagine the Ibrox side winning the 1964 League Cup without goal machine Jim Forrest in the side.

He had scored in every round of the competition (bar a 0–0 sectional match against St Mirren at Love Street), notching a staggering 18 goals in the other nine games.

And the Glasgow-born centre-forward was hardly a League Cup one-season wonder, as the season before he had scored in all rounds (again apart from one), amassing 16 goals. This included a four-goal haul in the final at Hampden against Morton, with 106,000 looking on. He also scored twice in a sectional match against Celtic at Parkhead – his Old Firm debut – when he was just 18 years old.

In the season in question, 1964/65, he fired 57 goals in all competitions – including six in the European Cup, against sides such as Inter Milan and Red Star Belgrade. Forrest was just two short of the British record held by Jimmy McGrory for the most goals scored in a season, which makes it absolutely criminal to think that his career was abruptly halted after Rangers' shock 1–0 Scottish Cup defeat at Berwick Rangers in 1967. Scapegoats, who needs 'em?

But back to the cup final and Rangers retained the League Cup with as gallant a performance as they had ever produced on the big stage, especially as they were forced to withstand a hefty Celtic challenge in the first half. At times they may have seemed fortunate, but they created goalscoring opportunities later which their opponents failed to do and, in the end, emerged as masters.

Behind their success was the influence of Baxter, who laid on the second goal for Forrest after 42 minutes, the centre-forward having 11 minutes earlier scooped up the ball after an indecisive clearance by Tommy Gemmell and swept it into the net.

When Jimmy Johnstone scored for Celtic in 71 minutes, after good work by John Clark and Stevie Chalmers, the stage was set for a grandstand finish which had the crowd of 91,000 in almost continuous uproar.

But Rangers, as they had demonstrated so often in the past, were extremely hard to beat once in front, and this Celtic forward line, weak in the inside positions and unable to take advantage of the prompting they received from the men behind, simply could not beat down the Rangers' defence.

John Hughes and Johnstone exchanged their outside-forward positions, but Baxter, Rangers' captain, cunningly countered this move by switching Davie Provan and Eric Caldow, so that Chalmers, ill-supported by Bobby Murdoch and Johnny Divers, never got the ball in such favourable positions as Forrest.

To begin with Celtic forced the pace but failed to capitalise on the chances which fell their way, their main stumbling block being Jimmy Millar, whose work in the middle of the park was superb – twice he baulked the elusive Johnstone in full cry for goal – and when Davie Provan headed a Divers effort off the line – which had Billy Ritchie beaten all ends up – the signs must have appeared ominous to the Parkhead team.

In the second half, with no goals on the scoreboard, Celtic's defence, not now so sure of itself, was in trouble early as Rangers' outside-forwards began to swing the ball into the middle, and John Fallon, who just before the interval had held a terrific drive by Baxter, had some anxious moments as his outfield colleagues showed signs of panic.

The scene was further transformed when Forrest scored the opening goal and, despite spirited retaliation by Celtic, in the course of which Ritchie saved from Murdoch and Chalmers, the issue was sealed when the same player grabbed the second.

By and large it was an engrossing game, in which fortunes alternated with astonishing rapidity. It had its rough and tough moments, in two of which Millar fell foul of the referee and had his name taken, but will be remembered as one of the great encounters between these two famous clubs.

Mind you, Celtic left Hampden bitterly resentful at being refused what they maintain was a perfectly good goal in the 55th minute, and at a time when Rangers were leading 1–0.

They were resentful to the extent of finding chairman, Bob Kelly, manager Jimmy McGrory and assistant manager Sean Fallon openly accusing referee Hugh Phillips and a linesman of a gross blunder.

Their vehement criticism arose from an extraordinary incident. Bobby Murdoch came on to a stray ball and shot for goal. The greasy ball spun from Billy Ritchie's arms and squirmed towards the line as the keeper made a desperate attempt to get to it.

Now the question is ... was the ball OVER the line before he grabbed it and cleared, or did he get to it before it crossed the white line?

Ritchie, like referee Phillips, had his lips sealed – by order of the League – and Scot Symon made it clear his keeper mustn't be quoted. But it's alleged Ritchie did say, on the quiet, to a respected journalist, that the ball was at least NINE INCHES on the safe side when he clutched it.

And the referee, also officially gagged at the end of the game, was overheard telling a Hampden official afterwards that he hadn't the slightest doubt the ball was still in play. In fact, he was taken aback that so much controversy had been placed on the incident.

Nevertheless, the fury of the 'Was it a goal?' saga raged long after the jubilant Rangers players had come back from their victory salute in the middle of the pitch, where captain Baxter was raised shoulder high after throwing the League Cup high in the air and catching it with a whoop of joy.

Rangers chairman John Lawrence said: 'It was a thoroughly wholesome match. I have congratulated Celtic on a very fine display against us. But I must say that to retain the trophy without our two regular wingers was unquestionably a tremendous achievement.' Celtic chairman Bob Kelly said: 'I am convinced in my own mind that the ball was over the line. I am also convinced we should have been awarded a penalty early on when Johnstone was brought down. Well, that's how things can go. We went out to play football but the breaks went with Rangers and though naturally disappointed, we must leave it at that.'

It was a massive day for Eric Caldow, who was returning to the top team after more than a year out following a leg break while playing for Scotland against England. He admitted to being nervous in the opening moments, but once he settled, felt as though he had never been away. Laughingly he remarked to a team-mate: 'Maybe I might even get my Scotland place back. I feel I could take it without a moment's anxiety.'

He, too, emphasised that the ball WASN'T over the line, and he was close to the Ritchie save.

The Celtic players, still searching for their first major medal, looked stunned in disbelief when the final whistle went and they were hit with the fact that once more they had lost out. Yet, it was handshakes all round, and even Stevie Chalmers came off the field with Jimmy Millar's arms around his neck.

Manager Scot Symon did not hide his anger at Millar's booking, and said: 'To me, there was nothing to warrant his booking.'

Meanwhile, controversial plans were afoot to remove five clubs from the Scottish League. It was the brainchild of the bigger clubs, and their endgame was fewer fixtures and, ultimately, a British league. However, the clubs under threat – which included Albion Rovers – took their case to the Court of Session and enjoyed a famous victory.

The bigger clubs reasoned that too many teams meant too many league games, and insufficient time to fit in the likes of European ties and glamour friendlies.

The British league proposal would've seen the eight leading clubs in the Scottish and English first divisions divided into two sections, playing home and away games in midweek from the qualifying to the semi-final rounds, with the final at either Wembley or Hampden.

It was an enterprising scheme which organisers believed would go some way to attracting back fans who were no longer prepared to suffer the tedium that went with the poor quality of so many of the domestic league games. It would also assure the continued efforts of those clubs no longer in with a chance of winning the league championship to fight for one of the eight qualifying places.

The plans might have failed in 1964, but ultimately they have never gone away.

Celtic: Fallon, Young, Gemmell, Clark, Cushley, Kennedy, Johnstone, Murdoch, Chalmers, Divers, Hughes.

Rangers: Ritchie, Provan, Caldow, Greig, McKinnon, Wood, Brand, Millar, Forrest, Baxter, Johnston.

Referee: Mr H. Phillips (Wishaw)

Attendance: 91,423

Rangers 1 Celtic 0

Wednesday, 27 April 1966
Scottish Cup Final replay

IS there a better stage to score your first goal than at Hampden Park in the final of the Scottish Cup – and it's the winner against your biggest rivals?

Probably not, so step forward Kai Johansen.

And the Danish full-back's achievements were all the more credible given Rangers were just about up against Celtic's European Cup-winning team in the replay, with just Willie Wallace absent.

So, when the final whistle sounded at the end of this pulsating midweek replay, you can imagine the joy in the Rangers end. It was raw and unharnessed.

Celtic had won the first of their nine successive league titles that season, and just 12 months later would be crowned kings of Europe – but for one night only they were second best to Rangers.

It was the Ibrox side's 19th Scottish Cup success, and it came during a rough, unpolished contest in which it was absolutely necessary for every single Ranger to stand up and be counted.

The vital goal was scored 20 minutes before the end of a relentless, ruthless battle.

It was a goal worthy of winning any trophy and its quality was matched only by its unexpectedness. Willie Johnston wriggled his way to the byline and when George McLean missed the ball a few yards out it ran through to Willie Henderson. The wee man's shot was cleared off the line by Bobby Murdoch, but only as far as Johansen, who let fly from 25 yards and the ball flew low and hard into the net.

Thus are cups sometimes won and in this instance the deed was done by a defensive member of a side whose forwards, compared with the opposition, had given little indication that they were capable of such damage by themselves.

Rangers' triumph, against all the odds, was built on a magnificent defence and some fortune since Celtic came close to scoring many times. Once again, the outstanding figure afield was Jimmy Millar, always there when he was needed most, supporting John Greig, Ronnie McKinnon and Johansen, and also finding the time and energy to urge his forwards on. Behind them Billy Ritchie was a safe pair of hands.

Celtic had their opportunities, but the fact is this was the fourth successive game in which they had failed to score a goal, and so all the effort and lead-up work, much of which was skilfully directed by Bertie Auld, came to nothing.

Jimmy Johnstone was again the most enterprising of their forwards. He made life tough for Davie Provan after the Rangers left-back had been booked for a third foul on the winger in the first half, a first period that had been most notable for the recklessness of many of the tackles. Bodies and boots flew in with scant regard for life and limb, and there were endless stoppages for free kicks.

The battle raged to and fro, and at one point Johansen and John Hughes held hands as they raced down the touchline, although neither was trying to be familiar!

Rangers struggled hard and unsuccessfully to find a rhythm, whereas Celtic, moving with cohesion and purpose, almost found the target more than once. Auld laid on three chances, of which Stevie Chalmers missed two and Hughes the other, while McBride had a shot diverted past the post.

Rangers' response was limited almost wholly to a shot from Greig which dipped over and another from Bobby Watson which was deflected for a corner by John Clark.

The start of the second half was almost identical to that of the first game as Celtic, now with the strong wind at their backs, swept down, looking for the goal which would break this agonising deadlock. Billy McNeill headed just wide, Ritchie saved a shot from Johnstone, and when McBride flicked the ball to Chalmers the centre-forward fired over the top.

Then came what proved to be the decisive goal, although immediately afterwards Ritchie, who had previously saved from Chalmers when he stuck out a leg to the ball, again saved from the centre and for good measure stopped a fine attempt from McNeill.

McBride, by this time limping, changed places with Hughes, but it was Rangers, in a breakaway from heavy Celtic pressure, who almost scored again, Ronnie Simpson thwarting Johnston with a splendid save.

Celtic kept up the pressure as they desperately sought the equalising goal and Hughes, Auld and McNeill weren't far away. But as the crowds melted away from the Celtic end, Rangers continued to hold out, sometimes just clearing their lines in an attempt to alleviate the pressure. But Celtic, who were so confidently expected to retain the trophy, instead saw it slip through their fingers.

For Rangers, McKinnon and Greig were simply impenetrable in the heart of defence. Nothing Celtic threw at this magnificent pair could get through, as they built a ring of steel around goalkeeper Ritchie.

Rangers' captain Greig was a happy man after the game, and said: 'This is the greatest moment of my career. On the two previous occasions I played in a cup final, we were favourites. But this time we were underdogs and victory gave me tremendous satisfaction. Most of the credit must go to manager Scot Symon, who planned the blueprint for success.'

Symon, not known for his long post-match press conferences, said: 'What more can I say than that I am delighted.'

Apart from scoring the winning goal – no mean feat for a defender in a cup final – Johansen had his finest game against bogey man Hughes, and arguably his finest ever in a Rangers strip. And the occasion almost became too much for him. Later, with tears in his eyes, he said: 'I honestly cannot say much tonight. I am overwhelmed. I didn't think my shot would reach the net as the goalmouth was too crowded. This is my greatest moment in football.'

It was Johansen's first goal for Rangers, and he was hardly likely to forget it.

The Great Dane was a 1960s trailblazer. Arriving at Morton from his native Denmark mid-decade, he stayed at Cappielow a season before clinching a £20,000 move to Ibrox. He had 20 caps before moving to Scotland, but would win no more, as the game in Denmark at that time was 100 per cent amateur and those who turned professional were excluded from representing their country.

But Johansen embraced his new life in Scotland and shortly after arriving, was picked to play in the Stanley Matthews testimonial match at Stoke, which was quite something. However, in his early days at Rangers it would appear that manager Scot Symon's definition of a defender – that he was there to defend and nothing else – stunted Johansen's growth and it wasn't until the shackles were removed that he was able to show just how adept he was at getting up and down the wing and posing a threat to opposition defences.

Johansen would go on to help Rangers reach the European Cup Winners' Cup Final in 1967, but while that one ended in defeat, he made 238 appearances for the Light Blues before announcing his retirement at the relatively young age of 30. After a spell coaching in South Africa, he returned to Scotland and was successful in turning his hand to many business ventures.

Later on, the players retired to the St Enoch Hotel and thousands of fans had turned up to wish them well, but as they showed off the cup from the balcony, hundreds of Celtic fans poured out from the nearby underground station – and charged straight at the celebrating Rangers supporters.

Fans cowered on the ground as bottles flew overhead, while many supporters were trampled.

By midnight hospitals had treated 60 fans for everything from bruises to a heart attack. Two were detained. Police said there had been 26 arrests – six at the game. One man collapsed and died at the ground, while three others had collapsed and died during the first game!

The first match had been as tough as they come, with both teams refusing to concede an inch. The result had seemed inevitable long before the end, and frankly it would have been a travesty had either of the teams lost. In fact, many reckoned it was one of the greatest games they had seen at Hampden, and certainly the closest. Both teams had chances, and perhaps the greatest of these fell to Greig, who had a terrific game, but on this occasion he failed to score.

Billy McNeill had also headed against the Rangers crossbar.

Rangers surprised many by switching wingers Henderson and Davie Wilson seconds after the start, but while neither side could find a goal, that wouldn't be the case in the replay, thanks to Johansen.

Rangers: Ritchie, Johansen, Provan, Greig, McKinnon, Millar, Henderson, Watson, McLean, Johnston, Wilson.

Celtic: Simpson, Craig, Gemmell, Murdoch, McNeill, Clark, Johnstone, McBride, Chalmers, Auld, Hughes.

Referee: Mr T. Wharton (Clarkston)

Attendance: 96,862

Celtic 2 Rangers 4

Saturday, 14 September 1968
Scottish League Division One

THE cheer which erupted from the Rangers end at Parkhead when Willie Johnston headed in a Sandy Jardine cross in 89 minutes was loud enough to rip the old roof from its fixings. In the ten minutes or so beforehand it had been touch and go as to whether Rangers could hold on to their slender lead. Now they would!

In those dying moments, when Celtic – who had twice been two goals down – were chasing a late equaliser, Rangers hit their rivals with a classic sucker punch and ensured both league points would be heading back to Ibrox.

The speed with which the Light Blues broke on the counter-attack was frightening, especially so late in the game when most were trying to conserve what little energy they had left. From Willie Henderson, out on the left, the ball was played across the edge of the penalty area to Johnston, who, in turn, whipped it out to Jardine on the right-hand side. The Celtic defence was completely caught out, and when the ball was played back into the middle, Johnston was on hand to nod home.

It was classic Rangers, and it was a goal from which Celtic had no time to recover. It also ensured Rangers' first victory in an Old Firm match for exactly 12 months, and their first at Parkhead since New Year's Day 1964. Moreover, it was a result which injected hope into the domestic game, for Celtic had been ruling the roost in Scotland and Rangers had already finished runners-up to their cross-city rivals in the previous three seasons.

But just as important as the victory itself was the manner in which it was achieved. Sure, the points were important, but Rangers' greatest need at that time was self-confidence, and by winning so convincingly at Parkhead, they achieved exactly that.

There was a Fair Cities Cup tie against Vojvodina just three days away and their confidence could not have returned at a more opportune time. In fact, the Yugoslavs would be sent packing from the competition as Rangers went all the way to the semi-finals.

For the match at Parkhead, manager Davie White had decided to engage Celtic in the fresh air of open conflict, and with the champions' defence more easily harassed than one might have expected it was a policy that paid off handsomely. With Celtic having to give best to Andy Penman and John Greig in midfield, Rangers strikers Orjan Persson and Johnston were able to enjoy a field day. During the Ibrox depression (three successive years of playing bridesmaid) those two had come in for their fair share of criticism, but this time they more than justified their selection. Tommy Gemmell had rarely a more uncomfortable afternoon than he had against the powerful Swede, and Johnston, showing the sharpness which made him the scourge of defences a season or two previous, was always there or thereabouts to carry the fight to Celtic keeper Ronnie Simpson.

It was Persson who first brought hope to Rangers followers that this at last was to be their day, when in 15 minutes he completely flummoxed Simpson with a header. Having failed to penetrate Celtic's right flank, Willie Mathieson changed the point of attack to the right, and when wee Willie Henderson crossed into the box, Persson sent it hurtling diagonally across Simpson and in at the far post.

Barely a minute later, Willie Wallace, having taken the ball to the byline, whipped it away from Norrie Martin and across an open goal, but Bobby Lennox was for once too fast off the mark for his own good and ended up in the back of the net instead of the ball.

It was a glorious chance missed and one which would be punished almost immediately, for a precision Penman pass caught Billy McNeill off balance and sent Johnston darting through the middle with only the goalkeeper to beat. This he did by gliding the ball past Simpson as he rushed out to intercept.

Thus, astonishingly, Rangers were two up, and to say that their supporters were ecstatic would be putting it mildly. Several even had to receive medical attention behind the goal after being caught up in the delirium.

But they were soon brought back down to earth. In 29 minutes George Connelly dispossessed Persson and sent a glorious pass out to Johnstone, who drew Martin towards him and then clipped the ball across to the waiting Wallace for a tap-in.

Johnstone then struck the bar following a mazy run, and Martin and Simpson pulled off one magnificent save after another as play swung from end to end, but there would be no more goals until after the break.

With 20 minutes of the second period gone, Jardine centred and Penman scored at the second attempt. It was 3–1 to Rangers, but Celtic were far from finished. Wallace immediately reduced the arrears, swivelling round on a Lennox pass and deceiving Martin with a shot which slithered underneath his body.

In the last five minutes, Johnstone and Johnston had their names taken, the former for apparently talking out of turn and the other for time-wasting.

And all that remained was for Willie Johnston to add the icing to the cake with that late goal.

In the aftermath of this great victory, it was probably the last thing on the minds of the vast Rangers following, but another Old Firm defeat would have been catastrophic. Celtic would have gained a huge advantage in the long race for the flag, but as it transpired Rangers played with a verve and confidence that had been missing for so long, and which earned them two well-deserved points. The vital difference was in midfield. Rangers played a 4–3–3 and Penman was the man who mattered most. He maintained a steady stream of passes which kept the Celtic defence fully stretched, and with Johnston and Jardine snapping at McNeill and Clark, it was a long time since the home defence had endured such an unhappy afternoon.

Persson too had a most effective 90 minutes, spending a lot of time in midfield, but pushing forward now and again to give Gemmell an uncomfortable time. Mind you, to Celtic's credit they made a fight of it. Twice they pulled one back when two down but never at any time did they produce the type of football they were capable of.

They were unlucky early on when a Wallace cross beat the entire Rangers defence and ran along the front of the goal. If Lennox had been a fraction slower off his mark he would have met it, but as it was he had overshot the runway.

And it was only a great save by Martin from a point-blank Wallace effort that stopped Celtic levelling matters. Johnstone too came close with a shot which Greig was happy to deflect off the crossbar.

Things were even closer at the other end with Simpson again confirming his undisputed talent with two second-half saves from Persson which were out of this world.

First he twisted to his right to hold with one hand what looked a cert after Gemmell had bungled a Johnston cross. Then he leapt with amazing reflex action to touch a 20-yard left-footer away when it looked as if the ball had beaten him. He was certainly on his toes all evening.

Thankfully, all the action remained on the field as opposed to off it, and much of the credit for that went to an earlier conversation between Celtic manager Jock Stein and Bailie John McElhone, Glasgow's senior magistrate. The duo came up with a scheme to prevent violence among rival groups of supporters by playing a schoolboys' match directly after the main event, and it was hailed a big success.

McElhone said: 'I would recommend this, or any similar scheme, to the Rangers directors, and ask them to consider doing this for the next game between the clubs, which will be held at Ibrox.'

After the match, the Celtic supporters stayed on to watch the schoolboys' game while the Rangers supporters dispersed without incident.

Just ten supporters were arrested inside Parkhead while four others were cautioned outside the ground. A police officer said it had been very quiet outside the stadium. Twenty-nine people were treated for injuries, with 11 taken to the Royal Infirmary.

Bailie McElhone said that, considering the type of game, tension and the number of people attending, the arrest count was 'reasonable'. He added: 'I was discussing the situation with Sir James Robertson, the chief constable, and there is an indication that the crowd, by and large, are prepared to cooperate with the police. This is a tremendous thing.'

Celtic: Simpson, Gemmell, O'Neill, Brogan, McNeill, Clark, Johnstone, Lennox, Wallace, Connelly, Hughes. Sub: Chalmers.

Rangers: Martin, Jackson, Mathieson, Greig, McKinnon, Hynd, Henderson, Penman, Jardine, Johnston, Persson. Sub: Smith.

Referee: Mr R. H. Davidson (Airdrie)

Attendance: 75,000

Rangers 1 Celtic 0

Saturday, 24 October 1970
League Cup Final

THE main image from this final will remain etched in the minds of all Rangers supporters present at Hampden that day. Derek Johnstone rising majestically like a phoenix to nod the ball past a despairing Evan Williams. Either side of him a Celtic defender, floundering in their duty to protect their goal.

But rather than criticise Billy McNeill or Jim Craig, one must congratulate the goalscorer, fresh out of school and still two years shy of being able to celebrate this historic achievement with anything alcoholic.

The match took place slap bang in the middle of Celtic's successful nine-in-a-row period, but perhaps someone forgot to inform the 16-year-old Dundonian. The Parkhead side were nailed-on certainties to continue their dominance of Scottish football and with John Greig unavailable for Willie Waddell's side, the task before the Light Blues looked insurmountable.

It would be a stretch to say Rangers were in disarray in the lead-up to the big game but the cultured Dave Smith was again overlooked while Waddell included two centre-halves (Colin Jackson and Ronnie McKinnon) and two centre-forwards (Colin Stein and Johnstone) within the starting 11.

Johnstone had made his first-team debut just a month beforehand, scoring twice against Cowdenbeath in a 5–0 league win. But apart from an appearance off the bench in a home game against Motherwell a fortnight later, the teenage striker's next domestic outing was in front of 106,000 Old Firm supporters at Hampden.

A watershed moment for the talented kid? You bet, but obviously manager Waddell had no doubts that his teen prodigy was made of the right stuff, and he was proved right as DJ's goal gave the Light Blues their first major trophy since 1965.

But it was Celtic who were on the attack right from the start, with Willie Wallace playing a perfect through ball to Jimmy Johnstone, who scampered down the right, rounded Alex Miller, took the ball to the byline and crossed. Thankfully big Peter McCloy was there to cut out the danger before it reached Wallace or Harry Hood.

Rangers hit back with a lovely combined move between Alex MacDonald and Willie Johnston which left Alfie Conn with just Williams to beat, but the keeper dived at the right-half's feet to save the day.

Another touchline dash by Johnston left Craig trailing, but his cross went out of play on the other side, while in yet another Ibrox foray, Willie Henderson cut the ball back to Johnstone, who lost a golden opportunity by delaying his shot.

It was 90 miles per hour stuff and the huge crowd were loving it.

Jackson then had a wonderful tackle on Jimmy Johnstone, when the wee winger raced past all before him following a perfect pass from Bobby Murdoch. And 'Bomber' Jackson was again in the spotlight when he rose to head a Johnston cross inches over the bar.

Big DJ lost another opportunity on a through ball from MacDonald by shooting wide, but by now Rangers were looking the more likely to break the deadlock.

However, George Connelly was booked in the 24th minute for a blatant foul on Johnston, after the left-winger had left him for dead.

Moments after this, police raced to the Celtic end of the ground when fighting broke out, and a number of fans were removed from the ground.

And with just five minutes until half-time, Rangers went ahead. Henderson began the move with a pass inside to Alex MacDonald, who sent it down the right-hand side to Johnston. Wee Bud centred on the run and there was DJ inside the box to head neatly inside the far post, past the despairing arms of Williams.

A minute from the interval, only a wonder save by Williams prevented Johnstone from nabbing his second of the afternoon.

Jimmy Johnstone was still Celtic's ace card up front as the Parkhead side went all out for an equaliser during the opening moments of the second period. And when the winger was fouled by Alex Miller, Bobby Murdoch swept the free kick to Lou Macari whose header flew just inches over the bar.

In a clear case of déjà vu, another free kick to Celtic for Miller impeding Johnstone was again taken by Murdoch and yet again Macari's header just narrowly cleared the crossbar.

Rangers then had a lucky break when Celtic had a penalty claim rejected. McCloy lost the ball when challenged by Macari. Both players fell and the ball broke loose, with Celtic insisting big Peter had held Johnstone down, but referee 'Tiny' Wharton waved away their claims.

Celtic were now at full throttle and the Rangers defenders were clearing the ball everywhere and anywhere just to keep out the eager Parkhead forwards.

In the 63rd minute, Celtic brought on Bobby Lennox for Hood. Wallace then squandered a golden chance when Murdoch beat three men in a mazy dribble before teeing the ball up for his team-mate, but to the chagrin of the Celtic followers, the Parkhead centre shot wildly over.

Ten minutes from the end McCloy denied Celtic by leaping through the air to turn a Wallace drive aside in spectacular fashion, and right at the end it was Celtic's turn for a lucky break when Colin Stein shot against the far post and into the arms of grateful keeper Williams.

There was no time for any more action and Rangers were ecstatic when Wharton sounded the full-time whistle. Their supporters were overjoyed, as were their idols on the pitch. Willie Waddell's men had won their first trophy for five long years.

All the credit went to the victorious Rangers side for upsetting the odds, especially as seven days before the final, Rangers had been in complete disarray after losing 2–0 to Aberdeen in a league match at Ibrox. Supporters voted with their feet, and a good 15 minutes before the end, the exits were packed with fans leaving the ground. The crowd of 39,763 had dwindled by two-thirds by the time referee Alistair Mackenzie brought the game to a halt.

It was the last thing Waddell wanted or needed the week before a cup final, but the manner in which he turned things round, and lifted his players, was to be commended.

It was a personal triumph for Johnstone, just three weeks short of his 17th birthday. He also became the youngest player to play and score the winning goal in a national cup final in Britain. In England the record had been held by Howard Kendall, who played for Preston against West Ham at Wembley in 1964 – 20 days before his 18th birthday.

After the match, Johnstone was carefully shepherded out of Hampden by coach Jock Wallace, and the youngster only had time to say: 'I felt great when the ball hit the net.'

And making sure DJ kept his feet on the ground, coach Wallace grinned and said: 'But what about the ones you missed?'

Also playing it cool was Willie Waddell. The Rangers manager who had led the club to their first major victory in his first year as manager, said: 'I was pleased with the team in general. The young lad did very well. As well as scoring goals – he has netted 13 in the reserve side – Johnstone has proved he has the right temperament. I told him yesterday he would be playing, so it had nothing to do with John Greig's absence. We were not reduced to 11 players.'

Asked if he had ever felt that Rangers were going into the game as underdogs, he replied: 'I've been in the game 30 years and I've never gone into any game feeling like that.' And when asked if there would be a big celebration, he added: 'There will be no celebration in the meantime. We have a lot in front of us yet.'

The best-kept secret of the week was revealed only minutes before kick-off when shocked Rangers fans learned that Greig would play no part. 'I went down with flu in midweek and was in bed all day Thursday and part of Friday,' said Greig.

'I was warned not to say anything, but I was only finally pulled out of the side just before we left Ibrox for Hampden. It was the right decision as I didn't want to let the boys down.

'It was twice as hard watching. I'm not normally bothered with nerves but my stomach was churning towards the end of the game.'

Greig's illness was a blow as it meant he missed the chance of leading his mates to League Cup triumph in his first final as skipper. The man to get his hands on the cup first was captain for the day Ronnie McKinnon.

Celtic: Williams, Craig, Quinn, Murdoch, McNeill, Hay, Johnstone, Connolly, Wallace, Hood, Macari.

Rangers: McCloy, Jardine, Miller, Conn, McKinnon, Jackson, Henderson, MacDonald, D. Johnstone, Stein, W. Johnston.

Referee: Mr T. Wharton (Glasgow)

Attendance: 106,263

Rangers 3 Celtic 2

Saturday, 5 May 1973
Scottish Cup Final

WHO can ever forget the goal that won this cup? Sure, it was no 25-yard thunderbolt, fit to win a handsome trophy, but by goodness it was every bit as important.

It was the last time a crowd of 100,000+ watched a football match in the United Kingdom as this clash of Glasgow's titans drew a cup final attendance of 122,714. And I don't think there was a single supporter who left the stadium complaining they hadn't had their money's worth.

It was therefore fitting that Tom Forsyth's winning goal should gain the royal seal of approval. The Queen's sister, Princess Alexandra, was present at Hampden and was beaming from ear to ear when she handed over the splendid trophy to victorious skipper John Greig. That moment sparked wild celebrations amongst the Rangers supporters.

Of course, the abiding and iconic memory of the afternoon is of Forsyth bundling the ball over the line from close range to win the cup for the Ibrox side, but there is one other image which captured the emotions of the afternoon perfectly.

As the final whistle sounded, and with bedlam all around, Rangers manager Jock Wallace had only one thing on his mind, and that was to track down his captain and give him a famous bear hug – and that's exactly what he did. There has been talk down the years that the pair didn't get on. Well, they certainly did that afternoon. Wallace sprinted on to the park to locate Greig and for a few moments the expression of sheer joy epitomised everything the pair had achieved together.

For too long, many football folk had thought of Rangers as merely the fittest and strongest team around – a group of players with the courage of a pride of lions who could run around all day without tiring. Well not any more. Throughout the game they had shown they also had the one other ingredient necessary for success … skill. And it wasn't in short supply either.

From the first kick of the ball, by Rangers centre Derek Parlane, it was soon apparent that we had a final which could become one to remember. The atmosphere inside the stadium when referee Tiny Wharton blew the first whistle was incredible. The noise was deafening and supporters on the tightly packed terracing were whipped into a frenzy.

There were early chances at both ends before Celtic eased into a 1–0 lead midway through the opening period, and when Kenny Dalglish shot past Peter McCloy, one half of Hampden came alive … and the other half followed, not in appreciation of Dalglish's fine strike, but to get behind Greig and co – and it worked, because ten minutes later the scores were level.

Alex MacDonald proved far too tricky for Celtic right-back Danny McGrain and when his cross came in it was met by the head of Parlane, and was soon nestling in the net. Cue the Rangers supporters going wild at their favourite's 27th goal of the season.

When the referee eventually brought the first half to a close, supporters breathed a collective sigh of relief. It had been a fast and furious first 45, but if the general feeling among the crowd was that the second period couldn't possibly eclipse what they had just witnessed, they were mistaken, for it got off to the most incredible start when Rangers scored within just 30 seconds. Winger Quinton Young, sitting deep in his own half, was the brains behind this strike. He sent a long ball through the middle. A touch on by Parlane and there was Alfie Conn sprinting past Billy McNeill to fire low and hard past Ally Hunter.

The posh punters in the main stand were still taking their seats when they heard the roar.

It was real end-to-end stuff, but the cheers were coming from the 'other end' when Greig turned goalkeeper – illegally – and punched a net-bound Dixie Deans shot off the line with McCloy well beaten. It wasn't a red card offence in those days but Celtic were awarded a penalty, which the ever-calm George Connelly slotted home.

We were back to square one, but only in terms of goals scored. Rangers then grabbed the game by the scruff of the neck and drove forward time after time. In one daring raid, Hunter did well to save from Conn. MacDonald then hit the post with a great header, and the general feeling was one of optimism in the Rangers end.

And then came the moment that cemented an image into Scottish folklore. Just after the hour mark, Rangers were awarded a free kick. Tommy McLean, king of the set pieces, shaped to take the kick. Inside the box, bodies pulled and pushed. Wharton was trying his best to keep an eye out for anything dodgy. McLean took the kick and aimed for his usual target. Derek Johnstone outjumped his marker, Connelly, at the back post and sent the ball goalwards. And that's the moment play switched to slow motion. The ball hit the post and rolled along the line before coming to rest. Who would react quickest? The answer was Forsyth, although in his great excitement and haste to get to the ball first, he almost missed, as his right foot seemed to get stuck on top of the ball for an eternity before he got it moving in a forward motion again and managed to persuade it to cross the line!

It's fair to say it wasn't a thing of beauty, but it was a vital goal. Forsyth was immensely popular among the Rangers support, and so there was no better time for him to score his first Rangers goal.

After the game, the goal hero said: 'I was so excited I nearly missed. Thank goodness it went in, because the atmosphere had been incredible throughout the game and it was a fantastic way to end it all. It's a moment I will never forget.'

The final was also the culmination of a tremendous 26-game unbeaten run in domestic competition. Rangers might have lost out to their great rivals in the race for the title but they proved that they were well on the road back to good health with their Hampden triumph.

Just 12 months before the final, the Ibrox side had won the European Cup Winners' Cup in Barcelona, the pinnacle – you may think – of many of the winning team's careers. However, moments after the Scottish Cup Final had ended, left-back Willie Mathieson insisted that the 3–2 win was 'right up there', and added: 'I was more nervous today than I was in Barcelona. The atmosphere and noise was incredible. I thought the final whistle was never going to blow!'

There wasn't a prouder man inside Hampden when the winning team was called to step forward and receive the cup from Princess Alexandra. John Greig, chest puffed out, climbed the steps to the presentation area and was beaming from ear to ear when he accepted the cup. The moment he raised the trophy aloft, thousands of supporters lifted the roof off the traditional Rangers end.

Jock Wallace had maintained throughout his team's great run that the players needed to prove themselves to many people by winning something. That they did at Hampden, and Wallace was delighted. He said: 'We won the cup and we won it well. Now it means we go into Europe next season as holders of the trophy, not as runners-up to Celtic. That has been our target this season. I'm particularly pleased for the players. They have worked far harder than anybody realises and this is a tangible reward for that. They deserve it.

'What a game it was too. All that is good in football was present. With matches like that every week there wouldn't be any complaints. Now, though, we must look forward to next season and our return to Europe.'

And it was revealed how a nice touch by Wallace prior to the final made an old friend's day. Wallace sent two tickets for the final to Sammy Reid, with the attached message, 'To the nicest wee guy who ever scored a goal against the Rangers'.

Sammy was, of course, the centre-forward who scored the only goal of the game when Berwick Rangers beat the mighty Rangers in a Scottish Cup tie in 1967. Wallace kept goal for Berwick that day and remained friends with Sammy.

Three days before the big match, Wallace was at Hampden to watch the Scottish Junior Cup Final between Irvine Meadow and Cambuslang Rangers. He had more than a passing interest in the game as Rangers had provisionally signed Meadow's outside-left Eric Morris. And he must've been suitably impressed as the winger scored twice.

It was quite a week for big Jock.

Rangers: McCloy, Jardine, Mathieson, Greig, Forsyth, Conn, McLean, Johnstone, Parlane, MacDonald, Young. Sub: Smith.

Celtic: Hunter, McGrain, Brogan, Hay, McNeill, Connelly, Johnstone, Murdoch, Deans, Dalglish, Callaghan. Sub: Lennox.

Referee: Mr J. Gordon (Inverness)

Attendance: 122,714

Rangers 3 Celtic 0

Saturday, 4 January 1975
Scottish League Division One

'PAR-LANE, Par-lane, born is the King of Ibrox Park' rang round Ibrox as the talented centre-forward headed home the third goal which confirmed extra festive cheer for the Light Blue supporters.

It was certainly a case of out with the old and in with the new as this comfortable win ensured Rangers had the advantage in the race for the last old-style Scottish League title.

Goals by Derek Johnstone, Tommy McLean and Parlane put Celtic to the sword just three days after Rangers had handed out a 4–0 pasting to Partick Thistle on New Year's Day.

There was certainly no better way to bring in the Ne'erday.

It was the days of two points for a win and before kick-off, Rangers trailed the Parkhead side by the same margin going into the big game. The majority of the 71,000 spectators who filed into Ibrox were hopeful of doing the double over Celtic, following a 2–1 win at Parkhead in the September.

But after a spate of matches affected by crowd unrest, there were pre-match concerns about how the 'big one' would go off. Rangers' officials and police needn't have worried, though, as the crowd remained good-natured from start to finish and just ten arrests were made inside the stadium – an acceptable number in 'those days'!

But to the action and while all 11 players in light blue – and substitutes Quinton Young and Alex Miller – played their part in a thoroughly deserved victory, the smallest man on the park stood head and shoulders above the rest.

Tommy McLean was outstanding. He scored one and set up the other two. A player who always relied on his quick thinking and skilful right peg, Mighty Mac conducted the orchestra and the rest played to his tune.

Conditions were far from perfect, with a howling wind making it difficult for players to get their foot on the ball, but not McLean, as every time the ball was played out to him, it stuck like Velcro, and when he set off on one of his many great runs, the ball was never more than a couple of feet in front of him. He was always in control of the ball.

With just six minutes on the clock, wee 'Tam' clipped in one of his trademark crosses. It was aimed at the far post, where Derek Johnstone was lurking with intent. And timing his leap to perfection, big DJ outjumped Celtic skipper Billy McNeill and Danny McGrain to power a header past Ally Hunter.

It was the perfect start for the Light Blues, and the scenes in just about every part of the ground were ones of real jubilation.

There were chances at both ends after this, with Stewart Kennedy showing exactly why he was keeping Peter McCloy out of the first team with a couple of excellent stops.

The teams trooped off the park at half-time with the cheers of the vociferous Rangers support ringing in their ears, and no doubt Jock Wallace's interval team talk centred around 'more of the same' after the break.

But as the players were heading into the dressing room for a half-time cuppa, walking in the opposite direction were four Old Firm legends. Brothers John and Billy McPhail were offered polite applause from the terracing and stands, but that was nothing compared to the noise when Rangers greats George Young and Willie Woodburn emerged from the tunnel.

To a man (and woman), the centre stand rose to show their appreciation of two former Light Blues who had racked up more than 800 appearances between them.

There was a real poignant moment when Young approached the traditional 'Rangers end' and stopped at one of the old-style square goalposts. He did what he had done on so many occasions and rubbed the post for luck. If you were a Rangers supporter of a certain age, then you knew! It was wonderful to see 'Corky' in the 18-yard box he had so valiantly defended on occasions too many to recount.

The reason for the appearance of the former players was to try and 'keep supporters cool at a time when they can become restless', and if that was the main purpose then it worked a treat.

The players took part in an impromptu keepy-uppy competition, before kicking signed Rangers and Celtic footballs into the vast crowd. They were shaking hands with the fans and clowning around, and the ten or 15 minutes they were on the park kept supporters focussed on the entertainment rather than their opposite numbers.

However, the second half was only minutes old when Rangers pivot Colin Jackson suffered a nasty injury. He received treatment but was forced to limp off and was replaced by Alex Miller. That signalled a move back into the heart of the defence for goalscorer Derek Johnstone, where he linked up with the irrepressible Tom Forsyth. But instead of the change forcing Rangers to lose their rhythm, they simply went up the park and grabbed a second goal.

In a simple, but highly effective move, Stewart Kennedy kicked the ball long and it was gathered by centre-forward Parlane. The 'King of Ibrox Park' controlled the ball in an instant and sent a sweeping pass out to midfield lynchpin Alex MacDonald. Wee Doddie spotted McLean making a great run towards the Celtic box and played an inch-perfect pass to the wee man. McLean cut through the Celtic defence like a knife moving through butter and drew Hunter from his line before picking his spot under the keeper. It was 2–0 Rangers, and at that point there wasn't a Bear in the ground who didn't believe they had just witnessed the killer goal.

But the Rangers weren't finished there. Ian McDougall, who was having a fine game in the middle of the park, went on a mazy run and fed the ball out to the diminutive man of the match. One look up and he floated a ball into the heart of the Celtic box, and there was Parlane arriving perfectly to meet the ball and head past Hunter.

It was the icing on the cake and as the ball was hitting the back of the net, three sides of the stadium erupted in a sea of red, white and blue and the band struck up the old favourite, 'Follow Follow'.

There was no further scoring and as the players shook hands, acknowledged the supporters and trooped back to the dressing room, Rangers fans filed out of the stadium comforted by the knowledge that they had just watched their team go top of the league at an important stage of the season. It might have been by virtue of a slightly better goal difference, but on top they were.

And the players had just shown the rest of Scottish football that they were in no mood to be shifted from their lofty perch.

When Jock Wallace looked back on his day's work, he said: 'What a terrific afternoon's entertainment it was. If every game is going to be like that when the Top Ten starts next season then it can't come quickly enough. I thought both teams played some tremendous stuff and, naturally, I'm delighted with the result. Essentially it was a superb team effort with every player doing his job well.'

Parlane's goal put him level at the top of the Ibrox scoring charts on 18, level with right-back Sandy Jardine (eat your heart out Tav!). Derek Johnstone's goal had him on 13, one more than Graham Fyfe.

Rangers would go on and win the last old-style Scottish First Division championship before the league changed to the ten-team Premier League.

The title-clinching match came on 29 March at Easter Road, when Rangers needed a point against Hibs, and Colin Stein, who had returned to the club a few weeks previously from Coventry City, scored with a bullet header. It was Stein's first goal of his second spell at Ibrox and it couldn't have been timed any better.

Rangers won the league with four matches to spare and in the process ended Celtic's domination of the Scottish First Division. The Parkhead side had racked up nine titles in a row but on this occasion the battle of the Jocks was won unequivocally by Mr Wallace. Rangers may have failed dismally in both national cup competitions, but that was small change in terms of the championship. Supporters had waited an eternity to see the title return and Jock Wallace and his players delivered in style, winning the league by seven points from runners-up Hibernian, while Celtic finished third, a distant 11 points behind Rangers.

There was a new king in town and Jock Wallace was already writing his name into the record books.

Rangers: Kennedy, Jardine, Greig, Johnstone, Jackson (Miller), Forsyth, McLean, McDougall, Parlane, MacDonald, Scott (Young).

Celtic: Hunter, McGrain, Brogan, Murray, McNeill, McCluskey, Hood (Johnstone), Glavin, Dalglish, Callaghan, Wilson. Sub not used: McDonald.

Referee: Mr J. Paterson (Bothwell)

Attendance: 71,000

Rangers 3 Celtic 2

Saturday, 10 September 1977
Scottish Premier League

THIS latest Old Firm confrontation was one that would be talked about for years with great pride by those whose allegiances lay at Ibrox, and perhaps even with grudging admiration by followers from the other side.

It was a match which set a standard for the season that would be almost impossible to maintain.

Rangers gave Celtic two goals of a start, sorted out their own problems at half-time and went on to win the points with a breathtaking display of attacking football.

'This team is on the verge of great things,' said Rangers manager Jock Wallace after the final whistle, and on the form his players had just showed, there was no arguing with big Jock. In fact, who would've argued with big Jock, period?

The encounter also proved that the Ibrox club might just have made the bargain buy of the decade in Gordon Smith, a £65,000 signing from Kilmarnock. Surely the Killie directors were already ruing the day they gave the player away for such a paltry sum. Smith scored twice, bringing his total to six in the last four games, and was just inches away from immediate immortality as a man who bagged a hat-trick on his Old Firm debut.

He started and finished the comeback in style.

Spitz Kohn, coach of Twente Enschede, due to meet Rangers in the European Cup Winners' Cup at Ibrox a few days later, was also impressed with Smith. Afterwards, he told Jock Wallace: 'Smith – he is like an automobile ... a Mercedes!'

Wallace, the protective father of the Rangers, growled back: 'You mean a Rolls-Royce!'

Certainly Smith was the man who could give Rangers a handsome lead to take to Holland for the second leg.

In analysing Rangers' victory, it could be said that the game was perhaps won in the first minute, when Derek Parlane went down with a bad knock on the face and looked to be in some distress. Parlane played out the rest of the first half, but was kept inside at the interval when it was discovered he had fractured a cheekbone.

Rangers, two goals down by that time, were forced to reorganise. Derek Johnstone, who had been posted missing when Johannes Edvaldsson grabbed both Celtic goals, was moved up front to take over Parlane's role, and John Greig, a substitute for the day, moved into the back four.

The change was dramatically effective. Rangers had started the game playing confidently, but it was confidence without any real aggression, and an Old Firm game needs plenty of the latter.

While the Ibrox men were stringing together some nice moves, Edvaldsson, in the 18th and 31st minutes, took magnificent passes from Tommy Burns to put Celtic firmly in the driving seat – and what appeared to be a winning position.

Then came the half-time break, an Ibrox reshuffle, and some words of gentle persuasion from Jock Wallace. 'Oh, I told them I didn't think they were doing well enough,' said Wallace. 'Maybe those weren't my exact words, but the players certainly got the message!' I'm sure they did, Jock.

In 53 minutes, with the Rangers supporters giving their team quite remarkable encouragement despite the deficit, Rangers got it all together. Greig found Bobby Russell with an intelligent pass, and in his own cool manner Russell clipped it to Davie Cooper, who hit the ball left-footed from the right side of the box. Johnstone, now switched from centre-half to centre-forward, stopped it, and chipped it in front of Smith who drove it low past Latchford. It was a sublime goal and Rangers were on their way.

Celtic quickly became units of disillusioned men as their midline of Ronnie Glavin, John Dowie and Burns cracked under the pressure of the Ibrox ball play.

In 61 minutes, Peter Latchford made a brilliant save from a typical left-foot drive by Cooper, throwing himself across the face of his goal to hold the shot. And two minutes later the Celtic keeper had another spectacular save from Coop and one wondered if Latchford was to be Celtic's saviour.

But it wasn't to be. Another smooth, crisp attacking move from Rangers involving Bobby McKean, Smith and Cooper ended with the latter slipping the ball in front of Johnstone, who smashed it into the net from point-blank range. The scores were level.

Nine minutes from the end tragedy struck for Latchford – and the points remained at Ibrox. Tommy McLean, who had replaced the injured Alex McDonald, flicked a superb pass to Russell as he made for the byline. Russell controlled it beautifully and crossed high into the box. Latchford was on the spot but quite inexplicably, failed to hold the ball, allowed it to spin over his head and off the crossbar, and there was Smith on the line to ram it home.

It was a personal tragedy for Latchford, but all's fair in love and war, and it did contribute to a Rangers victory, and a fully deserved one at that.

The look on Smith's face was a mixture of surprise and joy!

Jock Stein immediately introduced Bobby Lennox and Tom McAdam for Burns and Dowie, but for Celtic the game was all but lost. They had taken the lead in 18 minutes with a smartly worked goal. Burns, easily Celtic's most creative player, sent Paul Wilson down the left wing, ran on to take the return, then hit a delayed pass at the Iceman. With the Rangers defence in disarray, Edvaldsson drove the ball into the roof of the net.

Just 13 minutes later Edvaldsson scored again, this time with his head. Burns took off down the left flank after evading a Cooper tackle and saw Edvaldsson haring through the centre of the Rangers defence pointing to his head. Burns got the message. His high lob was perfect and, as McCloy hesitated, Edvaldsson headed strongly into the net.

Right then you wouldn't have given Rangers a chance, but the whole team were immense after the break, with Sandy Jardine, Russell, Smith, Johnstone and McKean the key players for the Light Blues.

Following the demoralising defeat, Celtic found themselves in their worst position for years at this stage of the season – just a solitary point from the opening four matches, and sharing bottom spot with Clydebank.

The blame couldn't all be attributed to the transfer of Kenny Dalglish to Liverpool, because Celtic did have other good players in their squad, although the fact remained that too many of them weren't producing the goods.

Celtic manager Jock Stein's most pressing case was the mystery of his vanishing defence. Twice in the last eight days he had looked on as his team had built up formidable leads (they were three up at Motherwell and lost two late goals) before collapsing.

Too many Celtic players faded in the second half at Ibrox, and the result was embarrassment for the club. Seldom had so many players been caught in possession, so slow in recovery or so completely out of touch with what was going on around them.

As far as Rangers were concerned, the win against Celtic meant they were firmly back on track. After starting the season with back-to-back defeats against Aberdeen and Hibs, they had followed up the 4–0 win over Partick Thistle with a stunning victory against their rivals. It didn't get much better, although Jock Wallace, I'm sure, would argue that a better first-half performance would have been easier on the old ticker.

But he couldn't argue with the result. It was a thoroughly deserved win against all the odds, as it looked as though Celtic had the game nicely wrapped up at the break. In fact, the points may even have left for Parkhead by courier at half-time! If that was the case then Mr Wallace was soon calling for their return when Gordon Smith struck the second of his magnificent double to seal the points.

Naturally it was early days in the championship race but the manner of Rangers' victory must have set alarm bells ringing down Parkhead way.

Match-winner Gordon Smith had a colourful football career. After five years at Kilmarnock, he won the treble in his first season as a Ranger – playing a huge part in the success and scoring 27 goals from midfield. Twenty of these goals came in the league, where he missed just a single game.

He stayed at Ibrox for just three years, moving to Brighton for £440,000, scored in the FA Cup Final against Manchester United, and had spells at Manchester City and Oldham, as well as in Austria and Switzerland, but one can't help thinking what he could've achieved at Rangers had he stayed a few more years.

Rangers: McCloy, Jardine, Miller, Forsyth, Johnstone, MacDonald, McKean, Russell, Parlane (Greig), Smith, Cooper. Sub: McLean.

Celtic: Latchford, McGrain, Lynch, Edvaldsson, McDonald, Casey, Doyle, Dowie, Glavin, Burns, Wilson. Subs: Lennox, McAdam.

Referee: Mr I. D. M. Foote (Glasgow)

Attendance: 48,788

Rangers 2 Celtic 1

Saturday, 18 March 1978
League Cup Final

THIS cup final may have taken place around six years after Rangers' dramatic win over Moscow Dynamo in the European Cup Winners' Cup Final in Barcelona, but in many respects it signalled a changing of the guard.

Sandy Jardine, John Greig, Alex MacDonald, Tom Forsyth and Tommy McLean were all involved as Rangers lifted the first trophy of the 1977/78 season. And while the 'veterans' played a huge part in the triumph, it was the 'new guard' of Davie Cooper and Gordon Smith who were on target for the Light Blues at the national stadium. Bobby Russell was unfortunately injured.

It was also another triumph for the Rangers manager Jock Wallace against opposite number Jock Stein. In fact, so annoyed and disappointed was Stein at his side's failure to capture the silverware that he left Hampden in a hurry, brushing past waiting reporters at the end of the game en route to the waiting team bus. In fact, it wouldn't be too much longer until he was leaving his post as Celtic manager, being persuaded to stand down by the Parkhead board.

He left to take up the managerial post at Leeds United, but lasted just 44 days before becoming manager of the Scotland national team.

For Jock Wallace, the story was similar, but altogether different. Wallace had successfully broken Celtic's domination of the game in Scotland and after lifting the League Cup, looked on as his side swept all before them in Scotland at the end of the 1977/78 season. It was Wallace's second treble in just three seasons and the colourful, and sometimes controversial, manager had put himself in a similar bracket to Stein thanks to his achievements in Scotland.

But there was a shock in store for the Rangers supporters when Wallace unexpectedly announced he was leaving Rangers at the end of the season. The reasons for his departure remain a secret to this day, although speculation suggested a bust-up with general manager Willie Waddell as one of the likely reasons for his eventual departure to Leicester City.

Before all that, though, there was a cup to be won, and that elegant mover Gordon Smith hurtled Rangers to a record-breaking ninth Scottish League Cup win at Hampden Park with his first goal in his first final. For a while, though, it had looked as though everyone was destined to reconvene at the Queen's Park ground on the Wednesday night when Celtic, a team in torment all season, took yet another punch to the gut.

This fidgety, careless affair, punctuated by what seemed an endless stream of fouls, had spilled over into extra time thanks to the head of Johannes Edvaldsson. Celtic were in the driving seat and Rangers the team fighting to survive. Then, with three minutes remaining, substitute Alex Miller swung a cross from the right into the Celtic goal area. Out came Peter Latchford, who had played superbly, and in went that gutsy little battler, Alex MacDonald. Latchford was fractionally late as MacDonald threw himself to make contact with his head. The Celtic keeper half parried the header. It broke away and in moved Smith to head the ball over the unguarded goal line. The winning goal, and once again Gordon Smith was a hero in his debut Rangers season.

He was submerged in blue jerseys, while Latchford was suddenly a man alone, kicking the ball from the back of his net, with only a couple of minutes remaining for his side to rescue the tie.

But the battle was over; Rangers had won, and Celtic had lost their third successive final. They perhaps deserved another chance, but this was a season in which nothing had gone right.

A strange game in many ways, with Rangers lacking their usual rhythm and Celtic continuously panicking the Ibrox defence by using the rampaging Edvaldsson as a main striker.

Celtic probably did everything right with the players they had at their disposal. They soaked up the Rangers pressure, had more shots than Rangers and more control of the ball in the opposition side of the field.

But in those temperamental Old Firm occasions it's goals that count. Nothing else.

Glasgow referee David Syme didn't have an easy ride in his first final. He booked MacDonald and McLean, of Rangers, and Andy Lynch, Johnny Doyle and Edvaldsson for petty fouls. He also warned several others. There were far too many stoppages for this to be an easy-on-the-eye flowing final.

Rangers should have taken the lead midway through the first half. Derek Johnstone drove the ball powerfully past Latchford from some 14 yards, but a linesman's flag was up, indicating that Rangers' skipper John Greig – who had taken the ball down the left side of the field before crossing – was infringing the laws of the game. He had apparently ran off the pitch to avoid straying offside and had stayed there. The goal was knocked off by the referee for what we must assume was ungentlemanly conduct.

Stewart Kennedy didn't know much about a 25-yard drive from Ronnie Glavin in 37 minutes which rebounded from his chest, and broke towards George McCluskey on the right. The keeper recovered to punch clear the predictable cross and so Celtic were denied.

One minute later, Davie Cooper also scored in his first ever final. Glavin should be embarrassed by this one as he tried to let the ball run over the line for a goal kick when that man of perpetual movement, Gordon Smith, swept in at his side to clip the ball across goal with his left foot. Cooper exploded the ball high into the roof of the net from ten yards.

Rangers were on their way.

Celtic shrugged off the goal and by half-time were again looking the better side. They were forcing the play, using the full size of the playing surface, and on the hour mark, Kennedy had a magnificent save from a head deflection from McCluskey, by one-handing the ball over the bar.

Edvaldsson had been booked. MacDonald had been booked. Then a shoving match between Lynch and McLean earned both the yellow card.

Not surprisingly, Celtic equalised with six minutes to go. McCluskey clipped a good through ball to young Alan Sneddon, overlapping on the right. His cross to the far post was crisp, and as Kennedy misjudged the flight of the ball just fractionally, in went Edvaldsson to pound it into the net, off the crossbar, with his head.

Extra time, extra moments of petulance as substitute Doyle was booked for kicking the ball away at a free kick. Then, with time running out, Smith brought it all to an end with his head. It was the perfect end to what had been a pulsating, rather than high quality, cup final.

Rangers certainly weren't at their best, but the club's roll of honour will show that the 1978 League Cup was heading for the Ibrox trophy room. Smith, Kennedy, Forsyth, Cooper and McLean were their most consistent performers.

Celtic didn't play badly, but lost. Sneddon, the unfortunate Latchford, McCluskey and Edvaldsson were their best players.

There was no hiding the joy of victory reflected in the faces of the Rangers players when the full-time whistle sounded. Rangers had just beaten Celtic after extra time and Jock Wallace leapt to congratulate goalscorer Davie Cooper, who had seen out the last few moments on the bench. His face was a picture, but the man with the biggest smile at Hampden was match-winner Gordon Smith, who said: 'That is the greatest moment of my life. To score the winner in a final at Hampden is unbelievable.

'If I had missed that one I'd have taken a lot of stick from the boys. I saw my chance when Peter Latchford deflected Alex MacDonald's header towards me. Fortunately I got it right. To get a winner's medal in your first final is fantastic.'

Jock Wallace praised both of his goalscorers: Cooper, bought from Clydebank for £100,000 the previous year, and Smith. He said: 'I was delighted they got the goals that mattered in their first final. It was a difficult game for us, but thankfully we won it. Even though Celtic came back at us, I never felt we would need an extra game. I had the feeling we'd win the contest right here, even when it went into extra time. Our players are trained to run for two hours and they finished strongly today. But it wasn't just our superior fitness that won the match. We were the better team on the day and we also competed very well indeed. I was pleased with every aspect of our performance.'

For Celtic, it was their third successive League Cup Final defeat.

Celtic: Latchford, Sneddon, Munro, MacDonald, Lynch (Wilson), Glavin (Doyle), Dowie, Aitken, McCluskey, Edvaldsson, Burns.

Rangers: Kennedy, Jardine, Jackson, Forsyth, Greig, Hamilton (Miller), MacDonald, Smith, McLean, Johnstone, Cooper (Parlane).

Referee: Mr D. Syme (Glasgow)

Attendance: 60,168

Celtic 1 Rangers 3

Saturday, 4 August 1979
Drybrough Cup Final

THE Drybrough Cup was a brewery-sponsored eve-of-season competition for the country's eight top scorers. It provided a welcome change from meaningless pre-season friendlies, but eventually fizzled out after five or six years.

However, this final in particular has given Rangers supporters many superb lasting memories. Who can forget Sandy Jardine's incredible run from the edge of his own box – and finish to match – or Davie Cooper playing keepy-uppy in the Celtic box before firing home a thing of real beauty?

But while the final would largely be remembered – and quite rightly so – for these two great cup-winning goals, there was another goal that day, and it also involved some wonderful play and a real cool finish.

Step forward John MacDonald. The youngster's was a quality strike after a quite sensational build-up, but sadly it would rate just third in the Rangers goal charts that afternoon, due to the incredible nature of the other two.

Although Celtic had been the busier side at the start, MacDonald struck first, in 13 minutes, which proved unlucky for Celtic.

Alex MacDonald played a great pass out to John MacDonald on the left. The youngster ghosted past Sneddon on the inside, side-stepped Roy Aitken and released the ball to Cooper. The winger stabbed it back to young John and, as Latchford came off his line, he steadied himself and drove the ball a foot inside the near post.

It was MacDonald's first start for the top team and boy how he enjoyed it – and his goal. And there was more, naturally. When Jardine whipped the ball away from Aitken at the edge of the Rangers box in the 28th minute there was a murmur of approval from one end of the ground.

Several moments later no one could quite believe their eyes. They had just witnessed arguably one of the finest individual goals ever seen at Hampden. Jardine, operating as sweeper alongside Colin Jackson, moved forward with the ball, resisted two Celtic challenges as he made the halfway line – then decided to go all the way.

He switched from left to right, took Tom McAdam on the inside at the edge of the Celtic box, and let fly with his left foot. Latchford, who must have been hypnotised by Jardine's mazy 100-yard sprint, got nowhere near the ball as it nestled in the net. A magnificent strike – and Jardine's team-mates made sure they celebrated a special goal in style as the goalscorer took his two-handed salute in the middle of the field.

The season had barely started, and already 50,000 spectators had perhaps witnessed the goal of the season!

After Jardine's goal, it was all Rangers to the break. The value of using him at sweeper with Alex Miller at right-back had been obvious. Jardine read the play magnificently, played the ball out of defence with control, and was a comfort and inspiration to the younger guys around him.

There were near things from Cooper and Kenny Watson at one end, and a good save from McCloy from a vicious Sneddon left-footer at the other. Celtic certainly weren't about to give up. They all but camped in the Rangers goal area for the opening ten minutes of the second half. McCloy had to make several instinctive close-range saves, from Johnnie Doyle and Aitken in particular.

Within an eight-minute spell Doyle was booked for an infringement on Cooper, and McAdam for a foul on the same player, as Celtic placed a stop-at-all-costs bounty on Coop's head. They had no alternative. The talented Ranger was dictating play from the middle of the park.

Then, 12 minutes from the end, we had another magnificent goal. Cooper took a short lob from Alex MacDonald inside the Celtic box. He held off a challenge from Roddie McDonald, then flicked the ball over the defender's head. As the ball dropped, Coop flicked it away from McAdam and, before Latchford could move, he had hurtled the ball into the net. No other way to describe it: sheer magic.

Deflated Celtic eventually managed to breach the Rangers defence in the 84th minute and, not surprisingly, the goal came from substitute Bobby Lennox. He blasted a Murdo MacLeod free kick high past McCloy as if to say to the young men around him, 'That's how you do it!'

Although Celtic couldn't find the net again, and persistently destroyed their own build-up by sloppy work in the final pass, it was an enjoyable game.

Rangers grew in confidence thanks to their early goal, had the best players on the field in Jardine, Cooper, McCloy, Jackson and Watson, and fully deserved their victory. And while in time supporters may forget the scoreline, one thing is for sure, they will never forget the goals that gave Rangers the cup.

Opening goalscorer John MacDonald belongs to a select group of Rangers players: those who scored more than 100 goals for the famous old club.

But MacDonald once revealed how he almost never made it to Ibrox, and that it was only a concerted 11th hour bid by Rangers to stop him signing for Ipswich Town that brought him to the club he had supported as a boy.

He recalled: 'When I was a kid, we stayed just along the road from Firhill so my dad used to take me to see Partick Thistle most weeks. We went there because it was handy, but once we moved home, and dad didn't want to go to the football anymore, I started going to the games with my mates. They were all Rangers fans and as I was a bit older by then, I was allowed to go with them to Ibrox.'

MacDonald will never forget the day he signed for Rangers, and insisted it was the proudest moment of his footballing life. He said: 'I was just 17 and when I signed my name on that contract I was made up – but it took a while to get there.

'I had been going down to Ipswich every school holiday. Their chief scout Ron Day had come up for one of the schoolboy internationals when I was 13 and showed interest in me so I started making regular trips south with a few of the other young Scottish players. Guys like Alan Brazil and I would meet up at the station and go down for the holiday weekends. I loved it, and the only thing I could see myself doing at that time was signing for Ipswich and playing at Portman Road.'

But MacDonald was called up by Rangers at 17, the start of an eight-year love affair – and one that has continued to this day. He made his league debut for Rangers against Hearts at Tynecastle in a feisty five-goal thriller in February 1979, and one other appearance that season in a 1–0 win over Partick Thistle in the second to last game of the campaign – his competitive Ibrox debut.

He also played in Glasgow Cup ties against the Jags and Celtic – the latter coming in a 3–1 final win – and showed genuine predatory instincts by scoring in both games.

He recalled: 'I would prefer to have gone to Ibrox a year earlier, because I'd outgrown school. I was persuaded to stay on and take my Highers but wasn't interested and just wanted to play football.

'Jock Wallace had left and John Greig was the manager. In fact, I was Greig's first signing. I signed pre-season and he took me up to Inverness for a friendly and I got on as a sub. It was a great experience and while I didn't score, we won 6–2. Billy Urquhart scored in that game – and we signed him straight after it!

'I had good times under Greig. He could have won the treble in his first year had it not been for one game against Celtic. He never managed to win the league, which was probably his downfall.

'As a player, I didn't win the league either, but I took part in seven cup finals – four Scottish Cups and three League Cups – and won three of the seven. I also scored in a few of them. Anywhere else and it would have been seen as success but at Rangers you're obviously expected to win the league. The likes of Dundee United, Aberdeen and Celtic were all vying for titles at that time, so it was a tough period for us.

'I think John Greig perhaps made too many changes too soon, and got rid of a lot of the guys he had played with, but I still thoroughly enjoyed my time working under him and made a lot of great friends at the club.'

Celtic: Latchford, Sneddon, McGrain, McAdam, McDonald, Aitken, MacLeod, Burns, Provan, McCluskey and Doyle. Subs: Bonner, Edvaldsson, Lennox, Conroy, Davidson.

Rangers: McCloy, Miller, Dawson, Jardine, Jackson, Russell, Watson, A. MacDonald, Cooper, Parlane, J. MacDonald. Subs: Kennedy, McKay, McLean, Johnstone and Smith.

Referee: Mr R. B. Valentine (Dundee)

Attendance: 40,609

Rangers 3 Celtic 2 (after extra time)

Sunday, 25 March 1984
League Cup Final

AS Old Firm games go, this one had the lot, with the most important ingredient being an extra-time Rangers winner. It was an epic struggle which produced three penalty kicks, eight bookings and a huge pay-off for the bookmakers – and that was because Celtic were red-hot favourites going into the match.

Thankfully, though, Rangers managed to reach the heights demanded of them by gaffer Jock Wallace, even though he had been forced to send out a patched-up side at Hampden for the only honour left to his side that season.

Wallace was just four months into his second spell in charge at Ibrox, but his players responded magnificently to win the League Cup in dramatic style.

The larger-than-life manager's conviction that the side he had cobbled together at the last minute would be good enough on the day was well founded. Rangers, with their tremendous commitment, fought harder and longer than their Old Firm rivals and took the silverware back to Ibrox, their first major trophy in two seasons.

But what an amazing final, with Celtic looking down and out only to come battling back from two goals down to equalise with a last-gasp Mark Reid penalty which sent the game into extra time.

But as was so often the case, Ally McCoist was the goal hero with a fine hat-trick, although the main man was midfield player Bobby Russell, who was head and shoulders above anyone else on the field, including 21-year-old McCoist.

Having lost two regular midfield men because of suspension, there was a belief that Rangers might be vulnerable in this area, but there was no chance of that with Russell in this kind of form. He was quite magnificent, and how well his mates responded, even when they must have felt like dropping from exhaustion.

Celtic deserve praise, too, for a fightback as dramatic as any seen at Hampden. And they did score a fine goal through Brian McClair. It was of the quality necessary to win a cup, but just not this one; as this had big Jock's name written all over it.

In such a short space of time, Wallace had done the job Rangers brought him back to do. No wonder he leapt from the dugout at the end, a huge fist raised in the air to salute a famous victory.

The match was far too tense and fierce to come anywhere close to being a classic, in terms of the finer skills, and referee Bob Valentine had his busiest afternoon for a long time, but he did well in a difficult situation.

Rangers settled first and in seven minutes they almost opened the scoring, thanks to a tremendous move sparked by Russell, who sent McCoist clear on the right. When his low cross came over Sandy Clark completely missed it right in front of goal and it carried on to John MacDonald whose first-time shot was blocked on the line by Tom McAdam.

Then in 11 minutes, Reid was booked for a bad tackle on Davie Cooper. Quite rightly the referee called him aside and, to be honest, the player was fortunate to remain on the park.

The game badly needed someone to slow it down. It was all too hectic with little football being played. Paul McStay tried his best, but the openings he created were squandered by his forwards.

The Celtic strikers were finding it tough against John McClelland and Craig Paterson, but in 28 minutes Frank McGarvey found space for a cross and McClair's header was only inches wide.

Seconds later, Clark had his name taken for lunging at Roy Aitken.

Another Celtic surge in 32 minutes also came close to producing a goal. McCoist fouled Murdo MacLeod, and when a short free kick was touched into the path of the Celtic midfielder he let fly from 20 yards but again his effort was off target.

Ten minutes before the break Celtic had Rangers pinned back in their own penalty area and McCloy brought off a fine save from a McStay header. Paterson then blocked a shot from Aitken before the danger was eventually cleared.

But there was joy for Rangers a minute from half-time when they took the lead from the penalty spot. Russell sped inside the box and when he went down under a heavy MacLeod tackle, the referee had no hesitation in pointing to the spot.

McCoist was handed the task of firing Rangers into the lead and he performed it admirably, slamming the ball inside Pat Bonner's left-hand post. The goal had come against the run of play but it was a tribute to Rangers' determination that they had hit the front at the halfway mark after absorbing so much pressure.

Two minutes after half-time Celtic were almost level when McClair took a pass from Burns and fired in a low shot which McCloy got down smartly to block.

Rangers then made the first change of the game, bringing on Hugh Burns for John MacDonald, and three minutes later Russell became the third player to be booked when he went in a bit late on Tommy Burns.

That disappointment was forgotten on the hour mark when Rangers scored a second. It came from a massive clearance by McCloy which had Aitken and Clark chasing the ball inside the Celtic penalty area, and when it broke from Clark to the unmarked McCoist, the clinical striker beat Bonner from a couple of yards out. There looked no way back for Celtic at this point.

McClelland was then booked for fouling Burns on the edge of the Rangers box in 67 minutes – and it proved a costly mistimed tackle. From the free kick, Celtic pulled a goal back: the catalyst for their fightback. Burns took the kick himself, putting his toe under the ball and lobbing it over the defence to McClair, who met it perfectly on the volley and fired it past a despairing McCloy.

With 14 minutes left, both sides made substitutions. Jim Melrose took over from McGarvey and Colin McAdam – brother of Celtic's Tom – came on to replace Clark. Dave McPherson was then booked for a foul on Celtic's Davie Provan.

Substitute Melrose was the sixth player to be booked as Celtic mounted a last-gasp effort to hold on to their trophy, and as the game swept into injury time the Parkhead side came up with a dramatic equaliser.

MacLeod looked certain to score as he had only McCloy to beat from a few yards, but he was pulled down by McCoist and the penalty was given. Reid showed no signs of pressure and hammered the ball high into the net.

The full-time whistle sounded shortly afterwards and both managers moved on to the famous turf to try and gee up their players for one final push. Who would prevail in the white-hot heat of Hampden?

Graeme Sinclair took over from a tiring Provan ten minutes into extra time, and just four minutes later Rangers scored the goal that would prove decisive. McCoist was sent crashing to the ground by a clumsy Aitken challenge, and while Bonner blocked McCoist's spot kick, Super Ally was quickest off the mark to clip the rebound into the net.

Aitken and McCoist brought the total of bookings to eight with a little bit of nastiness near the end, but the destination of the League Cup had been settled, and McCoist was the player smiling at the end.

The trophy helped Rangers fans forget all about their dismal start to the season. For now, it was time to party, and the supporters vowed to paint the city red, white and blue.

Alex Totten was Jock Wallace's assistant that day and recalled the match with glee. He said: 'It was the perfect afternoon in many respects. Don't get me wrong, it put Jock and I through the mill but the scenes at the end were amazing and it was a victory we celebrated long into the night.

'Old Firm games were certainly different from the others. Before any game, players react differently from one another, depending on the likes of nerves etc., but even the most experienced of players can come across as really nervous before matches against Celtic. These games were a huge deal for everyone connected with the club and that included the management team and players.

'But that afternoon at Hampden was amazing and it's one that will remain with me for the rest of my life. We were under a bit of pressure at the time but winning the League Cup, with, some might say, a below-par side, made the victory that bit sweeter, as if any win over Celtic wasn't!'

Rangers: McCloy, Nicholl, Dawson, McClelland, Paterson, McPherson, Russell, McCoist, Clark (C. McAdam), McDonald (Burns), Cooper.

Celtic: Bonner, McGrain, Reid, Aitken, T. McAdam, MacLeod, Provan (Sinclair), McStay, McGarvey (Melrose), Burns, McClair.

Referee: Mr R. B. Valentine (Dundee)

Attendance: 66,369

Rangers 3 Celtic 0

Saturday, 9 November 1985
Scottish Premier League

IF there is such a thing as the perfect preparation for an Old Firm game, it certainly isn't going into the fixture with two losses and two draws from your last four league games. But that was the sad state of affairs that preceded this one.

Manager Jock Wallace had presided over losses to St Mirren and Hearts, and draws against Clydebank and Dundee United. It was far from ideal with the visit of David Hay's Celtic looming.

But what was that they said about ripping up the formbook for this one?

Following a six-match unbeaten start to the season, which included a draw at Celtic Park, the next seven included four losses and the Rangers supporters were starting to lose patience with the man who had once been untouchable in their eyes.

As it was, Jock Wallace's faith in his young brigade paid off as techniques previously only seen on the training ground were paraded before a packed Ibrox and used to torment then finally obliterate a Celtic side experiencing a form slump of their own.

It was Rangers' most emphatic win over their oldest rivals for five years and the scoreline did not flatter them. Rangers were far too good for Celtic. They were ahead in every aspect of the game – more determined, more adaptable, and certainly much more competent in the basics of stringing together passes.

Weeks of misery for the Ibrox fans were blown away in a 90-minute spell in which Rangers at long last looked like genuine championship contenders. 'We were brilliant ... out of this world,' said Wallace afterwards, and no one could argue with him, even allowing for the fact that on the day Celtic were a shadow of their normal selves. Mind you, much of that was because Rangers made them look that way.

Wallace was also to be admired for refusing to take the opportunity to make a speech proclaiming 'I told you so'. For weeks he'd had to face the media, putting on a brave face as disaster followed disaster. This was his chance for a bit of drum-beating, but he declined, saying: 'I don't gloat at times like this, and I don't cry when things aren't going so well either.'

For vastly different reasons, Celtic manager Hay was just as short with his summing up of the afternoon. He said: 'The better team won – they wanted to win more than we did.'

The day belonged to Rangers from the moment referee David Syme started proceedings and Wallace's boys – whose average age was just 23 – gave as good a performance as any Rangers outfit in recent years.

The only question mark over their performance was the time it took to clinch the points. Mind you, from the early stages it was evident they wouldn't lose them.

Head and shoulders above anyone else on the field was teen midfielder Ian Durrant. He pointed the way towards victory with the opening goal on the half hour, his first at the top level for the club, but it was his overall contribution which raised more than a few eyebrows. The Kinning Park lad was outstanding. Durrant didn't just play when he had the ball. His work off the ball was a revelation and he showed how much of a bright future he had in the game.

Derek Ferguson, at just 18, was also outstanding in midfield until he had to be taken off injured. His was a refreshing performance which showed a maturity beyond his years.

At the back, 21-year-old Davie McPherson was commanding, both in the air and on the ground. He even had the confidence to surge forward with the attack on occasion, and was given tremendous backing in the middle of the defence by one of the older hands, Davie McKinnon, a man who seldom courted the limelight but who went about his job in a professional manner.

Another 'quiet man' was 23-year-old Stuart Munro, the only outfield player who had played in every Rangers match up to that point of the season. He kept a tight rein on Celtic winger Davie Provan, who normally sparkled in the Old Firm encounter, and, like Dougie Bell, had probably his best game since breaking into the first team.

Certainly one good win didn't mean Rangers' troubles were over but this victory would have gone a long way to restoring confidence. The win tucked them in just three points behind league leaders Aberdeen.

Celtic's experiment of playing three central defenders was a failure and the display of the entire defence emphasised just where Hay's problems lay, although everyone at Parkhead must have been aware of that for several years. Hay was in desperate need of at least one top defender.

The Parkhead men had shipped ten goals in their last three matches and it didn't take a genius to realise that if that trend continued they wouldn't win the title.

New striker Mark McGhee had a fiery baptism and admitted that while with Hamburg he had forgotten just how tough the tackling could be in the Premier League, but the former Aberdeen man battled well and would certainly be an asset to the club once he had a few matches under his belt.

But Rangers never looked back once they had taken the lead after half an hour. Davie Cooper set the goal up with a jinking run into the box and a shot that bounced off Pat Bonner's foot. The ball fell kindly to Durrant and, although he had his back to goal, he quickly wheeled and shot into the net.

With ten minutes left, Cooper himself clinched the points when he shot home after a drive from substitute Bobby Russell had come off a defender, and a couple of minutes later Rangers put a bit of sparkle on the result with a third. The enigmatic Ted McMinn moved quicker than the rest to push the ball over the line after a deft chip from McCoist had hit the crossbar and bounced down, although many supporters reckoned the ball had already crossed the line. In fact, after the game, McCoist insisted he was claiming the goal, saying: 'I spoke to the linesman and he told me that when the ball came down off the bar it bounced behind the goal line. So, as far as I'm concerned, it's my goal.'

Looking back on this fixture, the first thing that stuck out like a sore thumb was the status of the three scorers. Durrant, Cooper and McCoist: Rangers legends one and all. For supporters of a certain age, those three names were as good as it got. They rolled off the tongue.

But what a difference a week makes. Seven days previous, just 16,000 were inside Ibrox to see Rangers play out a turgid 0–0 draw with unfancied Clydebank. It was a tough watch for the diehards and did nothing to persuade those fans that they would whip their biggest rivals into submission the following Saturday.

Ten of the players who played against the Bankies were in the line-up for the Old Firm game, but these same players showed an aggressive drive against Celtic which left the Parkhead side on the back foot almost from the start and which gave Rangers a firm upper hand. In fact, the scoreline was a modest reflection of how superior they actually were. Had McCoist's left leg not argued frequently with his right in front of goal, Ally could have doubled their tally!

And by plumping for youth over experience, Rangers introduced a vitality that simply oozed out of their play. Durrant and Ferguson played without fear, and it showed. Both youngsters showed some delightful touches in the middle of the park and, apart from a glorious win to savour, the Rangers support were also given a glimpse into the future, and it was one that provided much optimism.

I'm sure Jock Wallace slept well for the first time in weeks, but sadly it would be the only decent night's sleep the big man would get that season. In fact, the 1985/86 campaign could be filed in the 'unmitigated disaster' column. Finishing fifth in the table was unacceptable and Wallace knew that. Perhaps this emphatic Old Firm win had papered over the cracks, because far too many lacklustre performances were lurking just round the corner.

There is absolutely no doubt Jock Wallace was a talented manager but, as we touched on earlier, the average age of the side was just 23, so perhaps if he had been given more time to see them blossom – and a few extra quid to spend – then things might have been different. I'd like to think so.

Rangers: Walker, Dawson, Munro, McPherson, McKinnon, Bell, McCoist, D. Ferguson, Williamson, Durrant, Cooper. Subs: Russell, McMinn.

Celtic: Bonner, W. McStay, Burns, Aitken, McGugan, McAdam, Provan, P. McStay, McGhee, Grant, McClair. Subs: McGrain, Johnston.

Referee: Mr D. Syme (Rutherglen)

Attendance: 42,045

Rangers 2 Celtic 1

Sunday, 26 October 1986
League Cup Final

IT was carnage at the end of this Skol Cup Final as a few moments of football threatened to break out amidst all the madness, but Rangers fans cared little as the fate of another piece of silverware was decided: destination Ibrox.

Let's face it, it's always good to get one over on your biggest rivals, and even better in a cup final.

The teams were locked at one goal apiece with just six minutes remaining when Derek Ferguson flighted a free kick into the Celtic box. Terry Butcher looked favourite to get to the ball first but was clearly impeded by Roy Aitken and referee David Syme pointed to the spot.

The Celtic players were furious and both Owen Archdeacon and Pat Bonner were booked for protesting, but Davie Cooper remained the coolest player on the park throughout all the crazy stuff, and when order was finally restored he made a perfect job of the spot kick.

2–1 to Rangers, and time was running out for their opponents … and then the match descended into an utter shambles as confusion and ill-temper reigned supreme.

After the winning goal Celtic striker Mo Johnston, booked earlier, was sent off for an alleged headbutt on Rangers left-back Stuart Munro, and the Celtic man's actions kicked off incredible scenes.

The Celtic players surrounded referee David Syme and his linesman, who had spotted the incident, and amid the protests the referee appeared to show Tony Shepherd the red card, but for some reason the Celtic midfielder stayed on the field until the end of the game. Such was the confusion that maybe Mr Syme thought that Johnston, who also had blonde hair, had refused to go.

Parkhead manager David Hay also got involved – on the one hand ushering his players back on to the field, and then making his own feelings known to the referee, in the strongest terms imaginable. It all marred what had been an exciting and well-fought contest, with the final tally of ten bookings and an ordering off a moderate reflection of just how keenly this match had been contested.

Oh, and just to compound the situation, Johnston thought it wise to bless himself in front of the Rangers fans before making his way up the tunnel. The player was subsequently fined by Celtic for bringing shame upon the club.

But what a marvellous day it was for Rangers player/manager Graeme Souness, who was forced to rule himself out of the match due to injury. In his first season as boss he had steered his side to their first trophy and there was the promise of more to come.

The Rangers goals may have come from Ian Durrant and Davie Cooper but the player who deservedly won man of the match was teenager Derek Ferguson, playing in the 'Souness' role. With young men like that around the future was bright for the Ibrox club.

It was a pulsating contest and both goalkeepers were quickly called upon to get involved in the action. Chris Woods twice got down to hold efforts from Shepherd and Brian McClair, but Rangers came even closer when Aitken fouled Cooper 25 yards out after just eight minutes. With everyone expecting Cooper himself to take the kick, Cammy Fraser stepped forward and hit a fierce low drive that Bonner brilliantly touched on to his left-hand post.

Seconds later another Fraser free kick found the head of Butcher but McCoist, with bags of time, hurried his shot and sent it straight into the Celtic keeper's arms.

Then came two Celtic bookings within a couple of minutes. The first was for Aitken, for a tackle on Cooper, and then Alan McInally for a foul on the same player. Once again, Coop was a marked man. After that Rangers seemed to take a grip on things and certainly there was more to their build-up play than Celtic were showing.

In 26 minutes Rangers produced a tremendous move down the right that caught Celtic napping. Durrant and McCoist worked a neat one-two that took them through the Celtic defence, but Durrant's shot cleared the bar.

As the first half drew to a close, Celtic forced their way back into the match and in 41 minutes they were unlucky not to take the lead. Aitken charged forward and released Johnston inside the Rangers box.

The striker did everything right, including beating Woods with his shot, but saw the ball come back off the post and Mark McGhee hit the rebound straight into the body of the stricken goalkeeper.

Johnston became the third player to be booked in 55 minutes for an off-the-ball incident involving Jimmy Nicholl and seconds later the Northern Irish full-back followed him into the book.

At that point Celtic made a substitution, Archdeacon replacing McGhee, but in 62 minutes it was the huge Rangers support who were celebrating as the Ibrox side shot into the lead.

Peter Grant fouled Cooper out on the right and when Fraser pumped the free kick into the box, the ball glided off the head of Butcher. It fell straight to the feet of Durrant at the far post and he wasted no time in smacking a low drive past Bonner.

Celtic's reply to the setback was a bout of intense pressure, which paid off with an equaliser in the 70th minute. Before that, however, McClair had chipped a free kick against the Rangers bar. So it was perhaps fitting then that he should get the goal. It all began with Aitken pushing the ball inside the box; Johnston touched it to the side, and from 15 yards McClair thundered a drive into the top left-hand corner of the net. Woods had no chance.

Three minutes later Davie McFarlane took over from Fraser, and in 77 minutes Derek Whyte became the fifth booking of the afternoon when he crudely hauled down the much-fouled Cooper. And when Grant brought the cautions to half a dozen – five Celtic players and a solitary Ranger – for a foul on McCoist, it was starting to get a little out of hand.

Then with just six minutes left Rangers grabbed the cup in the most dramatic of circumstances. Fergie swung a free kick towards the far post and referee Syme ruled that Aitken had pushed Butcher in the back. He seemed to take an eternity to point to the spot and when he did he was surrounded by protesting Celtic players.

After Cooper had despatched the spot kick, McCoist was booked for fouling Whyte, and in a most untidy finish came the Johnston ordering off, the booking for Rangers' Munro, and all the rest of the nonsense that followed.

As Rangers celebrated, there was a little sympathy for the losers, although perhaps they deserved at least an extra half hour despite the fact they had lost their discipline so poorly in the closing minutes.

After the game, Souness agreed that Celtic were slightly the better side, but after gaining his first honour as Rangers gaffer, said: 'It's great to win, but I cannot say I enjoyed it from the touchline. I knew when I went off in the Boavista game that I wouldn't be able to play, but I saw no point in giving our opponents an advantage by saying so.

'We still have a long way to go as far as I'm concerned. That was the start, and we must go on from here. Our priority is to win the league and as long as I'm here it always will be.'

Butcher added: 'I was going for the ball and was stopped from doing so. To my mind it was a penalty, although no doubt Celtic see it differently. They played well, but we took our chances. Ask me tomorrow how much I enjoyed it. Just now, I can't take it all in.'

Celtic manager David Hay was still fuming long after the final whistle, and said: 'If it had anything to do with me, I would apply for Celtic to join the English league tomorrow.'

Hay, however, had prefaced that remark by congratulating Rangers on their victory, adding: 'None of what I am saying is sour grapes. Good luck to Rangers.'

Hay had been fined £250 earlier in the season for requesting that Bob Valentine be prevented from taking charge of Celtic games, and he added: 'It does seem to me that in games against top teams, there are controversial decisions which always seem to go against Celtic. The referee is always right, or so I am told by the SFA. Yet Tony Shepherd seemed to be sent off. The referee presumably changed his decision. All I seem to be doing after major games is complaining, but I honestly felt it was an exciting, evenly matched game.'

Celtic: Bonner, Grant, MacLeod, Aitken, Whyte, McGhee, McClair, P. McStay, Johnston, Shepherd, McInally. Subs: W. McStay, Archdeacon.

Rangers: Woods, Nicholl, Munro, Fraser, Dawson, Butcher, Ferguson, McMinn, McCoist, Durrant, Cooper. Subs: McFarlane, Fleck.

Referee: Mr D. Syme (Rutherglen)

Attendance: 74,219

Rangers 2 Celtic 2

Saturday, 17 October 1987
Scottish Premier League

WHEN is a draw not a draw? When it's a moral victory. And that was the scenario at Ibrox in one of the most incredible and exciting games ever witnessed at the stadium.

Where to start with this one?

The game was moseying along at the usual Old Firm pace – frantic – when the ball was helped back to Chris Woods by his left-back, Jimmy Phillips. There were just 17 minutes on the clock and Woods routinely picked up the ball. Quite why Celtic striker Frank McAvennie felt the need to lunge in with a shoulder charge on Woods was beyond the comprehension of the majority of the crowd, but that's exactly what he did. And it set off a chain of events that was to reverberate around the stadium until the end of the match – and well beyond.

Naturally, Woods took exception to McAvennie's unnecessary barge – and an earlier lunge by the same player, long after Woods had tipped a dangerous Tommy Burns cross over the bar – and grabbed McAvennie by the throat. Enter Terry Butcher, who pushed the Celtic man away, and Graham Roberts, never one to watch a team-mate being jostled in silence. Roberts looked to be the peacemaker before taking exception to McAvennie, and then it was Butcher's turn to be peacekeeper. It was all very confusing at one point.

McAvennie then fell to the ground and the referee, Mr Duncan, raced to the scene.

When some kind of order was eventually restored, the referee sent off Woods and McAvennie and booked Butcher, perhaps for his incessant protests at his team-mate's red card. With Avi Cohen and Davie Cooper on the bench, Rangers settled down to play out the remaining 73 minutes with an outfield player in goals. Step forward, Graham Roberts. He donned that iconic red jersey and positioned himself between the sticks. This would be interesting.

One could be forgiven for thinking Celtic would immediately pound the Rangers goal with shots, crosses and the likes, but that wasn't the case. They continued to play their passing game in a bid to open Rangers up by conventional methods. And it didn't really work, as all they had to offer for the next ten minutes or so was a Peter Grant effort. But when Derek Whyte punted a long ball into Rangers territory in 33 minutes, Andy Walker outpaced Terry Butcher and smacked the ball under Roberts to put his side ahead.

Two minutes later, another long ball again had Rangers in bother. This time Walker touched the ball inside and, with Roberts off his line, Butcher and Grant were suddenly in a race for the ball.

Unfortunately, Butcher got there first and, attempting to clear, lofted the ball high over Roberts and into his own net. Both goals had been scored at the Celtic end and their fans were clearly enjoying what they thought was turning into a rout.

2–0 down in 35 minutes and with a sweeper in goals, things looked pretty desperate from the Rangers end. Even the most optimistic Rangers fan must have feared a trouncing, but Celtic then made the cardinal error of thinking they had done enough.

With an hour on the clock, it was still 2–0, and perhaps Graeme Souness sensed there might be some hope in the final third of the game – and then Butcher was sent off for a foul on Celtic goalkeeper Allen McKnight!

Even though their starting formation of 4–4–2 had been reduced to 3–3–2, Rangers were still the team taking the game to their opponents, and a change of tactics took £1.5 million defender Richard Gough up front to partner Ally McCoist – and boy how that move paid off, for within three minutes of Butcher being sent off, Rangers were back in the match with a real chance.

Young Derek Ferguson began the move with a fine run and pass to Gough, who touched the ball on to the unmarked McCoist, and he strode forward and sent a terrific shot in off the post.

Surely not … but suddenly there was belief among the vast majority of the crowd. They didn't see this as some meaningless consolation. Celtic were there for the taking.

There were chances at both ends, most notably when Celtic's Billy Stark saw his header come off the bar, but that apart there was no real pressure put on the home side, despite Celtic holding all the aces.

And the Parkhead men paid the ultimate price in the last minute when Rangers equalised.

Ian Durrant, who had practically run himself into the ground, found one last burst of energy to speed past Celtic substitute Anton Rogan on Rangers' right. He made straight for the byline and fired in a cross, which was headed straight back out to him by Mick McCarthy. Again he crossed the ball into the danger area, which completely baffled McKnight, McCarthy and Chris Morris. As they lay on the ground, along with Gough, it was the big Ranger who reacted first. He stuck out a foot to knock the ball over the line to give Rangers a draw which they absolutely deserved.

Three sides of the ground – bathed in glorious sunshine – erupted. The cheers could be heard at Govan Cross. There was delirium in the stands. Grown men cried as the remaining eight Rangers players chased Gough over to the Govan Stand. The scenes were too incredible for words.

It was the final minute of the match and there seemed no way back for Celtic. In fact, there wasn't. The visitors took centre and the ball eventually found its way back to Roberts in the Rangers goal. Defending the Copland Road end, the singing was incredible and, for a brief moment, Roberts dropped the ball at his feet, walked it along the edge of the box and conducted the Rangers choir in their 'victory' sing-song. Great stuff.

Rangers' player/manager Souness seemed happy enough with a point, but refused to discuss any of the game's controversial moments, which left very little to actually talk about, but he did say: 'It was an eventful game and I'm delighted we got something from it. Now we are looking forward to another difficult match on Wednesday when we play Gornik in the European Cup.'

Celtic manager Billy McNeill, who earlier in the season had watched his side throw away a two-goal lead against Aberdeen, said: 'We allowed Rangers to come back into the game from a dead position. They should have been running for cover and at half-time I told my players that they could only toss the game away. I didn't anticipate they would do exactly that.'

The nine remaining Rangers players gave everything they had to ensure a point was gained, but Gough, Durrant and Ferguson were outstanding.

David Mitchell: Captained Rangers in their first ever Old Firm victory

Jock Drummond: Insisted on wearing his trademark 'bunnet' while playing for Rangers!

John Taylor: The Rangers trainer was credited with having the players fit enough to land the 1893 Scottish Cup

RC Hamilton: Rangers' top scorer in Old Firm clashes

Davie Meiklejohn: Led the Light Blues to a historic Scottish Cup win in 1928

Torry Gillick: Was on target three times in Rangers' record 8-1 win in 1943

Willie Thornton: The classy front man was a 'thorn' in Celtic's side!

Johnny Hubbard: Scored a hat-trick against Celtic in 1955

Jimmy Millar: In action against Celtic at Parkhead

Rangers celebrating another Old Firm win – this time in 1963

Jim Forrest: A goal machine for Rangers in the 1960s

Jock Wallace: Celebrates Rangers' 1975 League Cup win over Celtic

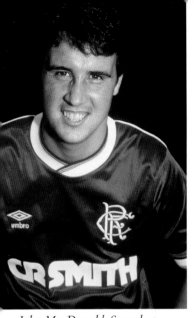

John MacDonald: Scored
a tremendous goal in the
Drybrough Cup Final

Old Firm players battle it out in the
passionate Glasgow derby

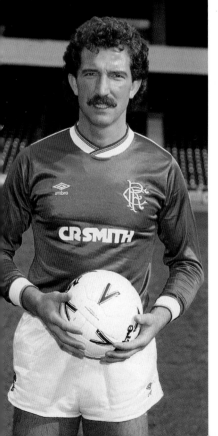

Dale Gordon: The Englishman takes on
Celtic's Dariusz Wdowczyk

Graeme Souness:
Relished the
opportunity to go toe-to-
toe with Celtic

Andy Goram: He broke many a Celt's heart!

John Brown: Is a veteran of many an Old Firm clash

Alexei Mikhailitchenko: Scored twice as Rangers thumped Celtic on their own ground in 1994

Ally McCoist: Super Ally doing what he does best – scoring the winner against Celtic, this time in the 1995 League Cup quarter-finals

Marco Negri: Thumps one into the Celtic net at Parkhead

Neil McCann: Celebrating an Old Firm goal at Celtic Park as Rangers clinch the title amidst utter chaos!

Pedro Mendes: In blue heaven as he scores at Celtic Park in August 2008

Ryan Jack: Celebrating with Andy Halliday after scoring the only goal of the Old Firm game in December 2018

There is no doubt the levels of excitement generated on the pitch were reflected in the stands, and even supporters leaving at the end were emotionally drained, but the manner in which a draw was salvaged from the ashes of a goals and personnel deficit was incredible.

Sure, there would be repercussions, as the events of the afternoon were dissected, but not even Mystic Meg could have foreseen the fallout, as three days later Glasgow's Procurator Fiscal ordered a police enquiry into the afternoon's events.

Woods, Butcher and Roberts, and Celtic's McAvennie, were all charged with Breach of the Peace and ordered to appear at court. It seemed a case of the law picking and choosing when to get involved in sport, although there was no doubt this case was without precedent in recent times.

Of course, there were 43,486 witnesses, none of whom would be cited. That would be left to the powers that be in their attempts to gain convictions.

The case dragged on and the eventual show trial lasted several days. Butcher and Woods were convicted and fined, while the verdict on Roberts was not proven. McAvennie was found not guilty of Breach of the Peace.

It proved nothing more than a charade, and if the authorities were attempting to make an example of some highly paid footballers then it failed miserably. Nothing changed and Old Firm matches remain highly competitive and full of incident to this day.

Before any court case was held, Rangers suffered by having Woods and Butcher suspended for the following Sunday's League Cup Final at Hampden. Nicky Walker deputised for Woods and Butcher's place was taken by Stuart Munro. In another highly competitive match, Rangers and Aberdeen shared six goals with Rangers eventually winning on penalty kicks.

Rangers would finish third in the league table, which was a great pity as they had won the title the season before and would go on to win the next nine. Eleven in a row would've been nice!

Rangers: Woods, Gough, Phillips, Roberts, Ferguson, Butcher, Francis, Falco, McCoist, Durrant, McGregor. Subs: Cooper, Cohen.

Celtic: McKnight, Morris, Whyte, Aitken, McCarthy, Grant, Stark, McStay, McAvennie, Walker, Burns. Subs: Rogan, Archdeacon.

Referee: Mr J. Duncan (Gorebridge)

Attendance: 43,486

Rangers 5 Celtic 1
Saturday, 27 August 1988
Scottish Premier League

THE previous week, Rangers played out a stuffy 0–0 draw with Hibs. Plenty of chances but an afternoon when our strikers couldn't hit a barn door with a banjo.

Fast forward seven days and no one – and I mean NO one – could've predicted the type of afternoon Rangers would have against Celtic. Supporters filed dutifully into the ground prior to kick-off with hope in their hearts, as they always do, but as the sun shone brightly in the sky, the afternoon would eventually turn into pure Roy of the Rovers stuff – the type of game you go to bed dreaming of only to be disappointed the following day.

Mind you, with five minutes played, it was soon looking like the stuff of nightmares for 35,000+ Bears.

Celtic ventured up the park and when a Peter Grant shot thundered off the post, Chris Woods and co felt they'd had a lucky escape. Nope. The ever-alert Frank McAvennie was waiting to pounce and like all good penalty-box predators he knocked the ball into the net.

But rather than let the shock of an early reverse stun them into silence, the Rangers supporters got fully behind their team, and it was the type of backing that might have wakened the dead.

A few minutes after McAvennie's opener, Graeme Souness's side were back on level terms. Ray Wilkins sent a free kick in from the right and when Bomber Brown saw his shot blocked, Ally McCoist pounced on it in a flash and fired past Ian Andrews.

It was exactly the type of response that was required, and gave Rangers the upper hand. Wilkins, Ian Durrant and Ian Ferguson started to run the show from the middle of the park with Ferguson, in particular, showing a real appetite for the game.

Rangers then turned their dominant possession into chances and Andrews' goal was soon living a charmed life. But it couldn't do so forever. And nine minutes from half-time, we were treated to a special goal from one of the best players ever to patrol a midfield. It was a goal 'Made in England' as Gary Stevens launched a long throw into the box and Terry Butcher nodded it on. It fell kindly for Wilkins 20 yards from goal and the technique used in the volley was top drawer. Andrews only appeared to catch sight of the ball as it was making its way back out from the net.

It was certainly a goal fit to win any game, but the home side had other ideas. Seeing out the game with such a slender advantage was the furthest thing from their minds. And if the first half had been a delightful starter served on a silver salver, the second would be a feast fit for a king.

It would've been nice to have been present in the dressing room for the gaffer's team talk, but I'm sure Graeme Souness calmly advised his players to 'start the second half the way you finished the first. Oh, and put the game to bed.'

It seems a fair enough assumption, because just a minute after the restart, Stevens caused confusion in the Celtic defence with a quickly taken free kick. Durrant knocked the ball back across the goal and McCoist sent a back header high up into the air and over the head of Andrews and into the net. Kevin Drinkell was on hand to ensure Andrews was under pressure as he attempted to claw the ball to safety. 3–1 Rangers and the players were just getting warmed up.

The pressure was then relentless and internationals such as Roy Aitken and Mick McCarthy were made to look second rate. And while Stevens was causing problems for Celtic down the right, Mark Walters was doing exactly the same thing on the opposite flank. And when Walters switched wings, he was equally as effective. Approaching the hour mark, he left Derek Whyte for dead and his cross was powerfully headed home by Drinkell in front of a packed and passionate Copland Road end.

Just four minutes later, and it was five. McCoist robbed a bungling Aitken on the edge of his own penalty box and when he was hauled to the floor inside the box, it looked a nailed-on penalty, but Walters was following up and found the net with a low, well-placed shot.

With 62 minutes gone Rangers were 5–1 up, but while the fans urged their favourites to go on and completely humiliate their opponents, there seemed to be an acceptance within the side that their afternoon's work was over and that they would settle for five, and the points.

Davie Cooper replaced Walters with 15 minutes remaining, and then five minutes later Souness came on for Durrant. Talk about replacing like for like! That was when Rangers supporters realised that a period of complete domination was on the horizon.

There wasn't a failure in blue that afternoon, but if one player deserved an extra helping of praise it was Ian Ferguson. He epitomised exactly what it meant to be a Rangers player as he worked his socks off defending the midfield – his midfield – while also providing bags of drive going forward.

Mark Walters was also given a lot of credit after the game for showing a different side of his game. He was asked by Souness to 'keep an eye out for Chris Morris bombing up and down the right-hand side of the park'. Walters obliged, adding: 'Souey knew the threat that Morris posed by getting to the byline and swinging balls into the box, a bit like our own Gary Stevens, so I was asked to backtrack a lot and keep his forward runs in check. I'd like to think I did a decent enough job, although my main priority was to get the ball into areas that could hurt Celtic. It was a brilliant afternoon and I'm sure our supporters enjoyed it just as much as we did.'

Boss Souness was also delighted with the afternoon's work, and said: 'We looked nervous for the first ten or 15 minutes but once we got the equaliser I felt we were the better side. We looked strong and positive in every department and if the players show that sort of attitude and commitment for the rest of the season we will be there or thereabouts.

'After just three league games it would be foolish to make any daft predictions, but I genuinely feel that if we can keep our strongest side on the park each week without any significant changes then things will get even better.

'The big thing for us now is to steer clear of injuries and suspensions. I know it's easier said than done but it can be the difference between success and failure.'

And Souness had a special word of praise for Ian Ferguson. He said: 'Every successful side needs a player like Ian. He gives us the kind of aggression and positive edge in midfield that we lacked recently against Hibs. There is no doubt he is a key man for us this season, and hopefully many seasons to come.'

After the game, Souness allowed Israeli defender Avi Cohen to rejoin his first club, Maccabi Tel Aviv, on loan. The 31-year-old defender still had a year on his Ibrox contract but was keen to return home.

There were two interested spectators at Ibrox for the game. First was Rangers owner Lawrence Marlborough, who had made the long journey from his base in the USA to take in the game and take a close look at an initiative called Rangers International, which was aimed at bringing expats closer to the club via live screening of games directly into their homes. Mr Marlborough and his team had identified more than 3,000 individuals that the scheme would be aimed at and he was keen to find out the thoughts of his board.

Visitor number two was England manager Bobby Robson, who was present to see how the many Anglos handled the white-hot atmosphere of an Old Firm game. Very well, I would say was the answer for the majority of them.

After the game, Mr Robson spoke at length to the likes of Terry Butcher, Chris Woods and Gary Stevens about the game and his plans for the England international team.

The two points garnered from the victory put Rangers joint top of the Premier League table on five points, the same total as Dundee United. Rangers' goal difference was superior to that of the Tannadice side, while Hibs were third on four points, with a goal difference of one for and none against – after THREE games!

Celtic were second bottom with just two points.

Rangers: Woods, Stevens, Brown, Gough, Wilkins, Butcher, Drinkell, I. Ferguson, McCoist, Durrant (Souness 80), Walters (Cooper 75).

Celtic: Andrews, Morris, Rogan, Aitken, McCarthy, Grant, Stark (Miller 57), McStay, McAvennie, Walker, Burns (Whyte 46).

Referee: Kenny Hope (Clarkston)

Attendance: 42,858

Celtic 1 Rangers 2

Saturday, 1 April 1989
Scottish Premier League

KEVIN Drinkell and Ian Ferguson scored the goals that assured Rangers of victory at Celtic Park on April Fools' Day, and the joke was on the home side when Chris Woods saved Joe Miller's late spot kick.

Rangers were two up at the break, and cruising, but while they weren't exactly hanging on at the end, it was starting to get a little bit uncomfortable.

There were two factors involved in the change of direction this match took. In essence, Celtic started playing at the same time Rangers stopped. Hence an almost total reversal of roles and the irresistible opportunity to describe this latest confrontation as the classic game of two halves.

The match might have taken place at Parkhead – and taken a huge twist after the break – but Rangers were so far ahead in the first half that Celtic almost required snookers. They really should have been more than two goals in front at half-time.

Celtic, on the other hand, will cite a missed penalty and disallowed goal as evidence of the misfortune which prevented them from at least grabbing a point.

Certainly, Rangers played with such command and swagger that they looked the complete team, heading for great things, which of course they were. Only Paul McStay, who was outstanding, looked in the same league during the first half.

Ray Wilkins was also marvellous – the ideal link between a solid, comfortable defence and the dashing, eager forwards. Among them Mark Walters was on fire, torturing Anton Rogan with his repertoire of dazzling skills and trademark changes of direction. There were times when it looked like Rogan might have to pay to get back in!

With his brilliance and the added assistance of Ian Ferguson operating in his most effective role, just behind the front men, Rangers looked a side of some class, bearing in mind they were giving this show amid the manic atmosphere that exists on these occasions.

They were helped to their interval lead by the uncertainty of their opponents, who seemed taken aback by the controlled mastery of Rangers. The warnings of their manager about conceding free kicks and thus giving Rangers opportunities to throw in their rear division clearly didn't sink in, because in no time at all, less than a minute in fact, they had given one away. However, it was the one taken by Wilkins in just four minutes, after Rogan had fouled Walters, which brought about the first goal. He pinged in a neat cross which reached an unhindered, unchallenged Kevin Drinkell, whose powerful header was diverted past Pat Bonner by the head of Celtic defender Steve McCahill. Rangers were one up and well in command, so early in the game.

As Billy McNeill was to indicate later, the opener left his team a mountain to climb, as he knew how stoutly Rangers could defend, and when the second goal was scored on the half hour, Celtic looked as if they might have to work hard to avoid a thrashing. Bonner did try magnificently to prevent that one, which came from another free kick. This time Ferguson hit one of the hardest dead-ball shots known to man and the fact Bonner managed even to halt its progress was remarkable.

It bounced from his hand and was chased by the ever-alert Ally McCoist as well as the despairing keeper, who seemed to get a hand to it on or just over the line. McCoist, too, got his head to it and, as is his wont, claimed the goal for his own. As McCoist had previous for that type of thing, we would have to wait until the goal was verified by an early version of VAR to see who would be awarded it! It was clearly Ferguson's goal.

Rangers might well have been awarded a penalty when Walters went down after a Rogan challenge, but when they went in for their half-time drinks they no doubt felt confident that two goals in their present mood would be a sound cushion for the next half, and perhaps even the catalyst for a few more.

But they were forced to revise that view almost immediately, as Celtic, within two minutes, were chasing only a single-goal deficit. Andy Walker turned quickly on a Morris cross and beat Woods in off the post.

Now it was a different ball game as Celtic, urged on by supporters who sensed a famous recovery, pushed Rangers into retreat. The Ibrox defence had to stand firm and disciplined as Joe Miller, who had replaced Billy Stark ten minutes before half-time, began to use his skill and pace to torment Rangers as Walters had done to Celtic on the same wing earlier.

It was from one of his crosses that Gough, who had been outstanding, was unlucky to concede a penalty seven minutes from time. As he tried to control the ball it bounced on to his arm and referee Douglas Hope awarded the spot kick.

Miller, clearly on a high, wrestled the ball from his captain, Roy Aitken, who had scored from the spot two weeks previously, strode forward confidently, but hit a weak shot which Woods, after having chosen the correct side, parried. Even then Miller was odds-on to score as he lined up the rebound. Enter Gary Stevens, and the Celtic man hit the ball high over the bar. It would've been interesting to get Aitken's thoughts on the matter.

That and the goal they had disallowed convinced Celtic it was not to be their day. The one that got away came when Morris stretched to reach the ball on the goal line near the corner flag. He put over a marvellous cross which sailed over the head of Woods, who was clearly claiming that the ball had been over the line, and landed in the net. Referee Hope signalled a goal, but after talking to his linesman gave a goal kick.

Just 48 hours after the Old Firm game, Celtic flew out to Dubai to face Liverpool in the unofficial British Championship. Chances were, it would be Celtic's last opportunity to take part in a glamour game like this for some time, because Rangers, after their Old Firm victory at Parkhead, would be required to drop at least four points in their six remaining games for them to lose the league – and we all knew there was little chance of that happening.

As it was, that nail-biting conclusion would be avoided as Rangers won their next five, with Motherwell, St Mirren, Hearts, Dundee United and Dundee all beaten for the loss of just a solitary goal.

In the final analysis, Rangers comfortably lifted the title by six points from their nearest challengers, Aberdeen, with Celtic a further four points adrift.

Manager Graeme Souness was also content to relish the first win at Celtic Park by Rangers under his guidance, indeed the first for nine years. Reasonably enough, he contended that no team could possibly dominate an Old Firm match from start to finish, but revealed that he had asked his players at half-time for more of the same. 'Don't do anything silly' was his parting shot. 'They then went out and did something silly, but overall I felt we played some good stuff all the way through and were worth the two points.'

At the post-match press conference, Celtic manager Billy McNeill insisted his side deserved a point after the way they had recovered from being outplayed in the first half. Others may have felt differently.

Joe Miller, who came on and played well after the interval, was now well aware of the fine line between heroes and villains. His insistence on taking the penalty kick, which could have given Celtic the equaliser, would have been extolled as the justifiable confidence of a hero had he scored. As it was, he missed and that precocity was condemned as foolish arrogance.

With the League Cup already in the bag, Graeme Souness prepared his side for the final push to what could still end up a grand slam domestic season. With the title virtually wrapped up, only St Johnstone stood between them and the Scottish Cup Final.

In the semi-final tie, played at Parkhead, the Perth Saints gave a sparkling account of themselves and almost pulled off a shock win. Under the guidance of former Rangers number two Alex Totten, they were a whisker away from winning the tie.

It was a different story in the replay at the same venue, though. Goals by Walters, Stevens, Drinkell and McCoist set up an Old Firm final – and sadly it was payback time for Joe Miller, who struck the only goal to deny Rangers a glory treble.

Still, the first of nine was in the bag!

Celtic: Bonner, Morris, Rogan, Aitken, McCahill, Grant, Stark, McStay, Walker, McGhee, Burns. Subs: Coyne, Miller.

Rangers: Woods, Stevens, Munro, Gough, Wilkins, Butcher, Drinkell, Ferguson, McCoist, Brown, Walters. Subs: Sterland, Cooper.

Referee: Mr D. D. Hope

Attendance: 60,171

Rangers 1 Celtic 0

Saturday, 4 November 1989
Scottish Premier League

RANGERS celebrated Guy Fawkes Day 24 hours early when they beat Celtic by a solitary goal – and sparks were flying in the away end when they noticed who had scored the game's only goal.

Maurice Johnston had joined Rangers at the start of the 1989/90 season, a decision which had split the home support down the middle, especially in the wake of his idiotic shenanigans in the League Cup Final just a couple of years before.

He took part in his first Old Firm game – wearing a blue jersey – at Celtic Park less than two months before the Ibrox game, and played his part in a 1–1 draw. He had scored five times in his 11 matches prior to the game at Ibrox, so no one was expecting miracles in front of goal.

But while we may not have received a miracle, more epiphany light, perhaps, it was certainly a defining moment in his short spell at Ibrox. With just a couple of minutes remaining, Gary Stevens picked up the ball out wide on the right. He drove towards the Celtic box, urged on by fans in the East Enclosure, and whipped in a cross which was only half cleared by Chris Morris. It fell at the feet of Johnston, virtually on the edge of the 18-yard box, and the 26-year-old striker took one touch to control it, and another to despatch it low into the right-hand corner of Pat Bonner's net.

And at that he was off and running towards the corner of the Copland Road stand and East Enclosure. This beacon of strawberry blonde hair was no doubt overjoyed at scoring for his new employers against his old ones. In fact, he might have looked upon it as some form of retribution given he had been pelted with objects by those who used to love him when he had gone to retrieve a ball.

We all knew it had to happen one day. There would come a time when Johnston would score for Rangers against Celtic. He was too good a striker not to. As it played out, he took part in 11 competitive games against Celtic, and he scored twice. Not the greatest of returns, but he was never really classed as an out and out goalscorer, like Ally McCoist. Maybe a more relevant statistic for this type of player is that of the eight league games he played against Celtic, Rangers lost just one.

In the match in question, the ramifications of his goal were significant, as it allowed Rangers to leapfrog Celtic and assume their mantle at the top of the Premier League table. They were ahead of Aberdeen due to a superior goal difference.

Although Billy McNeill and his players, who improved considerably in the second half, might have been aggrieved at being sent back to Parkhead empty-handed, it is fair to say they were fortunate to have reached the interval with their goal intact. Rangers dominated that period, although their lack of menace around goal was alarming, given the striking resources at their disposal.

Celtic played with their captain, Roy Aitken, at the back looking after Derek Whyte and Paul Elliott, a wise tactical move given the fragile condition of the defence which had been exploited by Dunfermline the previous Saturday. The intention was to have Morris and Tommy Burns driving forward in support of Mike Galloway and Paul McStay in midfield.

The intentions were laudable, but Rangers' four-man middle line assumed control. Morris, who could be such a potent force in supplementing Celtic attacks, was too busy wondering what Mark Walters was going to do next to even consider heading in the opposite direction.

Walters was in the mood, and after only a short period it was easy to see why Rangers' manager Graeme Souness had been fulsome in his praise of the winger prior to the match. Walters teased and tormented Morris, and any other Celtic defender who tried to stop him, including Paul Elliott, whose second-half challenge on the winger inside the box appeared worthy of a penalty.

There was a point late in the game when Morris actually offered the Englishman, who had fallen over, a helping hand. It was not exactly a gesture of defeat by the Celtic player, but enough to recognise that his opponent had won their individual contest.

Yet, while Rangers deserved their triumph, Celtic could have escaped from Ibrox with both points, if perhaps Dariusz Dziekanowski had been given a proper supply. Unfortunately for Celtic, just after they had started to come to grips in the midfield, their striker emerged lame from a tackle by John Brown and was taken off in 66 minutes to be replaced by Andy Walker.

Before then, however, Celtic had been presented with a gift. Terry Butcher swished at a long ball out of defence from Burns and Joe Miller was clear and homing in on Chris Woods, but his shot was far too straight and the ball squirmed away from the keeper straight to Tommy Coyne, but he could only knock it against a post, and with that went Celtic's best chance of getting anything from the game.

Rangers dominated the season's second Old Firm encounter for lengthy spells and although manager Graeme Souness had been concerned about a lack of goals at half-time, Johnston was able to ease the tension with his late counter, and while the Celtic supporters may not have been able to forgive him, when he left the stadium he didn't look too upset. He sauntered off into the evening, minder at his side, unconcerned that he had enraged tens of thousands of fans who not so very long ago had come to look upon him as some kind of hero.

But Souness, himself, had other concerns, most notably the immediate future of midfield lynchpin Ray Wilkins. The England international was outstanding against Celtic but it was known that he was unsettled and keen to head back to his native London. There is no doubt Wilkins had enjoyed a new lease of life when he moved to Glasgow, and Rangers supporters were treated to many vintage Wilkins displays. He had been a standout during his short spell at Ibrox, but would ultimately play just three more games for Rangers before indeed heading back down south to join Queens Park Rangers.

Souness needed support in a midfield which had suddenly become over-reliant on Trevor Steven. He also had the two Fergusons, Ian and Derek, the latter of whom was still recuperating after remedial work on a shoulder injury, while Ian had been having a difficult time with illness, and had still to regain the verve which was a characteristic of his game.

Ian Durrant was still a long way from Premier Division combat and although he was making steady, perhaps even impressive progress, there was still no guarantees of a return to his full glory.

The immediate problem for the Rangers boss was the second half of the season and a successful defence of the title. It's the type of thing that could have easily evaporated due to Rangers' long injury list, so Wilkins leaving was the last thing Souness needed.

But he had to find a replacement, and while Wilkins would be one of the hardest players to replace like for like, Souness came up with a very good second best. After a few hundred games in the blue and red of Chelsea and Liverpool, Nigel Spackman welcomed Ray Wilkins to Queens Park Rangers before immediately clearing out his locker and making the opposite journey to Glasgow.

The talented midfielder went straight into the team for the league match against Hearts at Tynecastle and was instrumental in a 2–1 win for Rangers. Spackman brought different qualities to the table than Wilkins but was cool on the ball and could pick out a pass. He was also known to make a tackle or two in his time at Ibrox. It was an excellent piece of business by Souness.

Four weeks after signing for Rangers, Spackman truly arrived when he scored the only goal of a tough Old Firm encounter at Parkhead. It would be his only goal of the season but that was by the way because the Light Blues would go on to successfully defend their Premier League title, the second of nine in a row.

The Englishman – who at one point looked like he would pull on the dark blue of Scotland – played in every league game from his arrival to the end of the season, and thoroughly deserved his championship badge. He would win another two before departing for a second spell at Stamford Bridge. Three league titles in three seasons wasn't such a bad return.

Rangers: Woods, Stevens, Munro, Brown, Wilkins, Butcher, Steven, Ferguson, McCoist, Johnston, Walters. Subs: Dodds and Nisbet.

Celtic: Bonner, Morris, Burns, Aitken, Elliott, Whyte, Galloway, McStay, Dziekanowski, Coyne, Miller. Subs: Grant and Walker.

Referee: Mr G. Smith (Edinburgh)

Attendance: 41,598

Celtic 1 Rangers 2

Sunday, 28 October 1990
League Cup Final

MARK Walters wasn't entirely sure what to expect when he agreed to join Rangers from Aston Villa in a half-million-pound deal.

Graeme Souness had been a long-time admirer of the skilful winger and was keen for Walters to join his 'English revolution' at Ibrox – and tendered an 11th hour bid to usurp Everton, just as it looked as though the Villa fans' favourite was on his way to Goodison Park.

So, 23-year-old Walters arrived in Glasgow just in time to make his debut against, guess who, Celtic at Parkhead in the traditional New Year game – and what awaited rocked him to his very core. The east-end ground was transformed into an arena of hate as racism in every shape and form was hurled at this brilliant young Brummy.

Of course, he survived the bananas, golf balls and pigs' feet that were chucked at him, and while it was a mighty shock to the system, Walters would soon learn to handle the 'unique' Old Firm occasion – thankfully they weren't all used as expressions of hatred – and, quite frankly, thrive on it more than the majority of Rangers' other imports from south of the border.

One clear example of how Walters lapped up the pressure games is the 1990 Skol Cup Final, which he helped Rangers edge in a cracking game against their old foes.

The only difference between the teams at the end of a superb 120 minutes was the colour of the medals given out in the Hampden presentation ceremony, with Rangers finally triumphing over adversity off and on the pitch to snatch a record 17th League Cup trophy that assured them of European football the following season.

Rarely had a game see-sawed quite so dramatically and ended with so little between the sides on play, but in the end, the men from Ibrox possessed that something extra that Celtic didn't, and that was the aforementioned Mr Walters.

Paul Elliott hurled Celtic into a dramatic 52nd-minute lead, Walters levelled and then halfway through extra time, Celtic's defence blundered badly and Gers' skipper Richard Gough grabbed the winner.

So the trophy, decked out in red, white and blue, was held aloft on the pitch afterwards by the victorious skipper – and then manager Graeme Souness led his players on a victory jig across the churned-up Hampden turf.

It was a joyous scene for a team who were at the wrong end of two contentious and crucial refereeing decisions, and had to play without the influential pairing of Mo Johnston and Terry Butcher.

Johnston was the surprise omission because of a groin injury, while it was decided that Butcher's match fitness might have been suspect after missing seven first-team matches.

The game was played in the best traditions of the Old Firm, full of determination, skill and, it has to be said, sportsmanship, and victory meant a fourth League Cup in seven years for the Ibrox side.

The winning goal was a lesson in persistence, and it sent scorer Gough hurtling over the advertising boards in his excitement, waving to the jubilant Rangers crowd.

Gary Stevens hit the ball firmly, fiercely and accurately, high into the area. Elliott and Mark Hateley failed to connect with headers and sub Chris Morris tried to shepherd the ball back to his goalkeeper Pat Bonner. But Gough rushed in from behind Morris and got between defender and goalkeeper to slot the ball away for the goal which won the cup.

So this titanic tie was settled by errors and opportunism as Rangers kept their cool despite a rejected penalty claim in 19 minutes when Ally McCoist tumbled as he was challenged by Bonner on the edge of the penalty area ... and despite a hint that Joe Miller elbowed the ball to control it as it came over from a John Collins corner kick on the lead-up to Elliott's goal.

In the first incident, referee Jim McCluskey, who had a decent first major final, signalled that McCoist had thrown himself to the ground. In the second, he ruled that the ball had come off Miller's chest.

Anyway, Dariusz Wdowczyk fired in a shot that looked to be going wide, but the massive frame of Elliott made a startling swoop to send the ball swirling away from Chris Woods and into the goal.

Rangers' equaliser was finished off perfectly by the dazzling Walters. Hateley leaped high to head the ball down to McCoist, who tried gamely to control it, couldn't, and it rolled into Walters's path for him to finish off with a beautiful swing of his left leg.

Chris Woods had three good saves on the ground from Gerry Creaney, Dziekanowski and skipper Paul McStay, and had an excellent game all round.

At the other end, Bonner looked unusually uncertain and even tumbled over the advertising boards as he was challenged by McCoist.

Both managers made changes to try to break the deadlock when the match was evenly poised at one goal apiece. Chris Morris came on for Miller on the hour, and three minutes later Dutch wide boy Pieter Huistra took over from the tiring Terry Hurlock.

Fourten minutes from the end John Hewitt replaced Steve Fulton and then Ian Ferguson was introduced to the game to replace McCoist – although Hateley went off first, thinking his number had been held up.

Hurlock and Hateley (Rangers) and Celtic's Dziekanowski were all booked, but for routine offences. Referee McCluskey stamped down efficiently on any trouble, but in the furious pace of the match the players more than not found time only to pursue the ball.

It really was a fantastic match, and one that kept supporters on the edges of their seats throughout – and they were even treated to an extra 30 minutes!

In the relative sanctuary of the Hampden press room, Richard Gough revealed the secret of his Skol Cup success. Rangers' stand-in skipper had taken giant steps towards Hampden glory thanks to a tip from absent Celt Charlie Nicholas.

After scoring the deciding goal, Gough pointed out: 'Charlie claimed in a newspaper article that I had lost my sting because I wasn't going up for set pieces. That's because my foot is still painful, but I decided to take a chance.

'It was a long free kick by Gary Stevens and Mark Hateley jumped up with Paul Elliott. As the ball bounced, I managed to get between Chris Morris and Pat Bonner and guided it home with the side of my foot.'

Gough's extra-time goal guaranteed Rangers European football the following season, but his sights were set a lot closer to home when he said: 'Now for the treble. It's great to win a trophy so early in the season, and this will give us a big lift for the return match against Red Star Belgrade.

'It's incredible, but a few days ago we were down in the dumps after our first leg defeat, but now we're on top of the world. Football can get you like that.'

Gough, who had taken over as skipper from Terry Butcher, added: 'It's the first time I've captained the team in a major final and I scored the winner. You can't ask for more than that.'

Mark Walters, who equalised after Paul Elliott had put Celtic in front, said: 'We've had a hectic time, but considering Celtic didn't have a midweek game we more than matched them all the way. It was a tribute to our pre-season training that we were able to last so well.'

Rangers' boss Graeme Souness was delighted with the final result, and said: 'There were quite a few players in my team who had a point to prove. In my book, this team showed the most character of any during my spell as Rangers manager.

'Considering the week we've had, starting with the loss of Oleg Kuznetsov and not playing all that well in our midweek European tie, the criticism the players received did us a favour.'

Souness revealed that Mo Johnston had been left out on medical advice after suffering a hamstring injury. He also said that deposed captain Terry Butcher had been close to playing, but he had decided to stick with the back four that had represented the club in the European tie. For apart from the Belgrade debacle they hadn't lost any goals in recent games.

Souness also praised Celtic's contribution to a cracking match, but added: 'We were just a bit too good for them.'

Celtic manager, Billy McNeill, meanwhile congratulated his rivals, but said: 'I was disappointed at the way we lost the goals. I thought when we opened the scoring it would be our day. We had a chance in extra time that would have made life awkward for Rangers, but we didn't take it.'

Celtic: Bonner, Grant, Wdowczyk, Fulton (Hewitt), Elliott, Rogan, Miller (Morris), McStay, Dziekanowski, Creaney, Collins.

Rangers: Woods, Stevens, Munro, Gough, Brown, Spackman, Steven, Hurlock (Huistra), McCoist (Ferguson), Hateley, Walters.

Referee: Mr J. McCluskey (Stewarton)

Attendance: 62,817

Rangers 1 Celtic 0

Tuesday, 31 March 1992
Scottish Cup semi-final

THE early red card for Rangers left-back David Robertson set the tone for this Scottish Cup last-four tie at Hampden to be played against a backdrop of driving rain and controversy.

Some would call it Rangers' finest hour and a half in Scottish Cup football, as they played 84 minutes with just ten men and still managed to beat Celtic.

But the truth is, quite frankly, that Robertson should never have been sent off, as his body check on former Aberdeen team-mate Joe Miller – who went down as though shot by a sniper – happened midway inside the Celtic half of the pitch, almost equidistant between 18-yard and centre line.

It was never a clear goalscoring opportunity and was, at best, a yellow card.

They say referee Andrew Waddell had a reputation as a stickler for the rules, but if that was the case then he should've stuck to the rules and issued a different colour of card. The same referee had sent off three Rangers players the season before in a stormy Scottish Cup tie at Parkhead. On that occasion, Mark Walters, Terry Hurlock and Mark Hateley had all managed to fall foul of this 'stickler for the rules'.

But Rangers got there in the end, thanks to Ally McCoist (who else?), who struck a minute before half-time to put Walter Smith's side into the Tennent's Scottish Cup Final. Coisty made the most of the opportunity after tenacious play by midfield ace Stuart McCall. Celtic duo Derek Whyte and Brian O'Neill banged into each other and McCall stepped in to win the ball and square it across the face of the goal. McCoist met it on the run and drove it with power and precision past a despairing Gordon Marshall, who could only touch the ball with the tips of his fingers as it headed for the corner of the net.

It was classic Ally McCoist, the predatory big-game hunter with an eye for goal. It's no coincidence the Rangers legend is the club's all-time record goalscorer.

It's easy to say that Celtic had wicked luck in this game. Sure, they might have hit both bar and post and perhaps should have had a penalty in the second half. However, the glory went to Rangers for recovering so well from the sixth-minute dismissal of Robertson, who as well as being a sound defender, was also a constant threat going forward.

No one is trying to pretend that his block on the 'mortally wounded' Miller wasn't deliberate. It was, and it was cynical, and every other adjective you care to use, but the bottom line is it didn't prevent a genuine goalscoring opportunity and therefore shouldn't have been red. If referees were to issue red cards for this type of foul in every game, we would regularly be playing five-a-sides.

Due to the nature of the game I would imagine there was a split vote on the rights and wrongs of the referee's decision, with the colour of the card depending on the colour of your shirt, but it was harsh, although the bottom line is Rangers were down to ten men.

And that was what so incensed those on the nearby Rangers bench. The moment the red card was brandished, Rangers players jostled the referee and were ushered away by skipper Gough, but manager Walter Smith and number two Archie Knox soon joined the melee and had to be moved away from the referee by a top cop.

One decision, after just six minutes' play, and the match was in chaos. To say Waddell's decision had proved unpopular with Rangers was an understatement. He was public enemy number one in the eyes of Walter Smith and co.

Smith had plumped for Stuart McCall and Dale Gordon, both of whom had recovered from injury. Scotland ace McCall did particularly well but the undoubted star of the show was Nigel Spackman. The former Chelsea star stepped back from the midfield to partner Gough at the heart of the defence after Robertson's untimely departure. The Englishman was immaculate and never lost his cool, even when Celtic were going through the gears and turning the screw.

The other true heroes of a pulsating 90 minutes were the supporters, the thousands who stayed to the finish in driving rain in the uncovered parts of the ground. It was awful in such an age that the draconian SFA expected thousands of paying customers to endure such spartan conditions. But stand in the rain they did, and many would no doubt have expected Waddell to point to the penalty spot nine minutes from the end when John Collins appeared to have his legs whipped from him by John Brown. Remarkably, the referee waved play on.

In a storm of pressure skipper Paul McStay hit the crossbar with a fierce 25-yard drive and a Gerry Creaney header was touched on to the bar superbly by Andy Goram.

When Mike Galloway replaced Brian O'Neill on the hour mark, he had two super shots at goal, but he just couldn't find a way past Goram. One of his shots almost knocked the keeper off his feet, but still the Rangers number one stood his ground to keep it out.

Just before O'Neill went off, he had a shot which skimmed off Brown and hit the bottom of a post.

It was probably at this point Celtic got the message that it wasn't going to be their night, while in adversity, someone up above was on the side of the Light Blues.

Having won at Ibrox in the league ten days previously, Celtic were full of confidence before the match, but very little went right for them. Against the verve of a robust Rangers they weren't able to play their normal passing game. Even Charlie Nicholas was below his best and was replaced by Tommy Coyne.

It was a bitter blow for the Celts, who hadn't won a trophy for three seasons, and this competition represented their final opportunity of the campaign.

Some observers felt that perhaps opposing ten men had rebounded on Celtic, but that would suggest Rangers merely dug in and defended from the trenches. Not true. Celtic might have failed to match the style and drive of their depleted rivals but Rangers still managed to carve out many fine opportunities of their own. It was by no means the Alamo, and Rangers were by no means mere observers.

One of the unsung heroes was Dale Gordon. The former Norwich attacker had been absent from the first team for some time due to a bad ankle injury, but he played exceptionally well and contributed much to the cause. Paul Rideout replaced Gordon with 13 minutes remaining and picked up where his fellow Englishman had left off.

The result, if not the match itself, would be remembered by Rangers fans for a long time – even to this day, because the resolve shown by the players epitomised the Rangers of that era. They genuinely didn't know when they were beaten. Even the most loyal Gers man might not have given the team much hope after losing Robertson so early in the match, but the players stuck at it and every one of a blue persuasion went home happy.

Super Ally's goal won the tie and more. It also clinched the *Daily Record*'s Golden Shot award for the first player to score 30 domestic goals in a season. As winner, McCoist collected the £1,000 prize, plus a case of champagne to celebrate.

Later, McCoist said: 'The team spirit was magnificent and we will sink a few sherbets tonight. I'm absolutely delighted. I've been runner-up a few times and I began to wonder if I would ever win it. It was even more agonising because I'd been stuck on 29 for a few weeks. The first guy to congratulate me after the game was Andy Goram – but only because I think he's after one of the bottles of bubbly.'

And at the end of an incredible match, Walter Smith raced on to the pitch to hug his players, and the first of those to receive the 'bear hug' was goal hero McCoist. The scenes were in stark contrast to those which took place after just six minutes' play.

The Rangers players shook hands with the beaten side and then rushed towards their own fans as rain teemed down and gusting winds swirled around the stadium. Having lost to Celtic in their last five Scottish Cup meetings – three of which were finals – it was a moment of real triumph for Smith and his players, and they milked it for what it was worth. They now had a final to look forward to.

Celtic: Marshall, Morris, Boyd, O'Neill (Galloway), Mowbray, Whyte, Miller, McStay, Creaney, Nicholas (Coyne), Collins.

Rangers: Goram, Stevens, Robertson, Gough, Spackman, Brown, Gordon (Rideout), McCall, McCoist, Durrant, Huistra. Sub: Spencer.

Referee: Mr A. W. Waddell (Edinburgh)

Attendance: 45,191

Celtic 0 Rangers 1

Saturday, 7 November 1992
Scottish Premier League

IF there was one thing that made Walter Smith spit feathers when he was manager of Rangers, it was talk of winning a title long before anything had actually been won. This season was no exception, with the media talking in terms of Rangers having the championship sewn up ... in NOVEMBER!

Maybe it was because this narrow win at Celtic Park was the Light Blues' tenth league win on the trot, or because they appeared to be streets ahead of their cross-city rivals. Either way, Smith was having none of it.

This latest success, while easing Rangers six points in front of Celtic, and with a game in hand, was anything but a one-way street. Celtic had the lion's share of the pressure and made a mammoth effort to grab an equaliser in a pulsating second half. But it simply wasn't enough, and the papers were speculating as to where any genuine championship challenge would come from. Perhaps Aberdeen, maybe Hearts ...

As far as Liam Brady's players were concerned, it was the same old Celtic story. Pile on the pressure and the agony will take care of itself!

After an uneasy start, Rangers had produced another European-like defensive performance, denying Celtic room inside the box by forcing them to play across the front of the defence. But as so often happens in an Old Firm game, one momentary lapse of concentration is all it takes to prove crucial.

A positive start gave Celtic fans hope that their side would be able to put one over on their old rivals, but Paul McStay's early shot was cleared off the line by Richard Gough and a genuine opportunity was gone.

Shortly afterwards, Andy Goram called on every ounce of his international experience to make a tremendous save, touching over a fierce free kick from Dariusz Wdowczyk. Celtic's early aggression and confidence looked like providing them with the opening, but at the same time they were reminded of Rangers' threat when Ally McCoist found space in the Celtic box, although his shot was aimed straight at Pat Bonner.

Celtic had a couple of other chances before the game's opening goal – but it was Smith's men who struck gold. The goal stemmed from Dale Gordon, a veritable revelation for the second game in succession, as he made one of numerous surges from midfield.

All credit, too, goes to McCoist who must have been tempted to add to his already growing goal tally, but who unselfishly squared the ball to big-game specialist Ian Durrant, who was better placed and who gleefully hooked the ball past the despairing Bonner.

After the ball bulged the net, the main questions requiring urgent attention were – where on earth was the centre of the Celtic defence, and would the goal be sufficient to see Rangers pick up the points?

The first half ended with Celtic still in outfield control but unable to penetrate the visiting defence. That said, Rangers appeared quite comfortable inviting their opponents on to them, and there was no panic in the Rangers rearguard.

However, Smith was forced to reshuffle his pack at the break as John Brown – who, alongside Gough, had provided an almost impenetrable partnership – took a knock and couldn't continue. Dave McPherson switched from full-back to team up with Gough in the heart of the defence, and Brown was replaced by Pieter Huistra.

But just 13 minutes into the second half, Gough was also forced to leave the field, and hobbled off to be replaced by Alexei Mikhailitchenko. That meant further reorganisation, with Mark Hateley dropping back to stand in for his captain. The fact that Celtic failed to score in the remaining half hour is definitely a reflection on how well the makeshift partnership quickly gelled. In fact, this latest tactical switch would later yield the famous quote from big Mark, who is reported to have said, 'When I'm finished playing up front I might revert to centre-half, as you just kick the ball the way you're facing!' Whether he said it or not, it was a cracker!

With both Gough and Brown off the park, Goram's goal was forced to endure an incredible second-half blitz, and at times it really was a case of all hands on deck.

The enigmatic Stuart Slater was the biggest threat to Rangers. He made a great run past three defenders but failed to hit the target from a promising position. He saw another effort touched over by Goram and then hit another shot over the bar – and all within a ten-minute period. The much-maligned West Ham recruit, who had linked up with Liam Brady – a former Hammers team-mate – at Celtic Park just a couple of months previously, had yet to win over the Celtic support, although it wasn't for the lack of trying. He also had shots which fizzed past both posts and he worked his socks off to try and find an equaliser, but all to no avail.

With Brown off at half-time, to be joined by a limping Richard Gough later, Rangers' changes were enforced, but it was a different story for Celtic. They were going for broke and pushed on Charlie Nicholas for Gerry Creaney, and then Brian O'Neill for Wdowczyk.

Rangers, however, dredged up all their character to withstand the pressure as the home punters headed grumpily for the exits, although despite the intensity of it all, the game was generally fought out in a sporting fashion.

Rangers had three players booked by referee Brian McGinlay, who handled the big derby match well. He yellow carded Gordon and Gough for fouls, and Durrant for dissent. They were joined by Celtic's Tom Boyd for backchat. Celtic's Mick Martin also received a dressing down in the dugout from McGinlay, but there wasn't too much of a nasty nature.

Brady made some early tactical changes, using Mike Galloway to pick up McCoist, and then putting Tony Mowbray on Hateley, with Gary Gillespie the spare man. It worked a treat – until that quite incredible lapse.

Celtic had a couple of penalty claims. McStay took a tumble in the box, which the ref rightly ruled as exaggeration. And if McPherson did handle a fierce late blast from Slater, it was totally unavoidable. He was far too close to be able to get out of the way in time, but at that point it was desperation stakes for the hosts.

Apart from the rejuvenated Gordon, Goram also provided inspiration for Rangers. He was a veritable brick wall and stood between Celtic and a certain equaliser at times. It's little wonder he is still hailed as Rangers' greatest keeper of the modern age.

As far as Celtic were concerned, if they could get a goal or two out of Slater, then they might just get their money's worth, as his outfield play had generally been very good in the period around the Old Firm game. Whether or not that in itself would be good enough to make life look good again in the east end was debatable. I suppose the fact he remained at Celtic for just 13 months tells its own story.

As a result of their narrow win, Rangers were able to consolidate their position at the top of the Premier League. Sure, it had been a really determined defensive display which ultimately won them the game, but it takes all types of different performances to win league titles.

Celtic had by far the bulk of the match and will consider themselves unlucky not to have won, but regardless of whether it was poor finishing on their part, or a great individual performance from Goram which thwarted them time and again, no one ever remembers the team that finished second.

Although it truly was a team effort that garnered the points for Rangers, they were best served by Goram, McPherson, Brown, Gough and Hateley.

The two points left Rangers well in control of the Premier League, and racked up a run of 28 league games without defeat, which was the catalyst for a fifth successive title. Aberdeen eventually finished second, nine points behind the champions, with Celtic in third place, 13 points behind rampant Rangers.

It was a busy season and Rangers just failed to make it to the Champions League Final, playing ten games and remaining unbeaten in every single one. Wins in the Scottish Cup and League Cup made it almost the perfect season for the Light Blues.

On the same day Rangers beat Celtic at Parkhead, 10,000 supporters were at Ibrox for the reserve league match between the Old Firm's second strings. Gary Stevens made his long-awaited return from injury but failed to inspire a victory. Rangers lost 3–0 but Stevens came through the challenge unscathed.

Celtic: Bonner, Wdowczyk (O'Neill), Boyd, Mowbray, Gillespie, Galloway, Grant, McStay, Slater, Creaney (Nicholas), Collins.

Rangers: Goram, McCall, Robertson, Gough (Mikhailitchenko), McPherson, Brown (Huistra), Gordon, Ferguson, McCoist, Hateley, Durrant.

Referee: Mr B. McGinlay (Balfron)

Attendance: 51,958

Celtic 2 Rangers 4

Saturday, 1 January 1994
Scottish Premier League

CELTIC were a financial basket case when Rangers arrived in the east end of the city for the traditional Ne'erday game. The Parkhead club – owned by two families for the greater part of 100 years – were in grave danger of going down the tubes, such was their perilous state.

The situation would reach a point of no return just a few weeks after the game when the Bank of Scotland demanded payment of £1 million within 24 hours or they would begin the process of winding up Celtic Football Club.

They didn't have that kind of money, and it looked to all intents and purposes that they were heading for oblivion when Fergus McCann, who had previously been denied the opportunity to invest in the club, offered up a lifesaving sum of money. Naturally it was accepted and the bespectacled Canadian began the arduous task of rebuilding the east-end club.

For some Celtic supporters, though, they'd had enough, and when Rangers scored their third goal of the afternoon, it was the catalyst for some of the ugliest scenes witnessed in recent Old Firm games. Small pockets of fighting broke out among Celtic fans and objects were thrown at the Celtic board sitting in the directors' box, and although some landed a little too close for comfort for Rangers chairman David Murray and manager Walter Smith, they were clearly not the focus of the fans' rage.

As the result of the match became a foregone conclusion, the visiting supporters were in full voice, and their jubilation must have seemed like an extra kick in the teeth for the dejected home fans.

After such a stuttering first half of the season, there was no better way for Rangers to get back on track than by first footing Celtic Park in such a confident manner. Playing their most exciting football of the season, Rangers were ruthless in the opening period and raced into a three-goal lead inside the first half hour.

As it was, John Brown and Richard Gough made virtually their first tackles of the afternoon with not a Celtic player in sight. They were called into action to wrestle with one idiotic Celtic fan who ran on to the pitch to attack Rangers goalkeeper Ally Maxwell.

It wasn't a day for the faint-hearted – but Rangers didn't lack bottle. They went into the game injury-ravaged and as underdogs but made a mockery of that within four minutes. With just 65 seconds on the clock, the tireless Stuart McCall sent Mark Hateley racing through on Pat Bonner and the big striker coolly slotted the ball into the far corner of the net. How Celtic must have despised Hateley.

The home defence were taking the season of goodwill just too far as three minutes later Gordon Durie dropped deep to send Neil Murray through on the keeper in a similar move which again exposed gaping holes at the back. Murray's effort was blocked by the feet of Bonner but Alexei Mikhailitchenko followed up to stroke the loose ball into the net.

Astonishingly, Miko added a third on the half-hour mark. Gary Stevens was magnificent in an unfamiliar left-back role as he thwarted the wing menace of Paul Byrne – and he proved his worth going forward too as he flung over a deep cross which Hateley nodded towards Durie. His effort on goal wasn't the greatest, but Miko followed up to poke the ball past Bonner, sparking delirium in the Rangers end and mutiny just about everywhere else in the ground as the home fans struggled to contain their anger.

Those were Miko's first two goals of the season and how he appeared to enjoy them.

However, it would be crazy to underestimate the role played by Durie in this game. He made one of the most impressive Old Firm debuts of recent seasons, his pace pulling the Celtic defence all over the place and his distribution and link-up play with Hateley and the midfield different class.

And both combined again to seal Celtic's fate in the second half. 'Jukebox' worked his way to the wing and pulled over a cross, which the defence were happy to scramble clear. However, the ball fell to sub Oleg Kuznetsov who cracked a magnificent volley from all of 25 yards into the back of the net to claim his first goal for Rangers.

And it was badly needed, too, following a period in which Celtic's bravery might easily have been rewarded. They hauled themselves back into contention a minute into the second half when John Collins executed a well-worked free kick, before firing a drive in off Maxwell's post from 20 yards.

And after an hour Charlie Nicholas was unlucky to see a left-foot shot smack the crossbar. However, Nicholas did offer his side a glimmer of hope nine minutes from time when he nodded home from a Byrne corner.

But Rangers were in no mood to give up their advantage and held on comfortably for a win which put them back on top of the table, a point clear of Aberdeen and four ahead of Celtic.

After the game, manager Smith said: 'If I could have a New Year wish it would be for an injury-free squad for a decent run of games to help bring that consistency back into our play. Our results so far show a lack of consistency and that's due to the changes we've been forced to make to team selection because of injury, not loss of form or anything else.

'No manager likes to change a winning team or formula but that has been forced upon us. However, hopefully the group of players who did so well for us at Parkhead continue to do so for a run of games and we can begin to add players back to the squad such as Duncan Ferguson, Ally McCoist, Ian Durrant, Andy Goram, David Robertson and Fraser Wishart, all of whom are getting ready to play again. If we can do that I'm sure we can find the consistency we've been looking for.'

Two wise men from the east had brought festive gifts to Parkhead for the Rangers supporters to feast on. They came in the shape of Old Firm goals from Mikhailitchenko and Kuznetsov, and they were also the perfect gifts for the players themselves, who were due to celebrate the traditional Ukrainian Christmas six days after the match.

Miko revealed how the duo were set to welcome family over from their homeland to help them celebrate – but tempered that with the knowledge that only a mild alcoholic drink could be taken as Kilmarnock were due at Ibrox the day after the Ukrainian Christmas!

He said: 'Oleg and I are looking forward to Friday, and the goals against Celtic will make it even better, but unfortunately not every day can be Christmas and we might have to go easy on a celebration drink.

'Personally, Saturday's goals felt twice as nice, not only because they were my first of the season, but because they were my first against

Celtic. I've had several chances to score against them before but never quite managed it. However, it was great to do so in the New Year's Day game, which I know is one of the most special games of the season.

'I was very happy to see Oleg score, too. His was a beautiful strike and was just what we needed at that stage as Celtic were coming back into the game.'

Even a player as experienced as Mikhailitchenko admitted he was shell-shocked at seeing Rangers sweep into a three-goal lead after just half an hour, and said: 'It's so hard to play against Celtic and these matches are traditionally such hard-fought affairs, so it did come as a shock, although a very pleasant one.

'I didn't sense any extra determination among the rest of the players before the game. Everyone knows these are the most important matches and so the manager and Archie [Knox] don't need to do much to encourage the players before kick-off. Thankfully we made a great start and we were able to build on it.'

Rangers followed up their Old Firm victory with a magnificent 3–0 win over Kilmarnock, and after draws against Dundee and Aberdeen, racked up six successive victories to put some daylight between themselves and main challengers Aberdeen.

Mikhailitchenko scored Rangers' goal in the final Old Firm game of the season – a 1–1 draw at Ibrox – and that was good enough to see Rangers crowned champions. Celtic had replaced manager Liam Brady midway through the campaign with Lou Macari, and Macari himself was sacked at the end of the season. Celtic finished fourth, eight points behind the champions.

Celtic: Bonner, Gillespie, Boyd, Grant, Wdowczyk (Biggins), McGinlay, Byrne, McStay, O'Neil (McNally), Nicholas, Collins. Reserve goalkeeper: Given.

Rangers: Maxwell, Stevens, Murray (Kuznetsov), Gough, Pressley, Brown, Steven, McCall, Durie (Huistra), Hateley, Mikhailitchenko. Reserve goalkeeper: Scott.

Referee: Mr D. Syme (Glasgow)

Attendance: 48,506

Celtic 0 Rangers 2

Saturday, 30 September 1995
Scottish Premier League

IT was the afternoon Gazza came of age in a Rangers jersey.

The most expensive signing in Scottish football history had made – by his own incredibly high standards – an inauspicious start to his career in Scotland.

But everything clicked into place at an eerie Celtic Park – one stand was closed for renovation work – 11 minutes after the break.

At the time, Rangers were 1–0 up and defending stoutly against an onslaught by the home team. And when Gordan Petric cleared the ball up the park, Gazza was standing on the edge of his own 18-yard box. Ally McCoist picked up the clearance and laid it off to Oleg Salenko, who raced off at a blistering pace up the wing. The Russian World Cup star played the ball back to McCoist, who looked up before playing a precision pass to the edge of the Celtic area, and who was arriving right on cue but Paul Gascoigne, who calmly despatched the ball into the Celtic net. 2–0 Rangers.

It was an astonishing show of desire and athleticism by Gazza, whose lung-bursting box-to-box run was vintage Paul Gascoigne, and he had the finish to match.

It was the moment every Rangers fan had been waiting for: Gazza's first league goal, and to come in an Old Firm match was extra special. Gazza ran straight to the 4,000 Rangers fans and stood there sporting his trademark grin as the Bears went crazy in the Rangers end.

The most perfect of counter-attacking goals meant the world to every single supporter, but deep down it gave Gazza a real sense of satisfaction. The Geordie master often spoke of how the football pitch was his only escape from a life under the microscope or, rather, in front of a paparazzi lens.

And after the game he opened up about how the harassment he had been receiving from journalists – mostly news reporters – was having a damaging effect on his mental health, as well as his ability to concentrate on his football.

Gazza said: 'I panicked when the ball arrived at my feet, as I didn't think Ally had spotted me making the run, but his pass was unbelievable. I was delighted to score and get my first league goal for the club. The goal helped me feel a lot clearer in my mind.'

A measure of Gazza's internal emotions arrived midway through the first half. He beat John Collins twice, and was fouled by the same player twice. But as he stepped away from the Scotland international, Celtic's Dutch striker Pierre van Hooijdonk clattered into him with a dangerously high lunge, which just missed Gazza's shin. A player who had suffered enough in the past from injuries could have been seriously injured, so how did Gazza react? He picked himself up off the Parkhead turf, glanced at the Dutchman and walked away.

It was 0–0 at that point and the game was swinging from end to end. Andy Goram – standing tall in the Rangers goal – had already saved a van Hooijdonk free kick, and beat away a Rudi Vata header. Celtic had enjoyed a lot of possession but those two efforts were all they had to show for it.

Walter Smith's 'Iron Curtain' central defence of Richard Gough, Alan McLaren and Petric had dealt with just about everything the Premier League leaders had thrown at them.

Even though we were just four games into the new season, there was a lot at stake, which there always is in Old Firm matches, and so tempers were easily frayed in the middle of the park. And just to prove this, Ian Ferguson, Gazza and Tosh McKinlay were all booked in a frenetic opening spell.

Meanwhile, Rangers were handed a real opportunity with an indirect free kick inside the box on 27 minutes when Celtic keeper Gordon Marshall scooped up a back pass from one of his defenders. The Celtic wall looked nervous as Petric lined up to have a go. When the ball was played to him, he let rip with a thunderbolt but it cannoned off the wall and out to safety.

Rangers had given their rivals a wee reminder.

Four minutes before the break, Salenko teed up Gascoigne, but his shot was saved by Marshall. Mind you, Gazza didn't have long to wait until he was celebrating for real.

With referee John Rowbotham close to blowing his whistle for half-time, Salenko's blistering turn of pace left both McKinlay and John Hughes for dead. His cross from the right was missed by just about everyone, except for the man that mattered most. Alex Cleland had ghosted in unnoticed and headed the ball back across Marshall and into the far corner of the net. What a time to score your first goal for Rangers!

Cleland's goal came as a result of his bravery. Vata had mistimed the flight of the ball, and drifted too far inwards, but in a desperate attempt to redeem himself, he took a wild swing at the ball with his boot, and almost took Cleland's head off. But credit to the plucky defender for still putting his head in where it was likely to hurt – although he got the greatest of rewards for his bravery.

Almost immediately after the restart, Rowbotham blew for half-time and it was a joyous 15 minutes in the Rangers end as the fans celebrated that late opener with an impromptu sing-song.

Those same fans would have been fully expecting Celtic to emerge after the break with bellies of fire and determined to make amends for losing the goal. Instead, for some reason they seemed resigned to the fact that the game was lost and restarted the game more with a whimper than a bang.

Rangers dominated and grabbed a second goal in 56 minutes when Gazza clipped the ball over the advancing Marshall after a sublime counter-attack.

There might still have been over half an hour to play but that mattered little to the thousands of Bears present as they started their celebrations earlier than planned.

A couple of minutes after the second goal, Celtic were awarded a free kick in a dangerous area. Dead-ball specialist van Hooijdonk shaped up to take the kick and looked to have placed it perfectly into the corner, only for Goram to come flying across and tip the ball round the post. It was a superb save, and if Gazza's goal hadn't knocked the heart out of Celtic, then that save certainly did.

Moments later, Celtic needed a desperate last-gasp tackle from Hughes to prevent Salenko making it three. It was a bittersweet moment for the Russian as he stayed down after the challenge and was eventually stretchered off and replaced by Charlie Miller.

The closing moments were played out to a backdrop of 'easy, easy' chants from the Rangers end as both McCoist and Cleland went close.

The final whistle signalled Rangers' second win at Celtic Park in just 11 days, with the other victory coming in the fourth round of the League Cup. On that occasion, Ally McCoist was the match-winner. Overall, it was Rangers' third successive victory at Celtic Park.

Goal hero Cleland, who had joined Rangers after eight years at Dundee United, admitted it had been 'the greatest day of my life'. He added: 'It is easily the best day of my career. Scoring in an Old Firm game is a dream come true, but I could have had another one late on but for a great save by Gordon Marshall.

'I had been saying to the lads that a goal was definitely coming so they were slagging me before the game because I hadn't scored. They said I was destined NEVER to score for Rangers, so getting the goal in an Old Firm game has definitely helped shut them up.'

The win saw Rangers leapfrog Celtic at the top of the table, but with only five games played, no one was getting carried away. However, by the end of the season, Rangers would clinch the title by four points from Celtic, with third-placed Aberdeen more than 30 points behind.

The league win was Rangers' eighth successive title victory, leaving just one more needed to equal Celtic's record of nine, which had been recorded in the 1960s and 70s.

As a footnote, Oleg Salenko – who made quite an impact in the game in question, and had cost £2.5m from Valencia at the end of July 1995 – moved to Turkish side Istanbulspor less than six months later. In return, we got Peter van Vossen! In his short spell at Ibrox, Salenko scored seven times in the league, as well as in a League Cup semi-final defeat by Aberdeen.

Celtic: Marshall, Boyd, McKinlay, Vata (Walker 73), Hughes, O'Donnell (McLaughlin 46), Donnelly, McStay, van Hooijdonk, Thom, Collins. Sub not used: Bonner.

Rangers: Goram, Wright, Cleland, Gough, McLaren, Petric, McCall, Gascoigne, McCoist, Salenko (Miller 79), Ferguson. Subs not used: Murray, Thomson.

Referee: John Rowbotham (Kirkcaldy)

Attendance: 34,500

Celtic 0 Rangers 1

Thursday, 14 November 1996
Scottish Premier League

THROUGHOUT the 1990s Rangers played in many unforgettable matches against Old Firm rivals Celtic. But when it comes to spine-tingling drama, few Gers supporters will argue that this victory at Celtic Park is up there with the very best.

Walter Smith's side were looking to include their names in the history books by securing a ninth successive league championship, but were always going to face stiff competition from an impressive Celtic side that featured guys like Pierre van Hooijdonk, Paolo Di Canio, Andreas Thom and Jorge Cadete.

Celtic boss Tommy Burns had every right to feel his side could snatch the league championship from Rangers' grasp and end the club's chances of equalling their feat of nine in a row. However, Gers also had a team littered with players best prepared to raise their game when the stakes were high.

Goram, Gough, Gascoigne, Albertz and Laudrup were always capable of turning in special performances in Old Firm matches and this game proved no different.

Both sides had made impressive starts to the season, but the Light Blues went into the match behind Celtic on goal difference. A win for either side would not only take them three points clear in the championship race, but also hand the victor a huge psychological boost.

Rangers got off to the best possible start when wing wizard Brian Laudrup gave them the lead after just seven minutes. A slip from Celtic defender Brian O'Neill allowed Laudrup to pick the ball up 35 yards out and race towards goal before unleashing a fierce shot beyond rookie keeper Stewart Kerr.

The Gers continued to dominate large portions of the match and had several opportunities to increase their lead. Paul Gascoigne, uncharacteristically, had a penalty saved by Kerr and Peter van Vossen – with an unguarded goal at his mercy – somehow failed to convert. It was an incredible miss and had to be seen to be believed. In fact, I still can't believe it!

The Rangers defensive unit of Richard Gough, Alex Cleland, Gordan Petric, Joachim Bjorkland and David Robertson performed heroically and gave Celtic few chances to get back into the match.

However, with eight minutes remaining, the Rangers support were stunned when the referee decided Gough had tripped Simon Donnelly inside the box and awarded the home side a penalty.

A confident van Hooijdonk stepped up but the magnificent Andy Goram had the last laugh as he dived to his right to palm the ball past the post.

It wasn't the first time the goalie had performed heroics against Celtic, but this save helped Rangers secure all three points and the club would never relinquish their place at the top of the league for the rest of the season.

Celtic boss Tommy Burns admitted that Goram's contribution to killing off his side's challenge was immense and famously stated that he would like the following inscription on his headstone: 'Andy Goram broke my heart!'

Goram has fond memories of that match, especially the penalty save. He said: 'I loved playing against Celtic but this has to be one of my favourites. I remember the game well as we had several chances to double our lead but couldn't get that all-important second goal.

'Gazza missed a penalty and Peter van Vossen missed a chance I'm sure he will have nightmares about for the rest of his life. However, just when it seemed we were going to hold on to our lead, we gave away a penalty with about eight minutes to go, and it seemed all the hard work that had gone into the match would count for nothing.

'I had watched van Hooijdonk taking penalties before but I decided to just pick a side and hope for the best. He hit the ball low to my right and I managed to turn it around the post. As you could see from my reaction I was ecstatic to make such a crucial save and it helped put us on the way to nine in a row.

'It was every schoolboy's dream to play in big games and I couldn't believe I'd managed to save a penalty at the end of such an important game. That sort of script was usually reserved for Ally McCoist, so it is a moment I will always treasure.'

Goram's save was the final twist in one of the most amazing Old Firm clashes ever, and put the seal on a night of high drama. Rangers number two Archie Knox was hit by a coin aimed at the Gers dugout, Celts gaffer Tommy Burns was sent off, Paul Gascoigne and van Hooijdonk missed vital penalties and both sides were guilty of unbelievable open-goal blunders.

Knox was unhurt by the coin-throwing incident, which took place when Rangers were awarded their penalty in the 68th minute after Kerr had hauled down Laudrup.

A police spokesman said: 'I am aware that the assistant trainer of Rangers was allegedly hit by a coin. He was examined but uninjured. No person has been traced.'

Burns was sent packing to the stand five minutes later for raging at linesman Eric Martindale's failure to give an offside decision against Jorg Albertz. And the Celts' gaffer admitted: 'I feel disappointed for the players and disappointed in myself for getting sent to the stand. I let them down but then everyone gets carried away in situations like that.

'We are disappointed to lose the game in that fashion. The result depended on a slip by young Brian and Laudrup took his chance very well.' Burns refused to criticise his players even though they had won only three of the last 17 Old Firm clashes. He said: 'There is only so much you can ask players to do. They played well against a team that defended very well in numbers and relied on the counter-attack. Rangers have their style of play and we have ours. We will not change.'

And he was full of praise for keeper Kerr – who brilliantly saved Gascoigne's penalty – and van Hooijdonk, who missed the penalty. Burns said: 'Stewart was magnificent and showed what a superb keeper he is going to be. And with just a few minutes left there wasn't exactly a queue of people waiting to take the penalty. It took courage but Pierre's missed it and great players have to put up with that. He will score many more important goals for us.'

Rangers boss Walter Smith also praised Kerr's performance, and added: 'I'm pleased to have won the game, but it was a strange encounter. I've never seen an Old Firm match with as many simple chances thrown away, especially from my own side.

'From our point of view we had by far the best chances on the break. Celtic put us under a great deal of pressure throughout the game but we defended well and in the end could have won by more goals if we had converted some of our simple opportunities.

'I was delighted with Brian Laudrup's goal and his performance. When you consider some of the chances we had, his was not among the easiest. It was a terrific strike.'

Goal hero Laudrup was pleased with the result and said: 'Celtic played the better football but yet again we have come away with the points. With the chances we missed and the penalty as well we could have scored a lot of goals tonight despite Celtic playing better.

'It was hard work playing alone up front. I thought when we missed the penalty it wasn't going to be our night, but thankfully we came through. I didn't want to take the penalty but I said to Gazza after the game, "Join the club!" I said, "You can maybe do a Pizza Hut commercial now too!"

'I have taken a penalty already this season and missed. Paul has taken a lot and scored a lot over the past 18 months so it was right that he took it. It was a good save by their goalkeeper.'

Meanwhile, Celtic were facing a battle with the likes of Inter Milan and Gothenburg to land £2m-rated Roma skipper Jonas Thern.

Thern said: 'My contract is up at the end of the season and I will definitely be leaving. I could easily return to Sweden but it depends what other offers come my way.'

Now, I wonder where he ended up!

Chilean goal ace Sebastian Rozenthal was hoping to seal a £3m move to Rangers in the days after the Old Firm game. The 20-year-old was said to be ready to snub Juventus to clinch a deal with the Ibrox club. His father Lazaro said: 'Sebastian wants to play for Rangers. Italy isn't right at the moment.'

Celtic: Kerr, Boyd, O'Neill (McKinlay), McNamara, Stubbs, Grant, Di Canio, Wieghorst, van Hooijdonk, Thom (Cadete), O'Donnell.

Rangers: Goram, Cleland, Robertson, Gough, Petric, Bjorkland, Moore, Gascoigne, McInnes (van Vossen), Albertz, Laudrup.

Referee: Mr H. Dallas (Motherwell)

Attendance: 50,009

Celtic 0 Rangers 1

Sunday, 16 March 1997
Scottish Premier League

IT may have been a few months after Christmas, but it was still the season to be jolly!

Four league wins out of four over Celtic gave the supporters far more than just bragging rights.

The 12 points gained from these matches also went some way to ensuring Rangers made it a record-equalling season as they bagged their NINTH successive title.

And yet just ten days earlier they had been pilloried by all and sundry after a poor display at the same ground meant a 2–0 Scottish Cup quarter-final loss.

But the players redeemed themselves in the best possible fashion with a gutsy victory against the old enemy.

As they edged towards a little piece of history, they created more with the first ever grand slam of Premier League victories in Old Firm encounters. And no one could deny they were worthy winners – despite a horrendous string of setbacks before and during the 90 minutes.

Out was Andy Goram and former THIRD-choice keeper at Manchester City Andy Dibble faced a baptism of fire.

Out went Richard Gough in his final match against Celtic as his calf injury flared up again just past the hour mark.

Off went comeback striker Mark Hateley following a needless clash with Celtic keeper Stewart Kerr five minutes later.

Yet, the Light Blues were always in control of this one thanks to a resilience and resolve sadly lacking in the cup tie. Dibble had a performance to be proud of and did everything asked of him throughout 90 torrid minutes.

Alan McLaren was outstanding in defence, especially after the departure of his captain, but there were 13 heroes for Rangers as they dug deep for a memorable victory against all the odds.

The visitors started confidently and held the upper hand for the opening half hour, winning the midfield battle and looking more like favourites than underdogs. Laudrup's lightning break after ten minutes set up a gilt-edged opportunity for Ian Durrant – starting his first match since November – but his shot was weak and wide.

There was a let-off for Rangers five minutes before the interval when Paolo Di Canio brilliantly volleyed a free kick against the top of the bar from 25 yards. And just as it seemed the home side was starting to take control, Rangers struck with a vengeance ... just 30 seconds before the break.

An Albertz free kick caused confusion as Hateley challenged Enrico Annoni, and Alan Stubbs's back header to Kerr was neither accurate nor firm enough. Durrant nipped in, lofted the ball goalwards, and Laudrup arrived on the scene to finish the job with Malky Mackay and Kerr found wanting.

It all got out of hand early in the second half when Laudrup was taken down by Mackay on the edge of the box and there followed an unseemly confrontation between Hateley and Kerr. The upshot was two Celtic cautions and an early bath for the big Rangers striker for a stupid head gesture towards the irate keeper.

With ten minutes remaining, Laudrup set off on another of his trademark runs but he was hauled down by Mackay, who received a second yellow card and took the long walk for an early bath.

And Albertz could have sealed it a minute later but was denied by Kerr, who also did extremely well to parry a Laudrup effort late on.

Di Canio showed the flawed side of his personality when the full-time whistle sounded as he appeared to lunge at just about everything in a blue jersey. The Italian acted like a petulant child, especially when he went for Ian Ferguson and appeared to gesture that he would break Fergie's legs, before offering the Rangers star a 'square go' in the tunnel. Of course, the players were separated long before then and Di Canio's words were hollow.

Walter Smith kept his cool, and his players cheekily mimicked the Celtic huddle, which didn't go down too well with the Parkhead faithful – at least those who were still inside the ground.

Afterwards, Smith said: 'I was very pleased to win the game after all the recent problems we'd encountered. The performance was secondary as we had to show more determination than in the cup game ten days ago and I don't think we were short of that out there.'

Goram had been ruled out of the big match after twisting his knee in a midweek game, and decided early on that he wouldn't be at Celtic Park. He explained: 'I booked into the Hilton Hotel with my wife and decided to watch the game on TV. I made sure I locked myself in the room on my own and I was nervous as hell when the game came on.

'If Jeremy Beadle had been there he would no doubt have got enough material for the whole of his *You've Been Framed* show. I must have looked ridiculous jumping about the room shouting at the TV and going crazy. It was a bad experience for me and as I'm sure you've already gathered, I'm not the best at watching our games when I'm not playing.'

He added: 'Ian Durrant called and said he wasn't going anywhere near Parkhead either. He asked where I was watching the game because he thought he wasn't going to be involved. The wee man said he'd phone me back at 2pm, but when I turned on the television and there he was doing his warm-up I thought, "Guess I'll be watching the game on my own then!"

'But it was a happy 90 minutes for me, although the obvious downside was I missed out. Watching on the box was difficult. But I think if I had gone along to Parkhead my heart wouldn't have held out. From the first minute of the game everyone expected a Celtic onslaught but it never materialised, and that was because we stopped it, not because they didn't do it.'

Goram also praised boss Walter Smith for his decision to re-sign Mark Hateley. He said: 'What a signing big Mark turned out to be. He may not be the same player he was five years ago but he caused so much bother in the Celtic defence. He's such a clever and talented player and the positions he found completely dumbfounded Mackay and Stubbs. Credit to the manager – bringing Mark back was a masterstroke.'

Durrant revealed how a behind-the-scenes 'battle' had developed – and the prize was the winning goal! He explained: 'So, did Brian Laudrup get the winner or was the goal mine? I was clearly the last person to touch the ball before Lauders and Malky Mackay got in each other's way!

'It would have been my first domestic goal of the season and I'm having a wee dispute with Brian about it. But we will save it for another time and agree that the most important thing was getting the three points.

'The match was quite unbelievable – the best I've been involved in. There wasn't an awful lot of quality football played, but for drama and excitement it definitely tops the lot.

'On a personal level, I was delighted to be included and from the first whistle I felt we were on top. The gaffer had a bit of a dilemma with injuries and I was grateful to get the nod.'

Durrant added: 'I was delighted to see big Mark Hateley back in a blue jersey. His appearance gave everyone a major boost and he did a brilliant job for us. He put himself about the Celtic defence and they didn't know how to handle him. He was disappointed to be sent off – we all were – but it's great to see him back up front doing damage again.'

After starring in the Parkhead encounter, stand-in goalkeeper Andy Dibble insisted it was 100 times better than playing in goal for Manchester City reserves.

He added: 'The move to Rangers on loan until the end of the season came totally out of the blue. I should've been playing for City reserves against Stalybridge Celtic, so you can imagine how surprised I was to find myself pitched into the action at Celtic Park.

'It's funny how football moves but this is one of these situations I have to take advantage of. I know I'm only filling in and it's not permanent, but I hope it's a springboard for better things.

'I aim to enjoy myself, because anyone not wanting to play for a club like Rangers would be potty. Andy and Theo [Snelders] have been unlucky with injuries, but I'll just wait and see how things go, although it was incredible to be involved in the Old Firm clash – especially as we won!'

Celtic: Kerr, Annoni, McKinlay, McNamara, Mackay, Grant (Hannah), Di Canio, McStay, Stubbs (Donnelly), O'Donnell, Cadete. Sub: Thom.

Rangers: Dibble, Cleland, Albertz, Gough (Miller), McLaren, Bjorklund, Moore, Ferguson, Durrant (McCoist), Hateley, Laudrup. Sub: Rae.

Referee: Mr H. Dallas (Motherwell)

Attendance: 49,929

Celtic 0 Rangers 3

Sunday, 2 May 1999
Scottish Premier League

THE word 'chaos' was invented to describe this game.

It was the afternoon when Rangers made a little bit of history by clinching the league title at the home of their greatest rivals, and they did so in magnificent style with a wonderful 3–0 victory in the most testing of circumstances.

As Celtic's grip on the championship they had won a year earlier loosened, the stadium became a cauldron of hate, but Dick Advocaat's men kept their heads and in the process proved themselves worthy champions.

Three players – Stephane Mahe, Vidar Riseth and Gers striker Rod Wallace – were sent off, seven players were booked, fans invaded the pitch, referee Hugh Dallas was struck by a coin and a Celtic fan took a tumble off the top tier of Celtic's huge North Stand. It was all going off.

With everything at stake, Celtic were desperate to prevent the Light Blues winning the title on their patch. And though many folk may remember this match for all the wrong reasons, Rangers fans and players will always recall it as the day they proved themselves the best in the country.

After the heartache of losing ten in a row just 12 months earlier, the Ibrox men were determined to gain revenge on Celtic and take their title home.

With Parkhead jam-packed and at fever pitch, it was Rangers who struck the first blow. And it proved to be a sucker punch that Celtic would struggle to recover from.

There were just 13 minutes on the clock – which was unlucky for the hosts – when Gers broke up a threatening Celtic attack and Jorg

Albertz took control. The talented German slipped a delightful pass through to van Bronckhorst, who flicked the ball on to Wallace. The wee man's inch-perfect cross was met in the box by the on-rushing Neil McCann, who stretched every muscle in his body to reach the ball, which he did and poked home much to the delight of the huge away support.

The early goal settled any Rangers nerves and they were soon running the show, while Celtic were left chasing blue and white shadows.

Just before half-time, though, the game turned nasty, the crowd turned ugly and Rangers turned the screw. Celtic left-back Mahe was sent packing by referee Dallas as the Frenchman collected a second yellow card.

Minutes later, as Rangers prepared to take a corner, Dallas was struck by a coin thrown from the Celtic support. Despite a head wound streaming with blood, the man in black picked himself up and when the corner was swung in Tony Vidmar was hauled down by Riseth, leaving Dallas no option but to point to the spot. Albertz was handed the task of putting Rangers two goals up and, as cool as ever, slotted the ball into the corner of the net. Even so early in the game was there any way back for ten-man Celtic?

In the second half, McCann clinched victory – and the title – when he raced clear of the chasing pack to seal a famous 3–0 win.

And then the madness continued.

Wallace saw red in the dying moments, although who could blame him as any sane person would have reacted furiously to such a reckless challenge by Riseth. But you cannot raise your hands and he had to go. Madman Riseth himself then went a minute from time. He had already been booked but his challenge on Reyna would've merited a red card by itself.

And while tempers were deteriorating all over the park in the dying moments, nothing could dampen the celebrations as Dallas finally blew the whistle to signal the end of the 'game'. What better way to celebrate Dick Advocaat's first season in charge of the club?

Sure, chaos ruled supreme, but it should never be forgotten that Rangers were unbelievable on the day and that they played the game, unlike their opponents. Nothing should detract from the effort, commitment and skill of Advocaat's men. They were immense.

And while two-goal hero, Neil McCann, was a happy man, he also revealed how he felt terrified after scoring the third and final goal.

He said: 'I knew as soon as I scored we were champions but I was also conscious of what was going on around me. I didn't want to cause a riot with my celebrations. My momentum was carrying me towards the Celtic fans so I slammed the brakes on, changed direction and ran towards the Rangers fans. It was only then that I let myself go a little. Scoring the goal that clinched the title for Rangers was a great honour and is something I'll never forget.

'I feared it might all boil over when Hugh Dallas was hit by a coin and a few fans came on to the pitch. I think we were all a bit scared as we thought about the consequences, but we had to retain our concentration and just get on with the game. To be fair, the majority of players managed to keep their cool, but a few definitely lost it. I didn't really understand some of the Celtic players who lost it because they must have known what was at stake for their club. Probably the pressure and the atmosphere on the night got to them but I was pleased that we managed to remain calm and in the end we deserved our win.'

The day after the game, Advocaat hailed his 'special relationship' with chairman David Murray as one of the main reasons behind the victory at Celtic Park. He said: 'It's important to have the support of your chairman and I don't think I could find better at any other club. We have a very special relationship. We keep the pressure on each other. I phoned him after the game and the first thing he said was "well done, but now for the cup final!"

'We are close and like each other very much, but can talk about things besides football which I think is important. But we are also both so focussed on achieving success that our chats are more often about Rangers than anything else.'

Advocaat was delighted with his players' committed performance and believed his first ever Old Firm win, not to mention the small matter of a league trophy, was no more than Rangers deserved.

He said: 'It was important we won that game for our fans and we are proud to have done so. I'm delighted with the way we played and also the way we controlled ourselves. I think we deserved the championship. We lost the first game, went top after the third match and from that point we stayed top of the league to the end, so we deserve credit for that.'

The win put Rangers ten points clear at the top with three matches remaining. Rangers had reclaimed their title from Celtic and the agony of losing out on ten in a row had partly been erased, and no one was more delighted than Jorg Albertz. But while he may have looked the calmest man on the park when he stepped forward to take the penalty, inside he admitted he was a quivering wreck – but NOT because he was afraid of missing the target from 12 yards.

He explained: 'It wasn't hard for me to concentrate on the penalty because I enjoy making these decisions. I knew that if I had missed we would probably have allowed Celtic back into the game. But I am physically and mentally strong enough to cope in situations like that and I was looking forward to taking it. It was definitely the most important kick of my life because of what was at stake.

'It was the best atmosphere I have ever played in but also the most dangerous. You must have respect for the Celtic fans because it was only one or two idiots who ran on to the pitch to take a swipe at Hugh Dallas and in hindsight it could have been a lot worse had others decided to follow them on.

'You get a little bit nervous when you see things like that, but the majority of fans would never think of doing anything like that. You always get shouts of abuse from away fans wherever you go but that's part of the game. It gets serious, however, when fans start trying to attack the referee.'

Albertz paid tribute to Dallas by saying: 'You must give him respect for the way he handled the situation because it was all going off around him when he awarded us the penalty. But I think when you saw it on television, every decision he made proved to be the right one. It was still brave, though.'

Celtic: Kerr, Mahe, Stubbs, Annoni, Riseth, Wieghorst (Healy), Marshall, Lambert, Larsson, Brattbakk (Donnelly), Viduka.

Rangers: Klos, Porrini, Amoruso, Hendry, van Bronckhorst, Vidmar, Reyna, Albertz (McInnes), Amato (Johansson), Wallace, McCann.

Referee: Mr H. Dallas (Motherwell)

Attendance: 59,918

Rangers 4 Celtic 0

Sunday, 26 March 2000
Scottish Premier League

TEN years after the major MC Hammer hit 'U Can't Touch This' included the line 'Hammer Time', Jorg Albertz brought the phrase back into vogue during a quite superb dismantling of Celtic.

On the back of the treble-winning season in 1999, Dick Advocaat's men were again racing to the title when Celtic came calling in March looking for their first Ibrox victory in ten attempts. Yip, ten attempts!

John Barnes had been sacked as manager the previous month – after Super Caley had gone Ballistic and knocked them out of the Scottish Cup – and under Kenny Dalglish's temporary stewardship the Parkhead side had fallen 12 points behind the runaway league leaders.

Desperately requiring a victory to claw their way back into the title race, Celtic instead suffered their heaviest Old Firm defeat in almost 12 years.

Rangers had won 1–0 at Parkhead only a few weeks earlier to install themselves as title favourites and this comprehensive victory merely underlined where the power in the city lay.

The game started in dramatic style when the flying Andrei Kanchelskis charged down the right, only to be stopped in his tracks by Stephane Mahe. Claudio Reyna swung over the resultant corner, and Kanchelskis, all alone in the box, played the ball across the face of Jonathan Gould's goal and Albertz nodded over the line from inches out to open the scoring after just four minutes.

It was a dream start for Rangers but to make matters worse for Celtic, Mahe injured himself in the challenge and was forced to hobble off soon after, with Olivier Tebily coming on to replace him.

Celtic had a few half-chances to equalise before Kanchelskis, with a little help from Giovanni van Bronckhorst – and Tebily – brought Rangers supporters back to their feet five minutes before the break.

The Ivory Coast defender tried to play a pass infield but van Bronckhorst was on to the loose ball in a flash, and released Kanchelskis. The Russian winger sped forward, drew Gould, and stroked the ball into the net to double Rangers' lead.

Celtic boss Kenny Dalglish faced a half-time dilemma. Would he reshape his team to take chances in pursuit of goals or would he try to avoid a more embarrassing scoreline? He opted to send out the same players for the second half even though far too many had underachieved in the first 45.

And Rangers might have been three goals up just after the break as Billy Dodds had the ball in the net. However, the wee man was flagged offside, although the chance had followed what appeared to be a foul by Rod Wallace on Johan Mjallby.

Celtic's afternoon was summed up early in the second half when Mark Viduka was booked for a dive in the Rangers box. The Aussie striker went down far too cheaply under a Scott Wilson challenge.

Rangers were dominant, and Gould was forced into action several times to deny van Bronckhorst, Dodds and Barry Ferguson in quick succession as Celtic were reduced to a rather shoddy support act.

It was as though fear was freezing the minds and limbs of Dalglish's players, who had more to worry about when Neil McCann came on to replace Dodds. His first contribution was an attempted lob which was too weighty, but he then landed a cross perfectly on the head of Wallace who delivered the ball tamely into the arms of Gould.

Six minutes from the end van Bronckhorst, McCann and Albertz combined to create the third goal. The Dutchman hit a wonderful pass out to McCann, who veered in from the left, skipped around Gould and then chipped the ball into the middle for Albertz to bundle it into the empty net.

The game was over; Rangers were in cruise control and Celtic had given up the ghost. But the hosts weren't finished. There was a fourth goal to come and it was fitting that man of the match van Bronckhorst would grab it. The talented Dutchman found the right-hand corner of Gould's net with a sweet strike, which was the cue for the huge home support to start celebrating again – just moments after they had finished cheering the third!

Van Bronckhorst was exceptional throughout and covered every blade of grass on the Ibrox pitch. He proved he had the skill to go with his exceptional engine and his goal was just reward for one of his best displays of the season.

In between the third and fourth goals, Albertz was taken off to make way for Tugay, but the German wasn't the only one to depart the scene. Celtic fans had also deserted their seats in the Broomloan Road stand – their afternoon and season over.

After the game, Advocaat revealed how Celtic's pre-match boasts had helped motivate his team to a convincing victory. He said: 'That win was very satisfying. In the newspapers in the week leading up to the game it was as if Celtic were the team who were 12 points clear at the top. They were talking as if they were the better side but we showed them on the pitch who was the best team in the league.'

Two-goal hero Albertz agreed with his gaffer. 'I don't have a hat or I would have taken it off for my team-mates. The build-up was good for us because the papers were talking about Celtic beating us easily. But we waited until we got out on to the park before we did our talking.'

As someone once said, careless words cost lives and Celtic were made to pay for theirs. Dalglish may even have been one of the offenders, although there was no 'Ibrox insider' to say as much.

It was a game Celtic realistically had to win if they were to have any say whatsoever in the destination of the Premier League title. But with a crushing defeat behind them, they fell 15 points behind Rangers with ten games remaining.

The Light Blues travelled to Pittodrie six days after the Old Firm win but could only draw 1-1.

However, after that game, Rangers won their next eight to take the title by a staggering 21 points from second-placed Celtic.

Rangers lost just two of their 36 league games, including the last one of the season – a dead rubber at Fir Park, Motherwell – to conclude a campaign which was just as memorable for the great football Advocaat had Rangers playing as it was for the invincibility of the champions.

Delighted Andrei Kanchelskis enjoyed his first Old Firm goal – and revealed how he had now found the net in Manchester, Liverpool and Glasgow derbies.

He also thanked Celtic's Johan Mjallby for providing Rangers with an added incentive just hours before the last Old Firm clash of the season. Mjallby had allegedly boasted in a Sunday newspaper that the Parkhead side were a cut above Rangers.

The Swedish international claimed Celtic were a better team and would win easy despite languishing 12 points behind in the title race. Kanchelskis said: 'Everybody played very well and this was an excellent result for us. Before the game Celtic players were saying they were the better team. But you see the 4–0 result and now who is better? Celtic? I don't think so.

'I don't understand them saying they are better than us but now Rangers are 15 points clear and I think we might be better. If the gap had been three points then maybe we could understand. I think it would have been better for Mjallby to speak after the game. That's what we did. We won 4–0 so I think Rangers are the best.'

The reality was, take away Mark Viduka and Paul Lambert from that Celtic team and it was clear as day that they were nowhere near good enough to stop Rangers – regardless of what Mjallby said. The Swede simply couldn't cope with Gers' pint-sized strikers Dodds and Wallace. He wasn't skilful or agile enough. Equally, Lubomir Moravcik and Stiliyan Petrov looked out of their depth in a midfield battle where the enemy combatants included Ferguson and van Bronckhorst.

Two days before the big match, Dalglish decided – against the better judgement of just about everyone with a vested interest – to hold the club's weekly press conference in Baird's Bar, in Glasgow's Gallowgate. Although at the time Dalglish said, 'We like to get out and show the fans how we prepare for the game, and they get to see a media conference,' journalists felt the Celtic manager was trying to prove who was boss. Regardless, it actually turned out to be one of the most appropriate pressers in history, as Celtic played like a pub team at Ibrox!

Rangers: Klos, Amoruso, Numan, Ferguson, Kanchelskis, van Bronckhorst, Wallace, Albertz (Tugay), Reyna, Wilson, Dodds (McCann). Subs: Charbonnier, Nicholson, Penttila.

Celtic: Gould, Riseth, Mahe (Tebily), Boyd, Mjallby, McNamara, Lambert (Burchill), Petrov, Viduka, Moravcik, Johnson. Subs: Kerr, Berkovic, Healy.

Referee: Mr W. Young (Girvan)

Attendance: 50,039

Rangers 3 Celtic 2

Saturday, 4 May 2002
Scottish Cup Final

ALEX McLeish had been in charge at Ibrox just six months – and 28 games – when he led his team out at Hampden for the Scottish Cup Final.

Facing a title-winning Celtic side, many had already written off Rangers' challenge when McLeish was appointed, but he had led Rangers to League Cup success by March and presided over an unbeaten run against rivals Celtic that had restored belief amongst a squad that had been underperforming prior to his arrival.

And it would take every ounce of that new-found belief for his side to carry themselves through one of the most dramatic Scottish Cup Finals of recent times.

When referee Hugh Dallas got the 14th Old Firm Scottish Cup Final under way, it was on a pitch which resembled a snooker table at the Crucible, rather than a fortnight beforehand, when it had looked like a second-rate National Hunt racecourse following a four-mile steeplechase.

Just 90 seconds into the game Johan Mjallby body-checked Claudio Caniggia, and from the free kick, Lorenzo Amoruso headed just over the bar. It was an early warning to the pre-match favourites. Neil McCann then went close with a free kick after Alan Thompson had fouled Fernando Ricksen.

But when Chris Sutton scythed down Caniggia, as Rangers went for the jugular, it was apparent Celtic were trying to stop them at all costs!

Mind you, with 20 minutes on the clock, it was Celtic who took the lead. Stefan Klos tipped a teasing John Hartson cross over the bar and from the resulting corner the Welshman headed home.

McLeish's men responded almost immediately. Mjallby failed to deal properly with a long ball out of defence, instead heading into the path of Lovenkrands, who fired it past Rab Douglas.

With the scores level, McLeish received a bitter blow when Caniggia was forced off after failing to recover from Sutton's crude challenge. He was replaced by Shota Arveladze.

Bobo Balde was then booked for a reckless challenge on Ricksen. The Celts defender had earlier clattered Lovenkrands from behind and got off scot-free.

Dallas was on the receiving end of abuse from the Celtic support when he refused claims for a penalty when Henrik Larsson stumbled as he was going through on goal. The referee was then forced to book both Hartson and Amoruso for fouls shortly after the restart, and just moments later Celtic were again in front. Neil Lennon floated the ball into a crowded penalty area and Balde rose unchallenged to head home.

Rangers were quickly back on the front foot and from a deep McCann cross, Amoruso headed just wide. Barry Ferguson then rattled the post with a 25-yard shot, after good work by Arthur Numan. It was tough luck on the Gers' midfielder, but an equaliser was coming, and it wasn't long until the Light Blue half of Hampden erupted. This time skipper Ferguson was on target. Amoruso was flattened on the edge of the Celtic box by Balde, and Fergie shaped up to take the free kick. His execution was superb and the ball flew into the top corner, leaving Douglas no chance. It was now anyone's game.

Celtic took up the cudgel and Craig Moore was booked for halting Hartson in his tracks as he made a beeline for goal. Thankfully for the Aussie, Numan was the last man or the card might have been a different colour.

With time running out, Lennon followed Moore into the book for a bad challenge on Lovenkrands – but there was late drama in the Celtic penalty area. McCann crossed, Douglas spilled the ball and could only look on as Ricksen hit a shot that was cleared off the line by Mjallby.

The big Swedish defender then appeared to foul Lovenkrands in the box, but Dallas waved away claims for a penalty. The Danish international had the last laugh, though, when McCann crossed into the box and the striker threw himself at the ball to head home. It was the last action of the match, and left the Rangers players in ecstasy as their dejected opponents slumped to the ground in despair.

There was no doubting Lovenkrands' contribution to the cause, but Ferguson was correctly named man of the match. Boss McLeish said: 'It's not fair to single out individuals. I think the star was the squad because everybody played their part. There are no secrets, it's down to hard work. We had increased the input in training because the fringe players and those coming back from injury needed to find a bit of sharpness.

'Once we won some matches and had some momentum I could see the dressing room spirit lifting. I imagined winning trophies, but for it to become a reality was a fantastic achievement when you consider we had been written off around Christmas.'

It was a sentiment echoed by McLeish's right-hand man, Jan Wouters. The Dutchman admitted he sensed victory was in the air before the squad had even reached Hampden – and it came in the shape of a rousing rendition of 'Follow Follow' on the team bus!

He said: 'It all started on the bus going to the game. We played the Rangers song and everyone was singing heartily. I have never had a feeling like it. I had goosebumps. I knew then the players were ready and they showed their commitment on the pitch.

'We were pleased on the bench because our tactics worked, but it was the endeavour of the players that made the difference.'

Those extra endeavours led to an astonishing finish to the game, and Lovenkrands' winner, but he admitted: 'I felt too tired to run anymore and was just desperate for the referee to blow the whistle so we could have a rest. But when I spotted Neil McCann sprinting down the wing I knew I had to give it one more push and managed to reach his cross. I just hit the ball and momentum made me run past the goal which meant I didn't see where it had gone.

'That was a nervous moment but when I heard the cheering I realised I had scored. I was so happy all I could think of was to run towards the fans and share the moment with them. It was an unbelievable finale – no one could have predicted it.'

McLeish picked out the second equaliser as the moment that helped the Gers find their extra reserves. He said: 'That goal by Barry was the inspiration we required. You need players like him in those games. It was an incredible match and to come back twice against Celtic speaks volumes for the character of my players.

'There aren't many teams who could do that against Celtic. It was a stunning performance and we deserved it. I will never forget this game. It was a fantastic day for me and the players.'

It was certainly special for Lovenkrands, who had already scored his side's first goal after 20 minutes to level the game after Hartson had exploited some poor marking to put Celtic ahead.

The Danish winger's pace was a problem for Celtic throughout the game and had already helped him score three times against them earlier in the season. He said: 'It's a dream to score two goals to win a final, especially after Celtic had twice taken the lead. In fact I think it was the best day of my life – it was definitely the most fantastic feeling I have ever had.

'You can't say what goes through your head when you score, but it's such a great feeling to see everyone so happy when you do. For the first one I just watched the long ball and saw Sutton and Mjallby both going for it and thought I would hang back a bit. It fell nicely for me and I just took a touch and had a shot, and I caught it perfectly.'

However, McLeish's pre-match concerns that Celtic's physical side may prove to be a problem were confirmed when Balde scored from another set piece to put the pressure back on Rangers. The gaffer said: 'We knew Celtic would be a big threat at set pieces, which they certainly were. But I thought it would be a shame were we to lose the game because we had played some really good football. We had played well despite going 1–0 and 2–1 down.

'I felt we had controlled the game reasonably well but the faith we had in the players and the backing from such a fantastic support prevailed and won it for us in the end.'

That win brought McLeish his second piece of silverware in an incredible first six months at the club.

Rangers: Klos, Ross, Moore, Amoruso, Numan, Ricksen, de Boer, Ferguson, Lovenkrands, McCann, Caniggia (Arveladze). Subs: McGregor, Vidmar, Nerlinger, Flo.

Celtic: Douglas, Mjallby, Sutton, Balde, Agathe, Lennon, Lambert (McNamara), Petrov, Hartson, Larsson, Thompson. Subs: Gould, Boyd, Moravcik, Guppy.

Referee: Mr H. Dallas (Motherwell)

Attendance 51,138

Rangers 3 Celtic 2

Saturday, 7 December 2002
Scottish Premier League

WHEN the Rangers players took to the field a couple of weeks before Christmas to face their old foes, little did they realise that the three points they were fighting for would go a long way to cementing their place in the history books.

For at the end of the season, when the medals were being handed out, this group of Gers players had just helped land the club's 50th league title – and the fifth star became a reality.

Victory in this five-goal thriller was an early Christmas present for Gers followers – and the stats which followed were impressive.

The match was played at lunchtime on a Saturday in front of a huge nationwide television audience, and by the end of the game, Alex McLeish remained undefeated in his sixth Old Firm match since taking over a year previous.

Rangers had won their first league match over Celtic since the 5–1 humbling they had dished out in November 2000, and, most importantly, the Light Blues had leapfrogged their old foes and now sat two points clear at the top of the league.

And yet, such a feat had looked unlikely after just 19 seconds when a sleepy home defence allowed John Hartson to skip into the penalty box and cross for Chris Sutton to bundle the ball past Stefan Klos to give Celtic an early lead.

Thankfully the setback only seemed to stiffen Rangers' resolve. They battled their way back into the match and had forged a 3–1 lead by the time the teams headed up the tunnel at the break.

Characterful was how McLeish later labelled the fightback but there were many other attributes present – determination, skill, bravery, persistence and a real will to win.

Craig Moore, no stranger to a battling comeback, embodied those traits in a match-winning performance. The Australian had come through a turbulent time at Ibrox but it now seemed almost impossible to imagine a Rangers side without him.

Moore was outstanding and brought McLeish's men back into the game following their dreadful start when he bulleted a header past Rab Douglas from Fernando Ricksen's corner in ten minutes.

You could see the goal meant as much to him as any Bluenose in the ground as he raced away to celebrate his equaliser.

He was also solid defensively, snuffing out the threat of Henrik Larsson to such an extent that you almost thought the Swede would sneak out of Oz's pocket when the Ibrox star talked to the press after the game.

'I'm really pleased,' said Moore with a toothy grin. 'If you're going to lose a goal, especially in a game like this, you're better doing it early. It gave us the kick up the backside we needed and we got ourselves back into the game. We took it from there and never looked back.'

However, there were escapes in the first half as Celtic pushed forward in a bid to re-establish their lead. Neil McCann was sloppy with a clearance in 17 minutes and Hartson redirected Stiliyan Petrov's mishit shot past Stefan Klos. Luckily the ball spun off a post and drifted agonisingly along the line before sliding out for a goal kick.

Rangers were forced to bring on Bob Malcolm for Maurice Ross, who had pulled up in pain and hobbled off. There seemed no adverse effect from the reorganisation and two goals inside five minutes emphasised just how superior the home side had been.

McCann made up for his early mistake by skinning Bobo Balde down the left and sending over a peach of a cross that Ronald de Boer volleyed high past Douglas. It was a goal of sublime quality.

Hartson was Celtic's most dangerous attacker and Klos pulled off a superb save when he expertly tipped a header from the Welsh international over the bar and to safety.

Rangers capitalised on their keeper's stunning save with a killer third goal. Ricksen, now covering for Ross at right-back, slalomed through the Celtic defence before sliding a pass to Shota Arveladze. The Georgian striker crossed for Michael Mols, who reacted with lightning speed and poked the ball under the Celtic keeper to silence the away support behind the goal.

As expected, the Parkhead side came back at Rangers in the second half as they tried to salvage something from a match that had, in all honesty, run away from them.

Alan Thompson came on for the anonymous Steve Guppy and almost made an immediate impact when his cross was knocked towards goal by Moore. But Arthur Numan showed superb commitment and razor-sharp reflexes to prevent an own goal. The Dutch defender lunged to hoof the ball off the line and took a kick in the head in the process.

Klos then denied Thompson with a fingertip save before Larsson laid the ball off to Hartson who scored with a low drive past Klos.

McLeish threw on the scourge of the Celts, Peter Lovenkrands, to see if he could add to the five Old Firm goals he had netted the previous season. However, the Dane was only an interested spectator when Ibrox almost saw what would have been a contender for goal of this or any other season.

There seemed little danger when Barry Ferguson nudged a free kick to Lorenzo Amoruso at least 40 yards from goal, but the Italian hammered the ball and only the width of a post prevented him from extending Rangers' lead.

Rangers, and Lovenkrands in particular, had further chances but the majority of the 50,000 crowd were delighted when referee Kenny Clark sounded the full-time whistle, and with it signalled a return to the top of the league for the impressive Light Blues.

Now, the task for McLeish and his squad was remaining there for the rest of the season and creating another piece of history to tell their grandchildren about. They certainly deserved it.

Mols was beaming with pride after scoring, and admitted he hoped his performance would help win him a new contract at Ibrox.

It was his fifth goal in eight games and it seemed that supporters were finally getting to see the best of the Dutchman, certainly more of the old form that had impressed them so much before the striker had suffered the serious knee injury three years previously against Bayern Munich in the Champions League.

He said: 'It's always nice to score but the most pleasing thing was getting a positive result. At my goal I saw the ball coming and thought there was a good chance I could get to it first. It went through the defender's legs and I managed to get it past the keeper – just. It proved to be the winner but I genuinely don't care who scores.

'To be honest, I wasn't that pleased with my performance. The way Celtic played and the pace of the game, especially in the second half, was quite tough. But I'm happy to be part of the team again and that's the most important thing.'

Mols' agent, Rob Jansen, said he hoped the popular Dutchman would now get the chance to extend his stay at Ibrox, and added: 'Michael and I are just waiting on Rangers to give the signal and we will be happy to talk. It's up to them what happens next. Michael is happy at Ibrox and the thing that has changed at the club since I last spoke to them is that he's performing again at the top level and doing the job that he loves for a team he loves.'

Mols would be offered a one-year extension to his contract, which he accepted.

Meanwhile, Rangers boss McLeish celebrated a year in charge at Ibrox in style, and was delighted to see his team sit proudly on top of the SPL table. He said: 'We have our noses in front and know we can't afford to make any more mistakes, but I'm confident we can hold on to our lead. If the lads play to the best of their capabilities and keep their organisation, shape and discipline, and we avoid any bad luck, then we can do it.

'Of course winning on Saturday is an excellent way to celebrate my first year in charge. I'll never forget coming in to take over as Rangers manager. It's a day that will stay with me forever.'

On the victory, he said: 'We played really well in the first half and ground it out in the second. Many times in the past the players might have surrendered but they showed a bullish resilience, as well as spirit and doggedness. We also showed we have a strong mentality within the squad.'

Rangers: Klos, Ross (Malcolm), Numan, Amoruso, Moore, Ricksen, Ferguson, de Boer, Arveladze (Lovenkrands), Mols (Caniggia), McCann. Subs: McGregor and Hughes.

Celtic: Douglas, Valgaeren, Balde, Laursen, Agathe, Lennon, Petrov, Guppy (Thompson), Sutton, Hartson, Larsson. Subs: Gould, Lambert, Maloney and Crainey.

Referee: Mr K. Clark (Paisley)

Attendance: 49,874

Rangers 3 Celtic 0

Saturday, 20 October 2007
Scottish Premier League

IT'S certainly a season that will live long in the memories of Rangers supporters. Mostly for positive reasons, but there will always be that nagging doubt, gnawing away and asking the same question on repeat.

What if the Scottish football authorities had bent the rules a little to help one of their member clubs out of a fixture pickle?

Especially when that member club had raised the profile of said association by qualifying for a European final.

But no, there would be no help, and Rangers would have to play their UEFA Cup Final and THREE crucial league matches in just eight days. It's no surprise the league title slipped from our grasp in those energy-sapping final days.

But to this specific Old Firm game, and even though we were just a few months into the season, it was a crucial match. Celtic hadn't beaten Rangers – or even scored against them – since the second coming of Walter Smith.

But it was points dropped against the likes of Hearts, Hibs and Motherwell that had the Light Blues lagging behind their biggest rivals in the opening months of the campaign.

If only Rangers could perform with the same levels of passion and determination in every match the SPL trophy would have been back at Ibrox before the Easter eggs had been handed out.

Following a cagey first half – notable for Nacho Novo's goal – Rangers were thoroughly dominant after the break. On the back of outstanding individual performances from Alan Hutton and Barry Ferguson, they simply cruised past the Parkhead men. At times Celtic couldn't get near them. In fact, the only thing Celtic 'won' was the yellow card count, racking up nine to Rangers' two.

Ferguson added a second goal to end any doubt about the destination of the result before a gleeful Novo rammed home a penalty to further underline Rangers' supremacy.

Smith, unsurprisingly, cut a contented figure come full time, and said: 'It was a terrific win for us and an essential one because we were under pressure going into the game. We had already lost two games and knew we couldn't afford to fall any further behind Celtic.

'It's a real boost because the consequences of losing were far more damaging for us than Celtic. It was great to get the second goal but as it was an Old Firm game you know that it is never ever finished at that stage.

'Celtic, being champions, were not going to allow us to sit back on that lead. But when we got the third it effectively killed the game.'

Novo had been a surprise choice in the starting 11, making his first start in the league – in a wide left role – for the first time in two months.

Fans from both sides had waited almost three months for this fixture to come around and it was predictably explosive from the start.

Scott McDonald, a name once worshipped in Govan following his heroics at the conclusion of the 2004/05 season, was the chief protagonist in the early exchanges. His acrobatic overhead attempt was tipped wide by Allan McGregor for a corner and, as the throng congregated waiting for the resulting delivery, McDonald lashed out at the goalkeeper with a sly kick.

It was an immediate challenge to Mike McCurry's authority and one the referee met with the curious choice of a yellow card, which led you to believe that he had seen the incident but not deemed it worthy of instant dismissal. Strange.

Shunsuke Nakamura then earned himself a soft free kick after collapsing at Davie Weir's feet following the weakest of nudges. It was within the Japanese winger's range but karma was at hand as he slipped just as he made contact and scooped his shot over the bar.

Rangers had looked comfortable without creating much to bother Artur Boric before forging in front with their first real attempt on target just short of the half-hour mark.

The goal owed much to the persistence of Novo and the athleticism of Hutton. The Spaniard started the move by passing inside to Ferguson, who failed initially to spot the overlapping Hutton making great strides down the right flank. As he tried to curtail his run to stay onside, Hutton slipped on the turf – to ironic cheers from the Celtic support – but was somehow able to get back to his feet almost instantaneously to meet Ferguson's belated pass. From there, the defender's tempting cross perfectly split Gary Caldwell and Stephen McManus allowing Novo space to nod a low header past Boruc for his fourth Old Firm strike.

Celtic's response was a vicious bad-tempered tackle by serial offender Scott Brown on Sasa Papac that earned the former Hibs man a deserved yellow card.

A frenetic first half came to a halt three minutes from the break when Daniel Cousin and McManus collided while challenging for a high ball. The Rangers striker was soon able to recover but, after a lengthy period of treatment, McManus was stretchered off and replaced by John Kennedy.

That was the last action of the first half but Celtic could, and probably should, have been level within 30 seconds of the restart. Caldwell's long ball forward was only partially cleared by Weir, falling kindly for Jiri Jarosik 12 yards out. The Czech player rushed his attempt and could only slice it tamely wide.

Opportunity then knocked for Caldwell shortly afterwards following Nakamura's free kick into the penalty box but, although his shot was well struck and on target, McGregor got down well to parry the attempt.

Just moments later Rangers doubled their lead, and Novo and Hutton again had key roles to play. The Spaniard initially robbed Nakamura to set up the charge into the Celtic half and then Hutton – the 'Blue Cafu' – thumped into a challenge with Massimo Donati to set up phase two of the attack after the initial danger had been half-cleared. Caldwell failed to put any distance into his clearance when the cross eventually came in and, after Lee McCulloch had forced the ball on, Ferguson was on hand to poke it past Boruc to send Ibrox into raptures.

It was down to Novo to add further shine to the scoreline after Charlie Adam had weaved his way into the box and was tripped by the otherwise anonymous Evander Sno. Novo grabbed the ball first and calmly slotted home the penalty to put Rangers three up.

And not even a late rammy or a McCulloch disallowed goal could take the sheen off a wonderful performance. It was quite clearly Rangers' day.

Smith surprised many by including Novo at the expense of Kris Boyd, who wasn't even on the bench, but he insisted he was still trying to find his best 11 given the large turnover of players in the summer, and added: 'We have a new group of players and we have to figure out how they best fit into the team. We know Nacho and what he gives us and really it's just a case of having a look at the whole squad.

'The problem is we have to do this in competitive games and it can be a little bit awkward in terms of team selection but we have had a good reaction when we have brought players in and we got exactly that when we brought Nacho in.

'We have been playing fairly steadily without being spectacular and we are still finding our way but I think there is the basis of a good squad there now. Hopefully we can now settle down over the next few months. If we can keep ourselves in touching distance over this period then we will be happy.'

The win put Rangers joint top of the league with Celtic on 22 points, with the Parkhead side top due to a single goal. Hibs were third, just one point behind the Old Firm.

After the game, Ferguson was in the mood to celebrate his first Old Firm goal in five years, and said: 'I tried to jump out of the way of big Lee's [McCulloch] shot, but it hit a couple of bodies and I managed to turn and get a shot on goal.

'There were a couple of defenders with me but thankfully it went in. It's always a special moment when you score, but ten times better in a match against Celtic. It gave us a cushion and allowed us to push on for the three points. It was a good result and a good performance. Sometimes I get criticised for not scoring enough, but it doesn't bother me who scores, as long as we win.'

Rangers: McGregor, Hutton, Papac, Weir, Cuellar, Thomson, Ferguson, McCulloch, Cousin (Beasley), Adam, Novo (Naismith). Subs: Carroll, Faye, Lennon, Emslie, Whittaker.

Celtic: Boruc, O'Dea, McManus (Kennedy), Caldwell, Naylor, S. Brown, Sno, Donati, Nakamura (McGeady), McDonald, Jarosik. Subs: M. Brown, Riordan, O'Brien, Bjarnson, Cuthbert.

Referee: Mr M. McCurry (Glasgow)

Attendance: 50,428

Celtic 2 Rangers 4

Saturday, 31 August 2008
Scottish Premier League

KENNY Miller scored twice for Rangers on his return to Parkhead – but Pedro Mendez took most of the plaudits for the manner in which he conducted the orchestra from the middle of the park.

Of course, he also scored with a rasping 25-yarder which helped fire Rangers to the top of the SPL table, although when the Portuguese playmaker insisted after the game that the Light Blues could remain at the summit for the rest of the season – even though it was only August – there were chuckles.

But come the month of May, Mendes would have the last laugh as Rangers reclaimed their title from Celtic, winning the championship by four points. In fact, Mendes scored in the title-winning game against Dundee United.

But his impact on the Old Firm scene was stunning. He was on top of his game at Parkhead as Walter Smith's team swamped the champions to leapfrog Kilmarnock at the top on goal difference.

The game started at a frantic pace and Kevin Thomson was booked early on for a late tackle on Shunsuke Nakamura.

A few minutes later the crime count was even when Stephen McManus stupidly drew a yellow card for throwing the ball at a linesman following a foul on Daniel Cousin.

Celtic were on top in the opening stages and Allan McGregor had to look lively to hold a header from Georgios Samaras following Nakamura's cross, before Aiden McGeady shot just wide from long range. But it was Rangers who took the lead on 37 when Cousin shrugged off Mark Wilson on the right flank before cutting in and slipping the ball inside Artur Boruc's near post from an acute angle. It was a finish of high quality.

Celtic were soon level through Samaras, but Miller regained the lead for Rangers seven minutes after the break when he got on the end of a Thomson cross and gave Boruc no chance with a fine volley.

And then came the goal of the game.

With just over an hour played, the quick-thinking Davis rolled a corner out to Mendes, who was lurking with intent 25 yards from goal. The Old Firm debutant hit the sweetest of shots and Rangers were 3–1 up.

With 15 minutes remaining, Rangers were reduced to ten men when Cousin was shown a second yellow for leading with an arm while jumping with McManus. Cousin had sarcastically applauded Dougie McDonald after receiving his first yellow of the afternoon and was a red card waiting to happen from that moment onwards.

But 60 seconds later, the numbers were level as Celtic sub Jan Vennegoor of Hesselink was shown a straight red for kicking out at Kirk Broadfoot, who was booked for his initial challenge. As Vennegoor of Hesselink disappeared down the tunnel, so did Celtic's chances of producing a realistic comeback.

Things went from bad to worse for Celtic when Boruc spilled a Broadfoot cross and Miller rolled the ball into the empty net. Rangers were in dreamland and even a late Nakamura free kick couldn't dampen the celebrations.

Of course, there were still 34 games to go in the long and winding title race but Mendes was adamant the win over Celtic had done wonders for dressing-room morale and given the players clear motivation to stay on top.

He said: 'We will do everything we can to remain in front. We don't want to lose it because it is so much better when you are leading. It's good for the atmosphere around Ibrox as everyone is happy.

'As soon as you go top and look down at the other teams it is all the motivation you need to do everything you can to hold on to what you have. There is always pressure, of course, but the teams below us know they need to win games to make up the difference and catch us. It is a good position to be top of the table to face the rest of the campaign.

'There is a long way to go but we had a tough start with three away games from four. This win is massive and we can take only good things from it.'

Rangers were full value for their success over Gordon Strachan's team and, naturally, Mendes had additional reason to smile.

'It was a great environment in which to play and confirmed what people told me through the week. We tried to play our game in the first half and it was disappointing to concede a scrappy goal after having taken the lead, but in the second half we played well and controlled the match. We passed the ball around the park, so, overall, it was good.

'It's always good to score and when you move to a new club you want to score as soon as possible to get confidence and motivation to build on. You can say scoring in this game is also a little bit special.

'We spoke of the corner kick. We always work to create the gap and Davis saw it. It was a good strike. But helping the team was most important. The third goal settled us because 2–1 is a dangerous score.

'But, of course, from a personal point of view it was all good and completed the perfect fortnight.'

The last comment referred to the whirlwind run of positive news he'd had in recent days. After completing his £3m move from Portsmouth, Mendes shone against Hearts and Aberdeen before starring in the Old Firm match.

In between came a shock recall to the Portugal squad by new national coach Carlos Queiroz for their World Cup 2010 openers. Mendes said: 'It has been quite a time. You can say I moved from the Premiership to the SPL, but Premiership to Rangers puts quite a different perspective on it.

'It all happened quickly but when I saw the facilities and squad, I could see how massive the club is. The Portugal recall came as a surprise as I have been away for five years, but good things always seem to happen in threes.'

Seven points from the opening three games against Falkirk, Hearts and Aberdeen laid the platform for the Old Firm win. To add to the mix, Mendes and fellow new recruits Madjid Bougherra and Steven Davis had settled in well.

And while on the subject of integration, the contribution of Kenny Miller may well have won over some of his critics. There was outrage among some when Smith announced the signing of the talented striker. But two Old Firm goals on enemy territory had the Light Blue faithful in raptures.

Mendes wasn't surprised by Miller's contribution, and said: 'Kenny showed what a good professional he is. It takes a strong character to come here, score and play as well as he did.'

Gary Caldwell was a different kettle of fish, though. He felt like he had just gone ten rounds with Mike Tyson, instead of less than 90 minutes marking football's equivalent. If Caldwell's pride hurt, so did his bones after a bruising encounter with Rangers battering ram Daniel Cousin. The striker was not willing to give an inch in the physical battle with Caldwell and McManus and had been warned by the referee before going into the book for decking the latter. Undeterred, Cousin belied his lazy look by continuing to throw himself into the challenges and when McManus was clattered again, McDonald flashed a red card. By that time, though, Cousin's work was done and Rangers had the points in the bag.

Rangers boss Walter Smith felt Cousin had been harshly treated and, to his credit, Caldwell made no attempt to heap disgrace upon his opponent and insisted Rangers had simply won the physical battle. The Parkhead defender had a burst lip and swollen right eye after the no-holds-barred encounter, and said: 'It's a man's game. The ref has got to sort it out and he did in the second half. There were elbows, there were knees, there was everything being thrown about. But it's an Old Firm game and you just have to take it as it comes. We didn't handle it too well today and we have to learn from this, get better at it and do far better next time.'

Artur Boruc in particular would remember the occasion with little relish. The Pole was outfoxed by Cousin for Rangers' opening goal when the Gabon international gave him the eyes for a cutback to Miller but instead swept a shot through the keeper at his near post. He also blundered badly for Miller's second. Not his most polished performance!

Celtic: Boruc, Hinkel, Caldwell, McManus, Wilson (Hutchinson), Nakamura, Hartley (Robson), S. Brown, McGeady, Maloney, Samaras (Vennegoor of Hesselink). Subs not used: M. Brown, Crosas, Loovens, O'Dea.

Rangers: McGregor, Broadfoot, Weir, Bougherra, Papac, Davis, Mendes, Thomson, Adam (Novo), Cousin, Miller. Subs not used: Alexander, Edu, Dailly, Lafferty, Niguez and McMillan.

Referee: Mr D. McDonald (Edinburgh)

Attendance: 58,595

Rangers 1 Celtic 0

Saturday, 9 May 2009
Scottish Premier League

STEVEN Davis was a hero at both ends of the park as Rangers took a massive step towards winning their first league title in four years.

The Northern Irishman scored the only goal of the game then knocked one off the line as Celtic threatened an equaliser. Both incidents would prove vital in the final analysis.

In terms of wrestling back power in the Glasgow football derby, this game was huge. Before kick-off, Celtic led the title race by a solitary point – by the end, Rangers were two points clear with just three games remaining.

Following 90 pulsating minutes of red-hot action, Rangers supporters were once again dreaming of seeing the league flag flutter at the first home game of the following season.

The victory owed much to the guts and courage of the home side, as the players knew that an away win would make it difficult for them to claw back a four-point deficit in such a short space of time.

Celtic were also slightly superior in the goals advantage column.

The rest of the clubs were also-rans; it was all about the Old Firm and while the result of this match would NOT determine the destination of the silverware, it would have a massive bearing.

On the day, Rangers' big players stood up to be counted, most notably Madjid Bougherra, Davie Weir, Davis and Kenny Miller. And although Kris Boyd missed two golden opportunities, his overall contribution was positive as he linked well with Miller and played with intelligence.

But Davis must have dreamed of this moment a hundred times while he was growing up. A childhood Rangers supporter, he had no doubt played out this scenario many times as a kid on the streets of his home town of Ballymena, in Northern Ireland.

And all his dreams came true in the 36th minute of an intriguing contest. It was brilliant work from Boyd and Miller in particular which created the opportunity and there was no way Davis was going to miss such a huge chance.

Boyd worked his way into the box on the left side and played the ball to Miller, who cleverly darted to his left to create some space. Looking up he saw Davis make his run and drove over a left-foot cross which eluded the Celtic defenders and found his target, who connected perfectly with his right boot. His momentum took him into the Celtic net as he celebrated right in front of the visiting fans.

It was a crucial moment in a match which had been tight up until that point. Indeed, if anything Celtic had enjoyed slightly better possession without ever doing anything with it.

But that changed just a minute before the break, when Davis once again proved to be the hero.

Celtic won a corner on the right side and Shunsuke Nakamura produced a good quality delivery. Jan Vennegoor of Hesselink won the header and beat Neil Alexander but, incredibly, Davis popped up behind the Rangers goalkeeper to scoop the ball off the line with his left boot.

It was his second valuable contribution of the afternoon.

The Celtic goal had come close to being breached in 20 minutes when everyone missed Steven Whittaker's whipped cross in from the left-hand side and it smacked off the post before being cleared to safety by grateful defender Darren O'Dea.

Seven minutes earlier, Miller had tried a spectacular overhead kick from a Christian Dailly cross, but it failed to trouble Artur Boruc too much.

Celtic were appealing for a penalty just after the half hour after a Whittaker challenge on Scott McDonald, but the Aussie striker had been looking for the award and thankfully referee Craig Thomson was well placed to call it.

Predictably, Celtic came out hungry at the start of the second half and put Rangers under a great deal of pressure, with the Light Blues hemmed in for ten minutes or so, and only some valiant defending stopped their lines from being breached. Mind you, Alexander was forced to make a smart stop from Vennegoor of Hesselink's header in 58 minutes when Andreas Hinkel fired in a cross.

Rangers needed something to ease the situation and manager Walter Smith must have thought he had the perfect retort a minute later. The ever-industrious Miller was the chief architect when he won the ball in the midfield, skipped away from two challenges and slid a great ball through to Boyd. The Rangers striker muscled his way past O'Dea and suddenly he was in on goal with only Boruc to beat. The angle was tight and he hit his left-foot shot well, but it came back off Boruc's chest and the chance was gone. Fortunately, it didn't have a major influence on the result, only making the rest of the second half a little nervy for the home defence.

Celtic continued to press but Rangers stood firm and then Boyd had another chance to settle it with a header from a Pedro Mendes corner in 84 minutes but missed the target completely. However, victory was eventually secured and the Rangers fans were left believing that the title was heading home.

Manager Walter Smith was beaming from ear to ear after the match, and said: 'We are delighted to have the situation that we're in at the moment and hopefully we can take advantage of it.

'We were in a good position last year but had a fixture pile-up, which didn't help us at all. We don't have that this year so we have to show that we have the ability to go on and take the championship.

'It was a great move for the goal and although Andrius Velicka had been doing well for us with four goals in four games I felt that Kenny Miller's pace would be important. I was also pleased for Maurice Edu, who has had to come in at a difficult time, but he acquitted himself well.'

Goal hero Steven Davis was in dreamland after the game. He said: 'As a Rangers supporter growing up in Northern Ireland it's a dream to score the winner in an Old Firm derby.

'It was a great ball in from Kenny and I couldn't really miss but it was a fantastic feeling to see the ball cross the line. We maybe didn't have as much possession in the second half as we would have wanted but we got the win and that was the most important thing.

'Hopefully we can now go on and win the title. We have three games left and if we win them all we are champions. Last year we had the chance and we didn't take it so hopefully we can learn some lessons and make sure we do it this time.'

Madjid Bougherra was a rock at the heart of the Rangers defence, and said: 'I'm so pleased with this victory because the destination of the title is now in our hands, and that is all any football team can ever ask. Of course we still have three hard games to play but we will look forward to them now. It was my dream when I came to Rangers to be a champion and I believe we can now go on and win it.

'We worked very hard in this game. Everybody defended well and that has given us great confidence. I had missed the last two matches against them so I was determined to do well in this one.'

On Saturday, 12 May, Celtic beat Dundee United 2–1 at Celtic Park to edge a point ahead at the top of the table. The following day, Rangers were in Edinburgh to face Hibs, and had to settle for a draw after Nacho Novo equalised a Derek Riordan goal.

Going into the penultimate weekend of the campaign, the sides were level on 80 points, although Celtic had a better goal difference of +2. It was that tight. This time, Celtic had to travel to Easter Road while Rangers entertained Aberdeen.

Rangers played their match 24 hours before Celtic and despite having Bougherra sent off in the first half, had enough in the tank to win 2–1 thanks to a Kenny Miller winner. The next day, Celtic and Hibs drew a blank, so Rangers were two points ahead with just one set of matches to play.

Celtic were at home to Hearts (which finished goalless) and Rangers made no mistake by going to Tannadice and thrashing Dundee United 3–0, with Kyle Lafferty, Pedro Mendes and Boyd scoring.

Rangers were champions and Steven Davis's Old Firm goal had indeed proved the turning point.

Rangers: Alexander, Dailly, Bougherra, Weir, Whittaker, Davis, Edu, Mendes, Smith (Lafferty), Miller, Boyd (McCulloch). Subs: McGregor, Novo, Velicka, Fleck, Wilson.

Celtic: Boruc, Hinkel, Loovens, Caldwell, O'Dea (Naylor), Nakamura, Crosas, Hartley, Maloney (McGeady), McDonald, Vennegoor of Hesselink (Samaras). Subs: Brown, Misun, Flood, Robson.

Referee: Mr C. Thomson (Paisley)

Attendance: 50,321

Celtic 1 Rangers 3

Sunday, 24 October 2010
Scottish Premier League

IT was the day Walter Smith became the godfather of the Old Firm; the day he became the most successful manager in this fixture since the Second World War, and his players did it with a touch of swagger and style.

It was also the day that Rangers chalked up nine in a row – that was nine successive league wins, which saw them maintain a strong position at the top of the SPL.

That said, going into the first Old Firm game of the season, both sides had won their first eight matches, so the game at Parkhead was vital, if not in terms of the destination of the title, certainly as far as any early psychological advantage was concerned.

And for the third consecutive season, Kenny Miller struck a double in the first Old Firm game of the campaign to help win the match for the Light Blues.

Manager Smith made two changes to the side which had played so well in the Champions League draw with Valencia at Ibrox just four days earlier. As he shuffled his pack to accommodate a 4–5–1 formation, both Richard Foster and Vladimir Weiss dropped to the bench.

In came the fit-again Lee McCulloch and Kyle Lafferty, with the Ulsterman handed a role on the left side of midfield.

It was Smith's 50th Old Firm game in charge of Rangers and he knew getting a win would take him beyond the tally of victories recorded in the fixture by 1960s iconic boss Scot Symon.

Smith's biggest concern in the opening stages was an injury suffered by Sasa Papac after less than a minute when he was hurt in a crude challenge by Anthony Stokes. The Celtic striker was extremely late as he slid in on the Bosnian and after the free kick was given, Stokes was the first name in the referee's wee black book.

When it seemed Papac might have to be replaced, he was able to come back on and take up his place on the left side of defence following treatment, although he appeared to be struggling quite a bit.

In a lively start, Steven Whittaker smacked a post with a shot from 16 yards as Gers got men forward in numbers. Then with only three minutes on the clock, McCulloch was shown the yellow card for a sliding tackle, when it appeared to all and sundry that he had clearly connected with the ball.

The visitors had made the better start and although Celtic tried to force their way into the game, their momentum was nipped when they lost their skipper Shaun Maloney to injury. Mexican midfielder Efran Juarez replaced the Malaysian-born Maloney and gave the hosts a more solid look.

Indeed, the game itself lacked rhythm but it was Rangers who appeared more composed and measured in their approach. That said, a good opportunity was wasted when Steven Naismith was fouled and Papac tried to swing the free kick into the box only to succeed in sending the ball out of play.

Rangers – SPL champions in each of the previous two seasons – began to settle and looked the more likely to do something when they came forward, with Davis becoming more and more influential.

The Northern Irishman had an early chance when he turned and fired in a fierce shot goalwards, from a Whittaker cross, only to see Fraser Forster gather comfortably. It was then Celtic's turn to move forward but like everyone else up to that point, Emilio Izaguirre couldn't find his range from 35 yards.

Rangers' advances upfield were more structured, but Naismith's lay-off only resulted in Madjid Bougherra putting the ball over from the edge of the area.

With half-time approaching, it seemed a lack of clear-cut chances would see it goalless at the break, but Celtic ended the first half with a series of corners and with each one, edged closer to breaking the deadlock. But just when it seemed Rangers had got to the break unharmed, they fell behind a minute into injury time. Ki sent in a cross and when the ball found its way beyond a ruck of bodies, Hooper was at the back post to nick it into the net.

Falling behind was nothing new to Rangers as they had clawed back deficits in each of their last three league games to come out on top, but it was almost six years since a team had gone behind in an Old Firm fixture and fought back to win, so they knew it would be tough.

Rangers made one change ahead of the restart with Kirk Broadfoot coming on for the injured Papac. And within three minutes the Light Blues were level, with Lafferty taking the credit for the equaliser after a Davis free kick was scrambled in. Replays showed the ball came off Loovens's chest but either way, the big Northern Ireland hitman claimed it as his first derby counter.

Just six minutes later, the match was turned on its head as Gers went ahead in dramatic circumstances. Forster's kick out was poor and was collected by Naismith, whose first-time touch played in Maurice Edu. Although he couldn't get his shot away, the attempt ricocheted off the American and into the path of the previously quiet Miller. Then, with as clean a connection as you're likely to see, the striker blasted in his 12th club goal of the campaign with a crisp low volley into the bottom corner from 15 yards.

In control of the match for the first time, Rangers were comfortable, while seeing their lead evaporate so quickly had visibly shaken the home team.

And their hurt turned to pure agony on 66 minutes as Broadfoot was brought down in the area by Daniel Majstorovic and referee Willie Collum pointed to the spot. It was a contentious decision, but shaking their heads in disbelief, home fans began streaming for the exits as Miller slammed his second of the game high into the net.

By contrast, there was sheer bedlam amongst the away supporters and they bounced up and down with delight as they sensed a first victory at Parkhead in more than two years.

Neil Lennon's team was slow to muster any sort of response but when they did, it took some spectacular goalkeeping to deny them. McGregor was at his very best as he threw himself across his goal to palm a good Juarez free kick around his post.

From there, it was a very muted Celtic who tried in vain to play their way back into the tie but with some very resolute defending, there was no way past the rampant visitors, whose one-touch football became more confident and if anything, only looked likely to add to their advantage.

After two minutes of injury time, the toothless hosts were put out of their misery when Collum signalled the end of the contest. It might only have been October, but Rangers were on their way to becoming champions once again!

After the game, the respective press conferences focussed mainly on the penalty decision by the referee, and Celtic manager Neil Lennon said: 'It looked soft to me. If you look at him [Collum], I'm not sure he saw it so I don't know why he has given it. He has a lot of questions to answer.'

Lennon also believed that Lee McCulloch, already on a yellow, should have been sent off for a foul on Georgios Samaras. 'I want to know why McCulloch was still on the pitch after a blatant obstruction when we were breaking. I'm not going to go on about the referee because I have my own problems regarding the team but you have to get the big decisions right and there's another big decision that has gone against us. I will be asking for an explanation.' But Walter Smith believed the home side's concentration on the referee in the run-up to the game had been unwarranted. In what was merely their latest battle with the SFA, Celtic had written to complain about the performance of the match officials during the game at Dundee United the previous weekend.

'There was unfair pressure on Willie Collum, there's no doubt about that,' said the Rangers manager. 'That is two out of the last three Old Firm games in which the referee has been placed under unfair pressure before the start of the game. We have got to stop and have a look at what is happening instead of blaming officials. If you look at it carefully, the majority of times the better team wins an Old Firm game. It's actually as simple as that.'

Smith added: 'There are a lot of games still to be played but I'm delighted at the position we're in.'

Celtic: Forster, Izaguirre, Wilson, Majstorovic, Loovens, Ki, Ledley, Maloney (Juarez), Hooper, Samaras, Stokes (McCourt). Subs: Zaluska, Cha, Towell, Twardzik, McGinn.

Rangers: McGregor, Whittaker, Papac (Broadfoot), Weir, Bougherra, McCulloch, Davis, Edu, Miller (Weiss), Naismith, Lafferty (Beattie). Subs: Alexander, Foster, Fleck, Hutton.

Referee: Mr W. Collum (Glasgow)

Attendance: 58,874

Celtic 1 Rangers 2

Sunday, 20 March 2011
League Cup Final

IT was the afternoon when Rangers' African import El Hadji Diouf contributed very little to the club's 27th League Cup win bar his iconic 'Dioufie' celebration at the end.

So often the wind-up merchant in these games, Scott Brown looked as though he was about to be physically sick when the Senegalese international popped up just 12 inches away, arms outstretched and clutching his winners' medal.

It was all good-natured banter on Diouf's part and the Rangers supporters lapped it up.

What they had witnessed beforehand, though, was 120 minutes of exciting, entertaining cup football, and great value for money.

And who will ever forget the agony and ecstasy of Nikica Jelavic's extra-time winner which spun into the net after hitting the post and rolling agonisingly along the line?

Or the cheer when Walter Smith hoisted up the trophy from the Hampden presentation area in his last ever cup final as Rangers manager – the gaffer's 20th trophy win of his Ibrox reigns?

Neil Lennon was banned from the touchline for the Co-operative Insurance Cup Final as more than 51,000 excited supporters waited eagerly for referee Craig Thomson to get the action underway.

Neil Alexander retained his place in the Rangers team, as he had done in every round of the competition, while there were also starts for Steven Naismith and Jelavic as the cup-tied Richard Foster and injured Kyle Bartley dropped out.

After the previous Old Firm match's highly publicised flashpoints, referee Thomson's first big decision arrived on the quarter-hour mark.

Mark Wilson burst into the Rangers box and went to ground as Davis and Sasa Papac closed the door but there was little contact and 'no penalty' was the correct decision.

Celtic almost went in front when Kris Commons sent over a wicked cross but Brown's diving header was well wide of Alexander's right-hand post.

It was Rangers who edged in front in 24 minutes when Davis pounced on Charlie Mulgrew's headed clearance, drove at the Celtic defence and guided a low left-foot shot into the net via the post.

But Neil Lennon's side drew level as Emilio Izaguirre's deflected cross was nodded on by Georgios Samaras and Joe Ledley glanced the ball past Alexander.

Rangers thought they had a penalty when Jelavic went to ground following Rogne's tackle, with Thomson initially pointing to the spot, but after speaking to one of his assistants he changed his mind and booked the Rangers striker for simulation.

The Ibrox side started the second period positively and Whittaker forced Forster into a save with a stinging drive. Maurice Edu then tried to force his way past Wilson and the Rangers players claimed in vain that the Celtic defender had used his arm to block the ball's path. Thomson said no, but Edu had a valid case.

The ineffective Brown was hauled off by Lennon and replaced by Ki, while Rangers made an enforced change when Madjid Bougherra was replaced by Kyle Hutton.

Vladimir Weiss came on for the final seconds of regulation time and, after the match moved into extra time, the winger would play a massive part in the final reckoning.

The Slovakian was fouled on the edge of the box and Jelavic's effort from the free kick was deflected off the wall but Forster reacted quickly to claw the ball over.

But Jelavic was not to be denied with his next attempt. Quick-thinking Weiss played a precision free kick to the Croat and he brushed off the challenge of Mulgrew to expertly slide a shot past Forster from the edge of the 18-yard box. The ball rebounded off the right-hand post and out around 18 inches, before spinning back and creeping over the line. It was the game's pivotal moment.

Jelavic tried to get the better of Mulgrew again as the pair went one on one at a Rangers attack and, though the Celtic man committed a foul on the edge of the box, referee Thomson produced a yellow card, judging that the offence did not deny a clear goalscoring opportunity.

Diouf replaced Jelavic for the closing stages and set up Weiss for a shot that required a last-ditch save by Forster.

Celtic pressed for a late equaliser and Gary Hooper was denied by an excellent sliding block by Whittaker. The Parkhead side were then reduced to ten men when Izaguirre was shown a straight red for cynically barging Weiss over as the Rangers player tried to take advantage of Forster's absence from his goal, minutes before the final whistle.

After the game, Walter Smith was beaming from ear to ear, but admitted he wasn't happy with referee Thomson for twice denying Rangers' appeals for penalties. He said: 'It's dangerous for a referee to do that. If it had happened in the other box … I don't know. I've talked before about Celtic mounting a campaign against referees, but I firmly believe that if you are good enough you will win despite a refereeing decision. Today we've won and I'm delighted.

'I felt aggrieved Jelavic was booked because the referee's first reaction was that he had been fouled. The referee gave the penalty and then didn't. But he must have thought there was something in it to give it in the first place. I don't know why he changed his mind but that's what he told the players.

'We went on to win so you might say everything is fine. Nonetheless it matters. That said, I hope both teams get a bit of praise for what they've done.'

Smith was referring to a number of appeals for calm before the final. The First Minister, police and religious leaders had all contributed their tuppence-worth but the match, while tough and uncompromising, was a thriller for all the right reasons.

Smith said: 'It was a terrific game. We deserved to win and I can't say if Kyle Bartley being injured worked in our favour in the way we had to set up. Steven Davis was man of the match but we had lots of good players out there.

'Our players have given everything for the club and I didn't see that they had anything to prove. Now they just have to keep winning but today was testimony to their desire to win. I never use what anyone says about us as motivation because motivation has to come from within yourself. You need to have the desire to go out and win.

'It was a nice trophy to win, and I know I'm leaving, but while I didn't want to go without another trophy the most important thing is the club. But will it help us in the remainder of the season? It might but we could still be badly affected by injuries. Steven Whittaker played in his EIGHTH position so far this season, and Maurice Edu finished the game at full-back. But we were here to win, and that's what we did.'

Rangers' skipper David Weir said: 'We set out our stall from the first minute to have a go at them and cause a few problems. Overall we thoroughly deserved to win. We were written off before the game and had a lot of accusations thrown at us but we answered in the best way. We don't need motivation as we're used to winning things. Perhaps some people need to eat their words.

'The ref made the decisions he thought were right – there were tackles but no damage to anyone. I actually got the feeling during game that it was going to be our day.

'Decisions maybe didn't go our way but the ref explained them and fair play to him for doing that. We felt some were wrong but we responded. We could have had sob stories and used it as a reason for us not winning the cup, but to be fair as a group of players we went and won it. They are now side issues because we got the job done.'

Vladimir Weiss insisted pre-match talk of a Celtic treble fired up the players to end their rivals' recent domination of the Old Firm fixture. 'We kept believing in ourselves. We showed a great desire to win the game and we played well. There has been a lot of talk about a treble for them but we are the first team to win something and hopefully we can concentrate on the title now. If we play like we played today, we will win it.'

And Rangers did indeed win the league, clinching it by a solitary point with a 5–1 win over Kilmarnock at Rugby Park, with Kyle Lafferty grabbing a hat-trick. It sure was a fitting way for Walter Smith to bring down the curtain on a dazzling career as Rangers manager.

Celtic: Forster, Izaguirre, Wilson, Mulgrew, Rogne (Loovens), Brown (Ki Sung Yeung), Ledley, Kayal, Samaras, Hooper, Commons. Subs: Zaluska, McCourt, Stokes.

Rangers: Alexander, Whittaker, Papac, Weir, Bougherra (Hutton), Wylde, Edu, Davis, Naismith, Lafferty (Weiss), Jelavic (Diouf). Subs: McGregor, Healy.

Referee: Mr C. Thomson (Paisley)

Attendance: 51,181

Rangers 2 Celtic 2
(Rangers won 5–4 on penalties)

Sunday, 17 April 2016
Scottish Cup semi-final

THE day before the game, bigmouth pundit Chris Sutton was all over the papers urging his former team to 'Smash Rangers all over Hampden!' Lovely. His opening line was, 'If I was still a Celtic player I'd think this isn't just about winning – it's about smashing Rangers all over Hampden.'

He then goes on to backtrack slightly by adding, 'I'm not talking about kicking people. It's about proving you are the top dogs, showing you are miles better and that there is a huge gulf between the teams.'

Too late. Bigmouth had struck, and 24 hours later I'm sure he was hiding under his duvet sobbing his eyes out as his beloved Celts made him look incredibly stupid. Hopefully he enjoyed Andy Halliday's early tackle on Patrick Roberts.

I know I did!

It was certainly quite a contest. You could say Mark Warburton had Rangers supporters believing that 'today might just be the day' as they converged on the national stadium from all points of the compass, but I suppose believing it will be your day and it actually being your day are two completely different things.

I would suggest that those with a more modest head on their shoulders hoped rather than believed. Of course, Rangers being the club they are – the most successful in the world – then you are always likely to believe you can win, although on occasions you just might not want to admit it. Perhaps this was one of those occasions.

Of course, there's no doubt Celtic were odds-on favourites with the bookies, TV pundits and just about everyone else, but odds are there to be upset, and even though it was the 'Championship team' against the so-called 'Invincibles', of course there was still belief in the Rangers end, because if you don't have belief …

Anyway, the game was a relentless affair from the start, with both teams desperate to stamp their authority on proceedings from the outset and, as a result, play swung from end to end in the opening stages.

Both sides had good chances and if Celtic's back four hadn't been aware of the threat they were facing before the game, they soon were when Barrie McKay played a sublime ball through to Kenny Miller, whose shot was well stopped by Craig Gordon.

Rangers began to impose their game plan, passing the ball swiftly and cleverly and taking the set pieces short, particularly corners, and for a time Celtic were restricted to playing on the break. On one such break, Scott Brown ought to have opened the scoring from the edge of the area, but dragged his shot wide.

And then the moment every Rangers supporter had dreamed of. The moment they took the lead – and it was well-deserved. James Tavernier delivered a corner kick and the ball broke to Andy Halliday. His cross cannoned off Brown into the path of Miller, who finished coolly. Cue delirium.

With Halliday and Jason Holt pushing forward in central midfield, Rangers were composed and assertive. The strategy was effective but Celtic could still rely on individuals to be bold and they should have equalised when Griffiths' shot bounced off the post and landed at the feet of Roberts. With an open goal in front of him – at the Rangers end – he shot horrendously wide.

Just what Celtic made of the way Rangers were passing the ball around them, even at close quarters, is anyone's guess, but it was a joy to watch.

Celtic started the second half the brighter and won four corners in quick succession – and scored with the last of them, when Roberts' delivery was headed high into the net by Sviatchenko.

The game then turned into a battle, in the best possible sense, and every ball was keenly contested.

And so to extra time: enter Barrie McKay. The talented, but enigmatic, kid picked the ball up 35 yards from goal, took a couple of touches and let fly … all the way into the top right-hand corner of Craig Gordon's net. It was one of the best goals Hampden had witnessed in a long time.

That goal deserved to win the match, but it didn't, sadly. Tom Rogic (remember that name) had other ideas and levelled it early in the second period of extra time.

And so to penalties. It was decided for some reason that they should be taken at the Celtic end. Not to worry, though, as Halliday, McKay, Nicky Law, Lee Wallace and Gedion Zelalem held their nerve to fire Rangers to a famous victory.

By the time Rogic's penalty was re-entering the Earth's atmosphere, the Celtic end was all but empty. One look at the other end, though, and it was party time. The unthinkable had happened: the 'Invincibles' had been neutralised.

The huge and jubilant Rangers support eventually started to make their way out of the stadium and on to their various ports of call. Many would be going straight home, others off to meet relatives who had been seated in different parts of the ground but, I suspect, the vast majority were headed to their favourite pub, to toast their heroes and indulge in a little choir practice.

For all his eventual shortcomings, Mark Warburton had given Rangers supporters back their swagger, and while it might have been nice to finish off the story with tales of another Scottish Cup victory, it mattered not a jot on Sunday, 17 April at around teatime, because Rangers had beaten Celtic. And please don't get the impression that little David had somehow managed to slay big bad Goliath, because it wasn't like that. It wasn't backs to the wall for 120 minutes of nail-biting terror. Nope. Rangers outplayed their apparently more illustrious rivals for large parts of the game and were worthy winners, although of course there were some nervy moments.

That said, the game should have been won within the regulation 90 minutes, but that mattered little in the final analysis, because there wasn't a dry eye in the house – on either side!

During the red-hot atmosphere of the penalty shoot-out, it transpired that Wes Foderingham's water container wasn't the only bottle to crash. Apparently, while waiting to face a Rangers spot kick, opposition keeper Craig Gordon fumbled around under Wes's towel, grabbed his water bottle and sneakily lobbed it over the advertising boards.

Quite what he hoped to achieve by indulging in such stupidity is anyone's guess, but sub keeper Cammy Bell spotted the gamesmanship, and ran the length of the pitch to find and return it to his team-mate.

Fod refused to be cowed, though, and went on to make a vital penalty stop from Brown, diving to his left, as Rangers made a nonsense of the suggestion that their seven Old Firm rookies would wilt in the Hampden furnace.

Foderingham said: 'Magically, I got my water bottle back. Craig probably had one eye on a little gamesmanship but it didn't work for him. I just tried to focus on the spot kicks. You try to research the takers, so I stepped up, picked my sides and thankfully it paid off on one of the penalties. It was a brilliant feeling.

'It's difficult to put our win into words. It was obviously a fantastic performance, which started with us going a goal up. It was a little bit of a rollercoaster of emotions with them getting back into the game, then it going to penalties at the end and winning in that fashion, but I'm just delighted we got the result.

'My save in the last minute of extra time from Griffiths was probably the most important I've ever made. It was so late in the game so obviously if that goes in we've lost the tie.

'It was a massive game, but the best of my career. We played some fantastic football, stuck to our guns and it paid off. I'm delighted for the fans as well because it has been a long time coming.'

Kenny Miller was equally as delighted, and said: 'This is the most emotional I've ever been after a game because I knew what it meant to the players, coaches, manager and fans.

'Watching extra time and penalties from the bench was torture. I kicked every ball but thankfully we got there in the end. It was a fantastic day – I have never felt anything like it. I was so close to tears.

'It is right up there with all I have achieved in my career. There was a lot of talk before this game about how far behind we were, but we showed we are more than a match for them.'

Rangers: Foderingham, Tavernier, Wilson, Kiernan (Zelalem), Wallace, Halliday, Ball, Shiels (Law), Holt, McKay, Miller (Clark). Subs: Bell, Burt.

Celtic: Gordon, Bitton, Brown, Griffiths, Mackay-Steven (McGregor), Boyata (Sviatchenko), Mulgrew, Lustig, Johansen (Rogic), Roberts, Tierney. Subs: Bailly, Kazim-Richards, Armstrong, Commons.

Referee: Mr C. Thomson (Paisley)

Attendance: 50,069

Rangers 1 Celtic 0

Saturday, 29 December 2018
Scottish Premier League

DREAMS and nightmares are two completely different things. The only thing they have in common is they mostly occur during sleep. One is a pleasant feeling, the other a feeling of terror. To give you an example, Celtic defender Michael Lustig would have nightmares about the way he was turned inside out by Ryan Kent in the lead-up to the Rangers goal.

Kent, on the other hand …

And so to the game. A win would see Rangers move level with Celtic at the top of the Premiership table, but to achieve that, Rangers would have to inflict Brendan Rodgers's first defeat in 13 Old Firm games.

It was over two and a half years since Rangers had defeated their greatest rivals and once again Celtic were favourites going into the game.

How it panned out, few could have predicted, because right from the start Rangers were on top, and in a relentless first half, Celtic goalkeeper Craig Gordon was busier than a supermarket checkout assistant on Black Friday.

Rangers' intent was clear from the moment Andy Halliday – filling in at left-back for the injured Borna Barisic – celebrated winning a crunching tackle on Olivier Ntcham in the opening minute as though he'd scored the winner.

The home side were urgent, imposing and dominant across the pitch, but the foundation for their success was built upon a midfield three of Ross McCrorie, Scott Arfield and Ryan Jack.

Celtic were hustled and bullied out of their rhythm, and they made a surprising number of unforced errors, mainly from the likes of Dedryck Boyata, Scott Brown and Calum McGregor, who either passed the ball straight out of the park or directly to an opponent.

It was a reflection on the dynamics of the game that Celtic's best player was goalkeeper Gordon, who kept the score down with early saves from a Daniel Candeias volley and Connor Goldson's header.

Before Rangers broke the deadlock, Alfredo Morelos and Brown competed for a Halliday corner, and sent the ball spinning off an upright.

Celtic were ragged, and that sense of disorientation eventually proved costly. Kent, a sprightly figure throughout, left Lustig grounded with a fine run down the left, and when he cut the ball back to Jack, the midfielder side-footed a shot through the legs of Brown.

The visitors had strength in depth on their bench, but by the start of the second half they had been forced into two defensive changes, with Kristoffer Ajer replacing the injured Filip Benkovic and Anthony Ralston coming on for Lustig.

The interval didn't disrupt Rangers' momentum, and they should have scored twice in the opening moments after Gordon underhit a pass to Boyata, allowing Kent to rob the ball. The winger's shot was saved by Gordon, and then Boyata blocked Arfield's follow-up on the goal line.

Even when Rangers' intensity levels dipped, Celtic were prevented from landing a decisive blow.

Ryan Christie's shot was deflected wide by Joe Worrall's challenge and in the final moments, Halliday defended stoutly to block a shot by Ntcham.

In between, McGregor ran in behind the Rangers defence, but was judged to be offside before firing the ball home.

Rangers' manager Steven Gerrard was delighted afterwards, and said: 'This moment is all about the supporters, they've been through a lot and they've been punished in these fixtures. But the players were outstanding. I asked them to win their individual battles and we were better to a man. We should have won it more comfortably. We played with courage and belief; we were brave and competed all over the pitch. I asked them to bring their A game and they did.'

Gerrard singled out Halliday for special praise, with the boyhood Rangers fan excelling at left-back. The gaffer said: 'He epitomised the whole squad. He was outstanding in our last game and earned the right to play in this one. Andy is my unofficial captain, I think the world of him and he deserves to have a great night.'

Halliday, himself, admitted he faced a major dilemma after the game: go on holiday with his girlfriend or head out to celebrate! Thankfully, for his relationship, he chose the former, saying: 'I virtually got straight on a plane after the game. It has been such a long season and we had played so many games in such a short space of time that I was looking forward to the break, but I celebrated on the plane, don't worry about that!

'I had actually said to my girlfriend that getting a flight the next day would be perfect as it would allow the opportunity for a bit of celebrating down Paisley Road West, but it didn't happen.

'The feeling at the final whistle was one of sheer ecstasy. The players who have been here a few years have been through some difficult times but we have stood up to the challenge and come back stronger, although not any more than the fans. They've been through hell but they have followed their club throughout the bad times so it was important to get that victory for them and you can see exactly what it meant to them. In fact, you'll be able to see that throughout Glasgow tonight.'

Halliday added: 'I heard my tackle early on went viral but it's important to set the tone in a derby match. I said to the boys if someone gets a chance to leave a marker then do it, and luckily it was me.

'There's no doubt it's the best fixture in the world. I've personally had some difficult times in past Old Firm matches with some heavy defeats, so it was good to give a bit back to the supporters. It might have finished 1–0, but it was one going on five. It was a bit of a doing.'

Celtic manager Brendan Rodgers was magnanimous in defeat, and said: 'I thought the best team won. Rangers played well. We had a lot of unforced mistakes and didn't create as much as we would like so there's no excuses.

'I think with players missing and one or two unfit, it took away a little bit of strength from us, but we brought pressure upon ourselves at times with poor decision-making. They will feel the hurt of losing an Old Firm game and hopefully it will make them better going forward.'

Ryan Kent was in the mood to lap up the adoration of the Rangers fans after inspiring them to a first Old Firm league win in almost seven years. But half an hour after John Beaton's full-time whistle, in the Ibrox tunnel, boss Steven Gerrard delivered his no-nonsense verdict on his star man. 'Shit hot,' he shouted as the on-loan Liverpool wide boy was being interviewed by reporters. It described the 22-year-old's performance down to a tee.

The manner in which Kent set up Ryan Jack's winner was sublime, and all the more incredible given the winger had managed just 45 minutes in almost two months prior to the derby after being sidelined with a hamstring injury.

His direct play was key to Gers' win and he admitted that was the aim after showing Celtic too much respect in the 1–0 Parkhead loss in September. He said: 'I just remember taking it down the line, cutting back and slipping Jacko in. He got the finish away and I was happy to get the assist. I missed a couple of chances, which was disappointing, but the most important thing was the win.

'It's an incredible feeling to come away with the points from such a big game. I would be lying if I said it's not the biggest derby in the world. It's most definitely up there, so to be part of a victorious team is an unbelievable feeling. You could see what it meant to the fans and to everyone associated with Rangers.

'There are people at this club who have been waiting a long time for this moment, so I could understand Andy Halliday being emotional at the end. Andy was outstanding. He's a real leader out on the pitch and you could see that as he put his body on the line near the end to block a shot.'

Midfield ace Scott Arfield turned in a stellar performance and insisted the win meant so much. He added: 'We have been battered from pillar to post and you have good days and bad days at this club but the belief never changes. These fans have stuck by Rangers through thick and thin and that is what it's all about.'

It may not have won Rangers the title but it laid down a marker that said 'Rangers are back, and gunning for 55!'

Rangers: McGregor, Tavernier, Halliday, Worrall, Goldson, McCrorie, Candeias (Coulibaly), Arfield (Flanagan), Jack, Morelos, Kent. Subs: Foderingham, Wallace, Lafferty, Katic, Middleton.

Celtic: Gordon, Lustig (Ralston), McGregor, Boyata, Benkovic (Ajer), Brown, Ntcham, Forrest, Christie, Sinclair, Johnston (Edouard). Subs: Bain, Hayes, Morgan, Tierney.

Referee: Mr J. Beaton (Motherwell)

Attendance: 49,863

Rangers' Scorers in Old Firm Games:

28: RC Hamilton

27: Ally McCoist

21: Jimmy Duncanson

19: John McPherson

17: Alex Venters

15: Willie Reid, Alex Smith

14: Jimmy Smith, Willie Thornton

13: Ralph Brand, Jimmy Millar, Willie Waddell

12: Sandy Archibald, Andy Cunningham, Torry Gillick, Billy Williamson, Davie Wilson

11: Derek Johnstone, Bob McPhail, Derek Parlane

10: Kenny Miller, Billy Simpson, Finlay Speedie, own goals

9: Willie Findlay, Jimmy Fleming, Mark Hateley

8: Jorg Albertz, John Barker, RG Campbell, Jim Forrest, George Henderson, Johnnie Hubbard, Jamie Marshall, Jim Miller, Alan Morton, Max Murray

7: James Bowie, Davie Cooper, Willie Johnston, Archie Kyle, Jacky Robertson, Mark Walters

6: Alex Bennett, Sammy Baird, Tommy Cairns, Charlie Johnston, Peter Lovenkrands, Tommy Muirhead, Robert Neil, Nacho Novo, Alex Scott, George Young

5: Ian Durrant, Jimmy Gordon, John Gray, John Greig, Willie Henderson, Brian Laudrup, Tommy Low, Alex MacDonald, John MacDonald, Hugh McCreadie, Willie Paton

4: Jim Bett, Ronald de Boer, Sandy Clark, Richard Gough, Sandy Jardine, Willie McIntosh, Jimmy Paterson, Gordon Smith, Jimmy Speirs, Colin Stein, Peter Turnbull, John Wilkie

3: George Brown, Jimmy Caskie, Alfie Conn, Harold Davis, Barry Ferguson, Ian Ferguson, John Graham, Billy Hogg, Colin Jackson, Mo Johnston, George McLean, Alec Mackie, John May, Alexei Mikhailitchenko, John Prentice, Dado Prso, John Walker, Rod Wallace

2: Gabriel Amato, Lorenzo Amoruso, Eric Bo Andersen, Shota Arveladze, Giovanni van Bronckhorst, Terry Butcher, John Cameron, Daniel Cousin, Steven Davis, Billy Dodds, Kevin Drinkell, Scott Duncan, Robert Fleck, Alex Forsyth, Cammy Fraser, Paul Gascoigne, Derek Grierson, James Henderson, Tom Hyslop, Nikica Jelavic, Kai Johansen, Neil Kerr, Don Kichenbrand, Colin Liddell, Colin McAdam, Neil McCann, Ian McColl, Tommy McLean, Alex Miller, Davie Meiklejohn, Michael Mols, Tom Murray, Steven Naismith, Orjan Persson, Bobby Russell, Eddie Rutherford, Ally Scott, Steven Thompson, Charlie Watkins

1: Charlie Adam, William J. Aitken, Sone Aluko, Scott Arfield, Mikel Arteta, Jan Bartram, Jim Baxter, Alex Beattie, Kenny Black, David Boyd, Kris Boyd, John Brown, Thomas Buffel, Eric Caldow, Daniel Candeias, Claudio Caniggia, William Chalmers, Jim Christie, Alex Cleland, Gordon Dalziel, J. Dickie, Charles Donaghy, Maurice Edu, Ugo Ehiogu, Alex Ferguson, Jimmy Fiddes, Tore Andre Flo, Tom Forsyth, Joe Garner, Neilly Gibson, Thomas Gilchrist, Carl Hansen, Brahim Hemdani, Clint Hill, Terry Hurlock, Roger Hynd, Ryan Jack, Jonatan Johansson, Joe Johnson, Andrei Kanchelskis, Ryan Kent, Davie Kinnear, Willie Kivlichan, Bert Konterman, Oleg Kuznetsov, Kyle Lafferty, John Law, Andy Little, Archie Macaulay, Billy McCandless, RS McColl, Murdoch McCormack, Andrew McCreadie, Lee McCulloch, Willie McCulloch, Alan McLaren, Robert McDermid, John McDonald, Ian McDougall, John McFie, Barrie McKay, George McMillan, Alex McMurray, Bobby Main, Andy Matthew, John May, Pedro Mendes, Craig Moore, Bobby Morrison, Marco Negri, Jamie Ness, Willie Nicholson, Arthur Numan, Jimmy Oswald, Jimmy Parlane, Andy Penman, Robert Prytz, Willie Rae, Claudio Reyna, Fernando Ricksen, Hugh Crawford Shaw, Nicol Smith, Nigel Spackman, Trevor Steven, Alec Stevenson, William Stewart, Derek Strickland, Scot Symon, James Tavernier, Jonas Thern, Kevin Thomson, George R. Thomson, Jim Turnbull, Gregory Vignal, Lee Wallace, David Weir, Steven Whittaker, Ray Wilkins, Bobby Williamson, Josh Windass, Jimmy Wilson, Quinton Young, William Yuille

Competitions used: Scottish League, Scottish Cup, Glasgow Cup, Glasgow Merchants' Charity Cup, Glasgow League, Inter-City League, Scottish Regional League (Western Division), Southern League Cup, Summer Cup, Scottish League Cup, Drybrough Cup.

Epilogue …

Victory over Celtic in the penultimate league game of season 2018/19 might not have brought the title back to Ibrox, but it served two useful purposes. First of all, it gave supporters a chance to celebrate and enjoy a rare recent success over Celtic. The 'Bouncy' that afternoon is something that will live long in the memory of all those who were 'bouncing'! There were smiles all around, almost everywhere you looked!

And because it was a second successive home league win over the old enemy it meant even more. It confirmed the end of Celtic's monopoly on the Old Firm fixture. The 1–0 victory at the end of 2018 had been the club's first league win in seven years, and this one proved we had the stomach for a fight – and the talent to usurp the so-called Invincibles.

The manner of Rangers' 2–0 win on 12 May was hugely satisfying. The match was won with a mix of swagger and skill. Take the second goal, for example. Glenn Kamara's cute change of direction left Celtic captain Scott Brown for dead and his pass – expertly dummied by Jermain Defoe – was gobbled up by Scott Arfield, who neatly slid the ball under the Celtic keeper to give the hosts a virtually unassailable 2–0 advantage.

Match that with events almost 12 months previous, when an Old Firm Scottish Cup semi-final tie was lost 4–0 at Hampden, and the difference was staggering. On that occasion Rangers weren't at the races. In fact, it seemed a case of damage limitation from the moment the players stepped on to the turf that day. But not now. Sure, the league was already won, clinched by Celtic the weekend previous after a routine win over Aberdeen, but if you're using the excuse that it was a dead rubber because of that, and therefore certain players wouldn't be trying, then you haven't been watching these games too long.

There is no such thing as a meaningless Old Firm game.

The win meant that league meetings were tied at two apiece, although Rangers were marginally ahead on goal difference. When was the last time that happened?

Rangers went into the final Old Firm match of the season with regular keeper Allan McGregor suspended, and top scorer Alfredo Morelos on the bench. Defoe was a worthy occupant of the centre-forward jersey.

There was a crazy start to the game when Rangers were awarded a free kick in a relatively safe zone, or so you might have thought. Not so, it appeared, as James Tavernier took the kick and deceived everyone – including painfully slow keeper, Scott Bain – to put Rangers in front after just two minutes. A 17th goal of the season for the Rangers captain and right-back. Yip, right-back.

Just after the hour mark, Kamara's defence-splitting pass which Arfield took full advantage of was the icing on the cake, and it also put some daylight between the sides.

As the Rangers players – accompanied by their children – went on the customary lap of honour after the final home game of a rather frustrating season, supporters were left to reflect on a fantastic performance: the complete performance, actually. It contained everything manager Steven Gerrard would have craved before kick-off. Wes Foderingham in goals was as safe as houses, pulling off an excellent save from Oliver Burke late on. It was Celtic's first shot on target – in 83 minutes – which said more about the way Rangers had defended than anything else.

The midfield four of Ryan Jack, Arfield, Kamara and Steven Davis completely dominated their section of the field and it was a joy to watch. Up front, Ryan Kent and Defoe gave the Celtic defence plenty to think about by way of their tireless running and inventiveness. It was a long time since we had seen such a dominant performance from blue jerseys in this fixture and the hope is it will become a regular occurrence.

It's far nicer to happily wander down the Copland Road than stomp down it grumpily!